The Law of Banking

CW01476691

For Hellen and our son Christopher

The M & E Handbook Series

The Law of Banking

David Palfreman
BA Grad Cert Ed
Senior Lecturer
Central Manchester College

Third edition

ME

Pitman Publishing Limited
128 Long Acre, London WC2E 9AN

A Longman Group Company

First published 1980
Second edition 1982
Reprinted 1983
Third edition 1986

British Library Cataloguing in Publication Data

Palfreman, David
  The law of banking.——3rd ed.——(The M & E
  handbook series, ISSN 0265-8828)
  1. Banking law—— Great Britain
  I. Title
  344.106′82   KD1715

  ISBN 0-7121-0682-0

Printed and bound in Great Britain.

Preface to the third edition

I wrote this Handbook specifically for students taking the Institute of Bankers' Stage 2 Examination in Law Relating to Banking and you will find that the scheme of the book follows that syllabus exactly. In addition, however, the book will provide a comprehensive account of Banking Law for both practising bankers and lecturers.

By incorporating the proven approach and format of the Handbook with my lecturing experience, my aim was to produce a concise, readable yet thorough treatment of the subject. The text should provide both students and lecturers with complete course notes for the Institute's examination, allowing more teaching time to be spent in discussion and other learning activities. Appendix 4 also contains some basic advice and suggestions on revision methods and examination technique.

Clearly, a great deal of information is contained in this book, and you are advised against trying to master the text on the first reading. A preliminary reading of the required section, followed by a more thorough study is the best approach. Once understood, the information can more easily be remembered. You will find *Cases in Banking Law* (Gheerbrant/Palfreman) in the M & E Casebook Series a useful and reasonably priced companion volume in this respect; it is also a recommended text for *Practice of Banking I*.

In the discussion of cases and their decisions I have used the following abbreviations:

House of Lords (H.L.)
Privy Council (P.C.)
Court of Appeal (C.A.)

In this third edition my main aim has been to update the text. I have endeavoured to incorporate all relevant new law up until the end of 1985. In particular, the Companies Act 1985 and the Insolvency Act 1985 are both fully incorporated, although those parts of the latter dealing with individual insolvency will not be fully in force until January 1987. Chapter 5 (now entitled 'Individual Insolvency') has been rewritten as has some of Chapter 4 ('Companies').

My thanks go to the Institute of Bankers for allowing me to reproduce their examination questions; and to Wolsey Hall for kindly allowing me to base the original text on the correspondence course that I wrote for them.

DP
March 1986

Contents

Table of cases

Table of statutes

1

Banker and customer

Definitions

1. Banker. A variety of statutes define a bank or a banker for particular purposes without actually explaining the term. For example, the Bills of Exchange Act 1882, s.2, states that a banker is "someone who carries on the business of banking". To say the least, this is not very helpful. The same is also largely true of the Banking Act 1979, s.3(1) of which states that "recognition as a bank" for the purposes of the Act is solely under the grant of the Bank of England.

NOTE: The purposes of the Banking Act 1979 are primarily the regulation of deposit taking and the control of deposit takers. Under the Act, only a "recognised bank" or "licensed institution" (institutions which have not been traditionally regarded as banks) can lawfully accept deposits. Thus, the Bank of England now has *formal*, rather than *de facto*, control of banks and control of other deposit takers where very little, if any, control existed before.

Recognition as a bank under the Banking Act 1979 is dependent on fulfilling the following five criteria:

(*a*) high reputation and standing in the financial community;

(*b*) the provision of a wide range of banking services (e.g. current and deposit account facilities, overdraft and loan facilities, foreign exchange, financing through bills, investment management and corporate finance), or a highly specialised service;

(*c*) satisfying the Bank of England that the institution's business will be carried out with integrity, prudence and professional skills consistent with its activities, and that there are at least two executive directors;

(*d*) assets of £5 million for a bank providing a wide range of banking services and £250,000 for a bank providing a highly specialised service;

(*e*) maintenance of paid-up capital, reserves and other financial resources as are considered appropriate by the Bank of England.

NOTE: For purposes other than those of the Act, the Act does *not* determine who is a bank or banker.

2. Use of the words "bank" or "banker". Under the Banking Act 1979, s.36(1), "no person carrying on a business of any description in the UK other than a *recognised* bank (and the Bank of England, the Central Bank of an EEC Member State, a trustee savings bank, the Central Trustee Savings Bank Ltd. and the Post Office in the exercise of its powers to provide banking services) may use any name or in any other way so describe himself as to indicate that he is a bank or banker or is carrying on a banking business for the purposes of the Act." Criminal sanctions are imposed for breach of this section.

Anyone who could call himself a banker under the old law (*see* below) can still do so for particular purposes, e.g. for the purposes of the Bills of Exchange Act 1882 and the Cheques Act 1957. He must not, however, use the name to suggest that he is carrying on business as such, i.e. provided the words "bank" or "banker" are not used, the whole of the previous law is unaffected.

In practice, s.36(1) only applies to *licensed deposit takers*. Indeed, if a person has a deposit-taking licence he can satisfy the *traditional* definition of a banker to be found in *United Dominions Trust Ltd.* v. *Kirkwood* (1966) (*see* below).

3. Traditional definition of a banker. This is currently to be found in the Court of Appeal's decision in *United Dominions Trust Ltd.* v. *Kirkwood* (1966), where the performance of three activities were identified as the definitive characteristics of bankers.

(*a*) They accept money from, and collect cheques for their customers and place them to their credit.

(*b*) They honour cheques or orders drawn on them by their customers when presented for payment and debit their customers accordingly.

(*c*) They keep current accounts, or something of that nature, in their books in which the credits and debits are entered.

These characteristics were stated to be very similar to those identified in Paget's *Law of Banking*, viz. "No one and nobody, corporate or otherwise, can be a banker who does not (*a*) take current accounts; (*b*) pay cheques drawn on himself; (*c*) collect cheques for his customers."

The Court of Appeal stressed that the definition was *not static* and would always depend on current practice. Indeed, the majority of the Court of Appeal accepted a secondary test of the reputation of the organisation in question with other bankers as a means of determining whether the organisation could be regarded at law as a bank.

4. Customer. There is no statutory definition of a customer, but cases show that a customer of a bank is *a person who has entered into a contract with a banker for the opening of an account in his name.*

It is not essential that a course of dealings has been maintained over a period of time: *Ladbroke* v. *Todd* (1914). The relationship is contractual and therefore arises when the customer's offer is accepted by the bank.

The existence of an account is essential, however, and no matter how many transactions have taken place between a bank and an individual, e.g. cashing cheques payable to that person, that person will not be a customer unless and until an application to open an account has been made and accepted.

NOTE: A banker may owe legal or fiduciary duties to another person before an account is opened, and even if an account is never opened. In *Woods* v. *Martins Bank Ltd.* (1959), for example, a bank manager who gave financial advice to a person who intended to become a customer, and who did so shortly afterwards, was held to owe him the same contractual duty of care as if he were already a customer.

The legal framework

5. The banker-customer relationship. The relationship between a banker and his customer is basically the contractual relationship of debtor and creditor. It is regulated by:

    (*i*) the general rules of contract;

(*ii*) the rules of agency (*see* Chap. 2) and bailment (*see* 7 below), where applicable;

(*iii*) banking practice.

(*a*) *Debtor-creditor.* The essence of the relationship is a debtor-creditor situation, with the position reversed where the banker has made a loan to his customer: *Foley* v. *Hill* (1848).

(*b*) *The implied contract.* The basic debtor-creditor relationship is made more complex by the imposition of rights and duties, similar to those which exist between a principal and his agent, by the implied contract between the banker and his customer: *Joachimson* v. *Swiss Banking Corporation* (1921).

EXAMPLE: In *Tournier* v. *National Provincial and Union Bank of England* (1924), it was held that in general a banker must not disclose information about his customer's affairs without his consent. The relationship between them is confidential. *Obiter dicta* in the case suggests that this duty extends to cover information acquired from sources other than the account itself.

(*c*) *A special relationship.* A banker is not presumed to be in a *fiduciary* position towards his customer, but it is quite possible for a special relationship imposing a very similar fiduciary duty, i.e. a very strict duty of good faith, to arise in his relationship with particular customers who have come to trust and rely upon him for advice. This duty is *independent* of the contractual relationship between them.

EXAMPLE: In *Lloyd's Bank* v. *Bundy* (1975), the defendant, an elderly farmer of little business acumen, twice mortgaged his home to the plaintiff bank to secure an overdraft to his son's company. When it was clear that repayment could not be made, the bank sought to exercise its right as mortgagee to sell the defendant's property. HELD (C.A.): it was not allowed to do so. The defendant had come to rely on the bank for advice and, on the facts, the bank owed a fiduciary duty towards him. The bank had broken this duty by not ensuring that he had had independent advice before mortgaging his home. (See also *National Westminster Bank* v. *Morgan* (1985): 10:**6**.)

(*d*) *Alteration of the contractual relationship.* Any alteration of the contractual relationship must be effected by a subsequent contract, i.e. the banker must bring proposed new terms and conditions to his customer's attention, and he in turn must assent to them.

EXAMPLE: In *Burnett* v. *Westminster Bank Ltd.* (1966), the bank had introduced automated book-keeping and cheques which bore magnetic ink characters for the automated branches. They printed a notice on the cover of their new cheque books stating that the cheques must only be used for the account for which they had been prepared. The plaintiff, an existing customer who had accounts at two branches one of which was automated, altered a cheque prepared for the automated account with the intention of drawing on the other account. He later countermanded payment but the magnetic coding took the cheque to the automated branch where it was paid. HELD: on the facts, the notice on the cover was insufficient to alter the pre-existing contractual relationship between the parties and the plaintiff could recover from the bank the amount paid. (*N.B.* The notice would probably have bound a new customer.)

(*e*) *Banking practice.* A full survey of the rules of banking practice is out of place in this book but one example will illustrate the relationship between banking practice and the law.

EXAMPLE: In *Baines* v. *National Provincial Bank Ltd.* (1927), it was held that a bank is allowed a reasonable period of time to complete its business after its advertised closing time. Thus, in this case the bank was allowed to debit its customer's account with a cheque (for £200) cashed five minutes after closing time and a countermand the following morning was ineffective (*see* also 12:**13**).

6. Rights and duties of a banker.

(*a*) *Rights.* A banker has the following rights.

(*i*) To charge his customer reasonable commission for services rendered to him, and to charge interest on loans made to him.

(*ii*) The right of *set-off* or of combining accounts. This enables a banker to reduce his liability to repay his customer on an account in credit by the amount his customer owes to him on an account in debit, or conversely to reduce the amount which the customer owes to him by the credit balance on the customer's account.

This right can only be exercised when the money owed is a sum which is due and where there is no agreement, expressed or implied, to the contrary.

(*iii*) To repayment on demand from his customer of any overdrawn balance which has been permitted on a current account.

NOTE: In *Williams & Glyn's Bank* v. *Barnes* (1980), it was held that a reasonable period of notice must be given to the customer where the terms and circumstances of the contract of lending clearly imply such notice.

(*iv*) To be indemnified by his customer for expenses and liabilities incurred whilst acting for him.

(*v*) To exercise a lien (*see* 2:2) over any of his customer's securities which are in his possession, other than those deposited for safe custody, for any money owing to him.

NOTE: (1) The lien covers not only negotiable instruments but also any document under which money will or may be payable to the customer, e.g. an insurance policy. (2) Where the lien is exercised over a *bill of lading*, it includes a right of sale of the goods that the bill represents; this probably also applies to a lien over a negotiable instrument which is payable to bearer, though the law on this point awaits judicial clarification.

(*vi*) To dispose of his customer's money as he pleases provided he honours his customer's valid cheques.

(*vii*) To expect his customer to exercise due care in drawing cheques: *London Joint Stock Bank* v. *Macmillan & Arthur* (1918) (*see* 11:28).

(*b*) *Duties.* A banker has the following duties.

(*i*) To abide by any express mandate from his customer, e.g. a standing order.

(*ii*) To honour his customer's cheques provided:

(1) they are properly drawn, and not stale or overdue;

(2) a credit balance or an agreed overdraft facility exists (*N.B.* if an account is £100 in credit and the customer draws a cheque for £101, the bank is legally entitled to dishonour the cheque—it cannot legally pay part of a cheque);

(3) there is no legal bar to payment, e.g. a garnishee order or an injunction;

(4) the customer has not countermanded payment;

(5) the banker has no notice that his customer has died, become mentally incapable of managing his affairs or had a bankruptcy petition presented against him;

(6) there has not been a bankruptcy order or winding-up order (as the case may be) made against him;

(7) he knows of no defect in the presenter's title to the cheque;

(8) there is no evidence to suggest that the cheque is a misapplication of funds.

(*See* 12:**11** for a consideration in greater depth of the termination of a banker's authority to pay his customer's cheques.)

(*iii*) Not to disclose information about his customer's affairs: *Tournier* v. *National Provincial Bank of England* (1924), unless:

(1) compelled by law to do so, e.g. to a guarantor under the Consumer Credit Act 1974, in evidence in legal proceedings, or under income tax or company legislation;

(2) he has a duty to the public to do so, e.g. where he knows that his customer is trading with the enemy in time of war;

(3) his own interests require disclosure, e.g. where legal proceedings are required to enforce repayment of an overdraft, or where a surety asks to be told the extent to which his guarantee is being relied upon by the bank (*see* 10:**7**);

(4) he has the express or implied consent of his customer to do so, e.g. banker's references (*see* below).

NOTE: The duty of non-disclosure survives the closing of the customer's account and possibly his customer's death.

(*iv*) To render statements of account to his customer periodically or upon request (*see* 1:**10**).

(*v*) To collect cheques and other normal banking instruments for his customer, and to credit the amounts collected to his account.

(*vi*) To exercise proper care and skill in carrying out any business he has agreed to transact for his customer. This duty is of most practical importance in relation to the collection and payment of cheques. This may extend beyond the traditional scope of branch banking, e.g. investment advice: *Woods* v. *Martins Bank Ltd.* (1959) *see* 1:**8**.

NOTE: Although no significant change is made to a bank's common law position, under the Supply of Goods and Services

Act 1982, it is implied that a supplier of services will show proper care and skill and complete the service within a reasonable time, if no exact time was agreed.

(*vii*) To give reasonable notice before closing a credit account. There are two reasons for this. First, it gives the customer time to make other arrangements. Secondly, the bank does not have to return cheques already issued by the customer, thereby preventing allegations that by so doing the bank damaged the customer's reputation.

7. Safe custody arrangements. The use of a banker's safe deposit facilities by his customer gives rise to a *bailment agreement*.

Bailment arises where one person (the *bailor*) deposits goods with another (the *bailee*) for a specific purpose on terms that the goods should be ultimately redelivered to the bailor or otherwise dealt with according to his instructions. The bailor retains ownership of the goods.

A distinction exists between the duties owed to the bailor by a gratuitous, i.e. unpaid, bailee and those owed by a bailee for reward. As the former, a banker, can be made liable in *tort* for loss of or damage to the property bailed, e.g. for conversion or negligence, but he is only expected to take the same care of the property as a reasonably careful person would take of similar property of his own. As the latter, however, he owes an additional *contractual* duty under which he must fulfil the high standard of care expected from a banker.

NOTE: In *Port Swettenham Authority* v. *T. W. Wu & Co.* (1978), the P.C. HELD that where goods deposited under a *gratuitous* bailment are lost, it is not up to the bailor to prove that this was the result of the bailee's negligence or misconduct, or that of any employee or agent entrusted by him with their care. The onus of proof lies with the bailee to show that this was not so.

Today, a banker who accepts property for safe custody can nearly always be regarded as a *bailee for reward*, i.e. the bailment is considered to be part and parcel of the wider contract with his customer, whether or not specific payment is made for the safe custody facility. In any case, the same high standard of care is always taken of property deposited for safe custody whatever the exact nature of the bailment agreement.

Night safe agreements expressly provide that the bailment which arises is gratuitous until the wallet is opened and the contents deposited.

NOTE: A bank cannot claim a *lien* over safe custody deposits, except to the extent of any unpaid fees for the bailment itself.

8. Bankers' opinions and references. When a banker gives a reference, an apparent conflict arises with his duty of secrecy to his customer. This can be reconciled, however, by implying permission from his customer to do so into the contract the banker makes with him.

A banker may incur *liability in tort* for an accurate opinion or reference.

(*a*) If the statement is deliberately false or misleading, the banker is liable for fraud. (*N.B.* the Statute of Frauds Amendment Act 1828, s.6, only allows an action to be brought if the opinion is in writing and signed—they are almost always unsigned.)

(*b*) If the statement was made negligently, the banker is liable in negligence unless liability was expressly excluded: *Hedley Byrne & Co.* v. *Heller Partners Ltd.* (1963).

EXAMPLE: In *Box* v. *Midland Bank Ltd* (1979), the defendant's manager failed to explain the difference between an ECGD policy and a ECGD Banker's Guarantee, failed to advise that there was no chance of such a guarantee being granted in the circumstances and failed to advise that, even if it had been, the Regional Head Office had indicated that there was no chance of the requested advance being approved. As a result of relying on the manager's advice, a business venture was unsuccessful, and a receiving order was eventually made against the plaintiff. HELD: The *Hedley Byrne* principle applied and the defendant bank was liable in tort to the plaintiff.

A disclaimer of responsibility is always made in the statement, but such disclaimers could be challenged under the Unfair Contract Terms Act 1977.

9. Advice on investments. While this is not considered as part of a branch's traditional banking business, if a banker advertises his willingness to provide such a service he will be liable should he give faulty advice: *Woods* v. *Martins Bank Ltd.* (1959).

10. Bank statements. A banker owes a duty to his customer to keep an accurate record of the transactions on his account. A customer has no obligation to check bank statements and inform the bank of any inaccuracy in them. Furthermore, if a customer does check the statements, he is not estopped (prevented) from subsequently challenging their accuracy: *Chatterton* v. *London & County Bank* (1890).

(*a*) *Over crediting the account.* If a banker over credits his customer's account, the excess credits can usually, but not invariably, be recovered.

EXAMPLE: In *Lloyd's Bank* v. *Brooks* (1951), the bank, over a period of time, credited to the defendant's account dividends for more shares than she in fact had. She used the money for her own purposes having relied on statements of her account in complete good faith. HELD: the bank was not entitled to recover the amounts wrongly credited to the defendant's account.

In *United Overseas Bank* v. *Jiwani* (1976), three conditions were outlined which must be fulfilled in order to defeat a bank's claim for repayment of excess credits.

(*i*) The state of the account must have been misrepresented by the bank.

(*ii*) The customer must have been misled by the misrepresentation.

(*iii*) As a result of the reliance, the customer changed his position in a way which would make it inequitable to require him to repay the money.

EXAMPLE: In *United Overseas Bank* v. *Jiwani* (1976) $11,000 were credited by telex to the defendant's Swiss bank making a total balance in his account of $21,000. The defendant issued a cheque for $20,000 in connection with the purchase of a hotel. Subsequently, written confirmation of the telex was received but the bank mistakenly treated it as a second credit and advised the defendant accordingly. The defendant then issued a second cheque, for $11,000, towards the hotel purchase. The bank sought to recover this amount from the defendant. HELD: the money was recoverable. On the facts, the defendant had alternative funds which he would have used for the purchase, irrespective of the mistaken credit. Thus, while the first two conditions outlined by the court were satisfied, the defendant failed to satisfy the third.

If the customer (a) is aware that the statement is incorrect: or (b) has not altered his position in reliance on the incorrect balance, e.g. the money is still in the account, the bank can always recover the amount of the mistaken credit.

(b) *Incorrectly debiting the account.* Whatever the reason for the incorrect debit, a banker is obliged to refund the amount (*see* 12:**12**).

If, as a result of incorrect debits, cheques are dishonoured for apparent lack of funds, a banker is liable for the wrongful dishonour of the cheques and must compensate the customer for the injury to his credit and reputation (*see* 12:**12**).

Progress test 1

1. State the three definitive characteristics of a banker. (**1**)

2. When does a person become a "customer"? (**4**)

3. By what rules is the banker-customer relationship regulated? (**5**)

4. List the rights of a banker against his customer. (**6**)

5. List the circumstances in which a banker's mandate to pay his customer's cheques is revoked. (**6**)

6. In what circumstances is a banker entitled to disclose information about his customer's affairs? (**6**)

7. Why may it be important to ascertain whether a banker is a gratuitous or a paid bailee in a safe custody arrangement? (**7**)

8. Explain the nature of a banker's possible liability should he give an incorrect opinion or reference about a customer. (**8**)

9. To what extent is a customer under an obligation to check the accuracy of his bank statements? (**10**)

10. In what circumstances can a banker not recover money mistakenly credited to a customer's account? (**10**)

2
The law of agency

The nature and creation of agency

1. The nature of agency. An *agent* is a person who acts on another's behalf, the other person being known as his *principal*. The essence of the relationship created is that the agent can alter his principal's legal position in relation to third parties by making contracts on his behalf.

Since an agent contracts on his principal's behalf, it follows that:

(*a*) the agent generally incurs neither rights nor liabilities on the contract that he makes;

(*b*) lack of full contractual capacity does not affect a person's ability to act as an agent, e.g. a minor may be employed as an agent. The principal, however, must have contractual capacity to make the particular contract his agent makes for him.

2. Types of agent.

(*a*) *Universal.* A universal agent is one appointed to handle all the affairs of his principal. Such an agent must be appointed by deed and his agency is a form of *General Power of Attorney* (*see* **4** below). A universal agent is rarely encountered.

(*b*) *General and special agents*. The distinction between a general and special agent lies in the extent of their authority.

(*i*) A *general* agent has authority to act on behalf of his principal in all business of a certain kind, e.g. a director is a general agent of a company, a partner is a general agent of a partnership.

A third party will not be affected by any limitation on a general agent's authority unless he is aware of it. This is because a general agent has *implied authority* to act in the ordinary course of his trade, business or profession. (The terms *usual* authority and *customary* authority are also used to describe this type of authority in particular circumstances.)

EXAMPLE: In *Watteau* v. *Fenwick* (1893), the manager of a public house was forbidden to order tobaccos by his principal but did so. HELD: the principal was liable to pay the seller because a manager of a public house would usually have authority to make orders of this kind. The seller could therefore rely on the agent's implied authority in the absence of express knowledge of the limitation imposed by the principal.

(*ii*) A *special* agent is appointed to effect a particular transaction which is not part of his normal business activities, e.g. where a bank officer is asked by a friend to act as agent in the sale of the friend's stamp collection.

Since a special agent's authority is limited to the particular transaction, his principal is only bound by authorised acts. Implied authority has no place in such an agency.

(*c*) *Factors*. A factor is a "mercantile agent", i.e. an agent who buys and sells goods for a commission.

By the Factors Act 1889, s.1, a factor "has in the customary course of his business as such agent authority either to sell goods, or to consign goods for the purpose of sale, or to buy goods, or to raise money on the security of goods."

A *bona fide* purchaser of goods from a factor which were in his possession with the owner's consent will obtain a good title to them, even where the factor did not have his principal's actual authority to sell them.

A factor has possession of his principal's goods and a *lien* over them for any unpaid commission. (A lien is a right to retain possession of the property of another in lieu of payment due from that other person.)

(*d*) *Brokers*. A broker is also a mercantile agent. While he is primarily the agent of the seller, his role is essentially that of a middleman between the buyer and seller. He has authority to act for both parties.

He differs from a factor in that:

(*i*) he does not have possession of the goods that he sells;

(*ii*) he cannot act in his own name; and

(*iii*) he has no lien over goods which come into his possession.

3. Creation of agency. The relationship of principal and agent can be created in four ways.

(*a*) *By contract.* The authority of the agent will be mainly determined by the *express terms* of the contract entered into between the principal and agent. However, the agent will have *implied authority* to do things which are necessary for the completion of his authorised tasks, e.g. an agent employed to sell land has implied authority to sign a memorandum in writing of the contract as required by the Law of Property Act 1925, s.40.

Where a bank's customer pays in cheques for the credit of his account, the banker-customer relationship gives the bank implied authority to collect the cheques on behalf of its customer.

(*b*) *By ratification.* Agency by ratification arises where the principal confirms and adopts a contract entered into on his behalf by a person who had no authority to act for him when he made the contract. The person purporting to act for the principal could be a complete stranger or, more likely, his existing agent who exceeds his authority by making the contract.

Ratification is most likely to arise in a bank's dealings with its customers where:

(*i*) It pays a company cheque on an unauthorised signature. The company can ratify the cheque.

(*ii*) Money is lent to a "company" before it is incorporated. Here the company cannot ratify and a bank would be unwilling to lend without adequate indemnity. (*See* below.)

Ratification is only possible under the following circumstances.

(*i*) The principal is fully aware of the material facts when he ratifies, or intends to ratify regardless of them.

(*ii*) The principal ratifies the entire contract.

(*iii*) The agent discloses his agency and names or otherwise sufficiently identifies his principal at the time of the contract (an undisclosed principal cannot ratify).

EXAMPLE: In *Keighley Maxstead* v. *Durant & Co.* (1901), an agent, without disclosing his principal or his agency, purchased wheat at an unauthorised price. His principal purported to ratify the purchase but subsequently refused to accept delivery and was sued for the price by the seller. HELD (H.L.): the principal could not ratify and was not, therefore, liable for the price. At the time of the sale, the seller had intended to sell to the agent personally.

(*iv*) The principal had legal existence, both when the contract was made and when he ratified it. Thus, a company after incorporation cannot ratify a contract made by its agent before incorporation: *Kelner* v. *Baxter* (1886). Before incorporation a company has no legal existence.

NOTE: The Companies Act 1985, s.36, provides that the person acting for the company in such a contract is personally liable upon it, unless otherwise agreed.

(*v*) The act is capable of ratification. Thus, a contract which is void *ab initio*, e.g. for illegality or mistake, cannot be ratified—it is a legal nullity. On the other hand, a contract which is merely voidable, e.g. for fraud or misrepresentation, can be ratified *before* the party entitled to rescind does so.

A company cannot ratify a contract made on its behalf which exceeds its powers as laid down in its memorandum of association (*see* 4:7). Such a contract is said to be *ultra vires* (beyond the powers of) the company. It is, therefore, void *ab initio*.

EXAMPLE: In *Ashbury Railway Carriage Co. Ltd*. v. *Riche* (1875), the company had been incorporated with the power to make and sell railway carriages and other railway plant and equipment. The directors, however, bought a concession to construct a railway in Belgium and made a contract with Riche for its construction. The directors repudiated the contract when the company ran into financial difficulties, even though the shareholders had all subsequently assented to the contract. Riche sued for breach of contract. HELD (H.L.): since the contract was *ultra vires* the company and void, the directors could repudiate it, and even the subsequent ratification of the contract by the shareholders could not make it binding upon the company.

Thus, a company cannot ratify a contract made by one of its directors if, in doing so, the director exceeded the company's powers as laid down in its memorandum of association: *Ashbury Railway Carriage Co. Ltd*. v. *Riche* (1875).

NOTE: Ratification operates retrospectively, i.e. it dates back to the time when the contract was made by the agent. Thus, if after discovering the agent's lack of authority the third party attempted to rescind the contract, a prior ratification would prevent him from doing so: *Bolton Partners* v. *Lambert* (1889).

(c) *By estoppel*. Such agency results from the principal's words or conduct, not from an agreement between the agent and the principal. It occurs where the principal allows a person to appear to be his agent to third parties. Where a third party relies on this appearance and deals with him as the principal's agent, the principal is estopped (prevented) from denying that person's authority. Agency by estoppel is also referred to as an agent's *ostensible* authority.

Agency by estoppel requires three specific things:

(i) an unambiguous representation by the person who it is sought to hold liable as principal;

(ii) a reliance on the representation by the person to whom the representation was made;

(iii) an alteration of his position by that person because of the reliance.

EXAMPLE: In *Panorama Development (Guildford) Ltd* v. *Fidelis Furnishing Fabrics Ltd.* (1971), the defendant company's secretary had entered into car hire contracts on the company's behalf. HELD: the company was bound by the contracts. While a company secretary is not an agent of his company, the defendant company had held their secretary out as having authority to act on its behalf in a wide range of administrative matters. They were, therefore, estopped from denying his authority to enter into these contracts.

Two situations where a bank could maintain agency has been created by estoppel are where:

(i) A customer's clerk is regularly sent to collect an envelope containing the customer's bank statements and on one occasion examines the statements, the customer subsequently objecting.

(ii) A customer becomes aware that his or her signature is being forged on cheques but does not immediately inform the bank: *Greenwood* v. *Martins Bank Ltd.* (1933).

(d) *By operation of law*. Such agency is the product of the law and arises neither from agreement nor from conduct. There are two types.

(*i*) *Agency of necessity*. This arises where the agent acts in excess of his authority in an emergency to save the principal's property. The classic example is that of a master of a ship acting to save his cargo or his ship.

The person claiming agency of necessity must show:

(1) that it was impossible to obtain his principal's instructions: *Springer* v. *G.W. Railway* (1921);

(2) that there was a real commercial necessity for his action, e.g. perishable goods were endangered: *Prager* v. *Blatspiel Stamp & Heacock Ltd*. (1924);

(3) that he acted bona fide in his principal's interests.

(*ii*) *Agency from cohabitation*. A wife (or mistress) living with her husband is entitled to pledge his credit for necessaries (e.g. food, clothing) which fall within her domestic responsibilities in the relationship.

4. Methods of creation. Agency can normally be created orally, although commercial practice will inevitably mean that many appointments will be in writing.

A *power of attorney* must be given *by deed* as prescribed by the Powers of Attorney Act 1971. Power of attorney is necessary if the agent is to *execute deeds* but it is also used for more general matters. It may be either *specific* (for a particular purpose) or *general* (for a specified period). The latter is usually encountered where the donor is ill, going abroad or where a trustee or personal representative delegates his power. Under the Enduring Powers of Attorney Act 1985, a power of attorney can be created which is not automatically revoked when the donor becomes mentally incapable of looking after his affairs. A bank must be alert to possible abuse of any power of attorney.

It is usual for the donor's bank account to be specifically mentioned and authority given to the attorney to operate the account. Specific clauses must be included if the attorney is to collect, draw and indorse bills of exchange; borrow money; charge the donor's property as security and withdraw safe custody items.

A bank's security forms may give it irrevocable power of attorney to transfer title to mortgaged property on the mortgagor's behalf.

NOTE: Provided a document intended to be a deed and executed as such bears the letters "LS" (Locus Signi) within a circle upon it, the absence of a wax or waifer seal will not prevent the document from being a deed: *First National Securities* v. *Jones & Another* (1978).

A bank will always require a *written mandate* from its customer when an agent is to be given authority to operate his account.

The principal and agent relationship

5. Duties of the agent.

(a) *Obediency.* An agent must obey his principal's lawful instructions.

(b) *Care and skill.* A paid agent is expected to exercise professional competence. An unpaid agent's actions are judged against the skill that he actually has.

NOTE: A gratuitous (unpaid) agent is liable to his principal only for *misfeasance* and not for *non-feasance*, i.e. he may be sued for negligence committed in the course of his agency, but he cannot be sued if he fails to perform his agency at all. No contract exists between a gratuitous agent and his principal on which to base an action for non-feasance.

(c) *Personal performance.* An agent must personally perform his task, he may not delegate it (*delegatus non potest delegare*—a delegate cannot delegate): *McCann* v. *Pow* (1974). There are exceptions:

(i) where the agent is expressly authorised to delegate: *De Bussche* v. *Alt* (1878);

(ii) where the agent has implied authority to do so in the circumstances, e.g. where a customer asks a bank to sell shares on his behalf, the bank has implied authority to employ a stockbroker to do so;

(iii) Where the task delegated does not require the exercise of skill and judgment, e.g. signing documents or sending notices;

EXAMPLE: In *Allam & Co.* v. *Europa Poster Services* (1968), it was HELD that an agent who was told to revoke certain licences could delegate to his solicitor the task of actually sending the notices of revocation.

(*iv*) where an unforeseen situation makes delegation necessary.

NOTE: Where delegation is allowed, the agent is liable to his principal for the sub-agent's acts.

(*d*) *Good faith.* An agent must not allow his own interests to conflict with those of his principal. This fiduciary duty applies whether or not the agent receives payment.

In particular, an agent must not disclose or misuse *confidential information* which he acquires in the course of his agency, nor must he make a *secret profit* over and above his agreed commission in any of his activities. If a secret profit is made and discovered, it may be claimed by the principal and the agent loses his right to commission.

EXAMPLE: In *Turnbull* v. *Garden* (1869), an agent was employed without payment to purchase clothes for his principal's son. He was allowed a trade discount on the transaction by the seller, but sought to charge his principal the full price. HELD: he had to account to his principal for the discount that he had received.

The duty of good faith is very strict.

EXAMPLE: In *Boardman* v. *Phipps* (1967), a solicitor while acting as agent, acquired information relating to the value of certain shares. Acting in good faith he used this information for his own benefit after the principal had declined to use it for his. HELD (H.L.): the agent was accountable to his principal for the profit made because the information that he had acquired and used for his own benefit belonged to his principal.

If an agent *takes a bribe*, the principal is entitled to the inducement, or to damages against either the agent or the third party. The principal may summarily dismiss the agent. Both parties to the bribe are liable to prosecution.

(*e*) *To account.* When required to do so, an agent must render to his principal an accurate and comprehensive account of his transactions. He must pay over to his principal all sums received on his behalf.

6. Rights of the agent.

(*a*) *Indemnity.* An agent is entitled to compensation from his principal for any loss or expense incurred by him in the performance of his agency: *Adamson* v. *Jarvis* (1827).

An agent loses this right where he acts negligently, in breach of his duty, or unlawfully.

(b) *Remuneration*. The principal must pay his agent the agreed commission provided:

(i) the event has happened upon which payment was made conditional;

(ii) the agent was the effective cause of that happening.

NOTE: No term will be *implied* into a contract of agency to restrain the principal from preventing his agent earning his commission, e.g. by deciding not to proceed with a sale or purchase: *Luxor (Eastbourne) Ltd.* v. *Cooper* (1941).

(c) *Lien*. An agent has a lien on his principal's goods in his possession for commission owed to him.

His lien is lost when payment is made or tendered by his principal, or where he relinquishes possession of the goods.

NOTE: Generally an agent's lien is a *particular* lien, i.e. it is limited to moneys owed on the transaction under which he has possession of the goods. Some agents, however, have a more extensive *general* lien arising from trade usage. This latter type of lien covers all moneys owed by the principal to the agent and is not limited to moneys owed on a particular transaction. Banks, factors and solicitors are entitled to general liens.

Relations with third parties

7. Introduction. Since an agent acts on behalf of his principal, he generally drops out of the transaction once he has made the contract. Privity of contract exists between his principal and the third party.

However, the exact legal position depends upon whether or not he disclosed his agency and/or the name of his principal.

8. The agent discloses his agency and his principal. The contract made is the principal's contract, and not that of the agent. Thus, the agent drops out immediately and generally incurs neither rights nor liabilities under the contract.

EXCEPTIONS: (1) Where the agent agrees to accept personal liability. (2) Where the agent signs a deed he is personally liable upon it. The principal incurs no liability unless the agent was himself appointed by deed. Where this is so, the agent drops out and the principal alone is liable. (3) Where the agent signs a bill of exchange in his own name without indicating that he is signing on behalf of his principal: Bills of Exchange Act 1882, s.26(1). It is insufficient for an agent to merely describe himself as such, he must clearly indicate that he signs on behalf of a specified person, e.g. by using the words "for and on behalf of X" or "per pro X": *see* 11:**33**. (4) Where trade custom makes the agent personally liable. (5) Where the agent is in fact the principal, e.g. where the contracting party describes himself as an agent but in truth makes the contract for himself: *Schmalz* v. *Avery* (1851); alternatively, there may be no other person who can be responsible as principal: *Kelner* v. *Baxter* (1866).

9. The agent discloses his agency but not his principal. Subject to the exceptions in **8** above, the agent drops out in the normal way and does not incur personal liability under the contract.

10. The agent does not disclose his agency. This is usually referred to as the *Doctrine of the Undisclosed Principal*. The agent appears to be acting on his own behalf when he enters into the contract. He discloses neither the identity nor the existence of his principal.

The third party may consequently enforce the contract against the agent. Alternatively, he may enforce it against the principal after discovering his existence and identity. He may not, however, enforce it against both; an unequivocal election must be made.

Commencing proceedings against one of them is only *prima facie* evidence of such an election, it is not conclusive: *Clarkson Booker* v. *Andjel* (1964). Obtaining judgment against either principal or agent even if it is unsatisfied is, however, conclusive evidence of an election and bars subsequent action against the other.

Unless the agent acted without authority (an undisclosed principal cannot ratify), or the principal's identity is a material factor in the contract, the principal can enforce the contract against the third party.

EXAMPLE: In *Said* v. *Butt* (1920), the principal wished to buy a "first-night" ticket for a play but the theatre's managing director, with whom he was on bad terms, would not sell him one. A friend therefore bought one for him but he was refused admission on the night. In the ensuing action, his claim against the theatre failed. His identity was important to the theatre and he could not, therefore, enforce a contract made indirectly on his behalf when he would not have been able to make the contract directly.

11. Breach of warranty of authority. By professing to act as an agent, a person warrants by implication that he has his principal's authority to act.

Should he lack the authority he professes, he is liable to the third party for any loss he causes him. However, his liability is *not* under the contract he made but for his breach of warranty of authority: *Collen* v. *Wright* (1856).

The agent is still liable if he exceeds his authority while acting in good faith, e.g. in ignorance that his authority has been terminated by the death or insanity of his principal or through the fraud of a third party.

EXAMPLE: In *Starkey* v. *Bank of England* (1903) (C.A.), a stockbroker, by virtue of a power of attorney forged by one of two joint holders of stock, but which the stockbroker believed to be genuine, instructed the Bank to transfer stock. This they did, and the proceeds of the sale were applied by the forger of the power of attorney to his own use. The Bank was obliged to transfer a like amount of stock to the true owner and its claim to be indemnified by the stockbroker was allowed on the grounds that the stockbroker had given an implied warranty that he had authority.

The agent does not incur liability if he exceeds his authority when acting in good faith following *ambiguous* instructions from his principal, or where the third party is *aware* that the agent is exceeding his authority.

NOTE: If the agent knows that he lacks authority to make the contract, the third party may bring an action against him for the *tort of deceit* for any loss he is caused.

12. Liability for an agent's torts. A principal is jointly and severally liable (*see* 3:7) with his agent for any fraud or other tort committed by the agent in the course of his agency, provided the act was within the scope of his authority.

This is so whether the agent acted for his principal's benefit or his own.

EXAMPLE: In *Lloyds* v. *Grace, Smith & Co*. (1912), S, the managing clerk of the defendant solicitors, fraudulently induced a client to sign deeds transferring title to certain properties to him. S then mortgaged the properties and absconded with the money obtained. HELD (H.L.): his principals were liable because S was acting within the scope of his authority, and it made no difference that he was intending to benefit himself and not his principals.

Termination of agency

13. By act of the parties. Agency can be terminated by:

(a) mutual agreement,
(b) revocation by the principal, or
(c) renunciation by the agent.

If unjustified, however, revocation of renunciation will amount to a breach of contract.

To avoid the possible operation of *estoppel*, the principal should notify any revocation to persons who have previously dealt with the agent.

In certain circumstances agency is *irrevocable*, e.g. where revocation would cause the agent personal loss.

A power of attorney cannot be revoked where it was granted to secure a proprietary interest held by the agent, or the performance of an obligation owed to him. (In bank security forms a mortgagor may give the bank irrevocable power of attorney to transfer title to the mortgaged property on his behalf, thereby enabling it to realise the security far more easily if repayment of the advance is not made.)

14. By operation of law. Agency is automatically terminated in the following circumstances:

(a) by completion of the contract;
(b) by frustration of the contract, e.g. where the contract subsequently becomes impossible to perform or illegal;
(c) by the death or mental disorder of the principal or agent;
(d) by the bankruptcy or liquidation of the principal;

NOTE: The bankruptcy of the agent does not terminate his agency nor give the principal the right to revoke his authority, unless his insolvency affects his fitness or ability to act as agent.

(e) at the end of a specified period of time, where the agency was created to last for that period.

Banking aspects of agency

15. Agency and banking. For two reasons *Agency* is a branch of commercial law which is particularly relevant to banking.

(a) A bank will often have to deal with people who are agents, e.g. directors of a company, partners in a firm and occasionally a person who has power of attorney.

Thus, it is important for a banker to ascertain and understand the scope and extent of an agent's authority before dealing with him.

(b) An important aspect of the banker-customer relationship is a banker's role as his customer's agent in collecting cheques paid in by his customer for the credit of his account. In addition, a bank may act as an agent in dealing with securities on his customer's behalf and in connection with the numerous other services that a bank can provide or arrange for its customer.

16. The operation of an account by an agent. Where an agent is to operate an account for his principal, or have authority to sign on it, a bank will normally insist upon a *written mandate* from its customer.

The agent is a *special agent* and the bank must ensure that he does not exceed his authority (*see* 2:2). For example, an authority for an agent to draw, accept and indorse cheques does not imply authority to draw, accept and indorse other forms of bills of exchange. Nor does it imply authority to negotiate new overdraft facilities or to give or withdraw security.

If there are two or more parties to the account, all must authorise the delegation. For example, where A and B operate a joint account, both must authorise C to sign cheques in place of B.

17. Borrowing by an agent. If an agent borrows money from a bank without authority, the debt cannot be enforced against his principal unless the principal (a) ratifies the loan, or (b) is estopped from denying the agent's lack of authority.

This is potentially of most importance in relation to borrowing by a director of a company which is *ultra vires* (beyond the powers of) the company. The company cannot ratify the contract (*see* 2:**3**), nor will the bank be able to rely on the Companies Act 1985, s.35. However, the company can ratify the borrowing where it is within its powers and merely *ultra vires* those of its director.

Should the company be unable to ratify the contract, or should it decline to do so, the bank has two important remedies which may enable it to recover the money lent.

(*a*) An action for breach of warranty of authority against the director concerned.

(*b*) Subrogation.

NOTE: This topic is discussed in depth in 4:**27**.

18. Agency and bills of exchange.

(*a*) *Agents signing bills.* An agent who signs a bill of exchange in his own name is personally liable on it unless he clearly indicates that he acts on behalf of another person: Bills of Exchange Act 1882, s.26(1) (*see* 11:**33**).

(*b*) *Agents collecting bills.* An agent must exercise care and skill when presenting a bill of exchange for acceptance and/or payment. The rules relating to notice of dishonour require similar care (*see* 11:**40–6**).

Cheques demand particular care in their collection and a bank should ensure that it follows accepted banking practice when doing so: *Foreman* v. *Bank of England* (1902).

Whenever an agent handles cheques for his principal, the possibility that he may be exceeding his authority arises. For example, he may, without authority, draw cheques on his principal's account payable to himself or he may indorse cheques payable to his principal and pay them into his own account. A bank must always ensure that it does not lose its statutory protection under the Cheques Act 1957, s.4, when collecting cheques for known agents (*see* 12:**19**).

Progress test 2

1. Define an agent. What is the essential feature of the principal-agent relationship? (**1**)

2. Distinguish between: (*a*) general and special agents, and (*b*) factors and brokers. (**2**)

3. List the requirements which must be satisfied for agency to arise by: (*a*) ratification, (*b*) estoppel and (*c*) necessity. (**3**)

4. List the duties and rights of an agent. (**5–6**)

5. In what circumstances can an agent appoint a sub-agent? (**5**)

6. In what circumstances will an agent incur liability when he discloses both his agency and his principal to the third party? (**8**)

7. Explain the position of a third party with whom an agent contracts on behalf of an undisclosed principal. (**10**)

8. List the situations in which the agency will be terminated by operation of law. (**14**)

9. Explain why agency is particularly relevant to banking. (**15**)

10. When is a principal bound by his agent's unauthorised borrowing? (**17**)

3
Partnership

The nature and formation of a partnership

1. Definition. "Partnership is the relation which subsists between persons carrying on a business in common with a view of profit." Partnership Act 1890, s.1.

A partnership is at law a very different form of business organisation from a registered company (*see* 4:**1**). A registered company has a separate legal identity, a partnership does not.

2. Possible tests for establishing a partnership. The Partnership Act 1890 does not lay down a specific test for establishing whether or not an organisation is a partnership. In particular, s.2 states that the following circumstances do not in themselves create a partnership between two or more persons.

(*a*) *Co-ownership of property.* This is so whether or not the co-owners share any profit derived from the use of the property.

Among other important legal distinctions between co-ownership and partnership, are that the latter is (*i*) always the *product of an agreement* while the former is not, e.g. co-ownership may arise under the terms of a will; and (*ii*) it involves *working for profit* which may not necessarily be the case with co-ownership of property.

(*b*) *Sharing of gross returns.* This is so even if it is coupled with co-ownership of the property producing the return.

(*c*) *Sharing of profits.* This is, however, *prima facie* evidence of a partnership, but it may be rebutted on the facts.

In particular, a person receiving a share of the profits is not a partner where the share is received:

    (*i*) in repayment of a debt;

    (*ii*) as payment by an employee or agent of the business;

    (*iii*) as an annuity by a widow or child of a deceased partner;

    (*iv*) as payment of interest (varying with profits) on money lent to the firm for business purposes;

    (*v*) as payment for the goodwill of the business.

NOTE: By the Partnership Act 1890, s.3, persons receiving payments under (*iv*) and (*v*) are deferred creditors in the event of the firm's bankruptcy.

Where two or more persons share both the profits and losses from the business, the evidence for the existence of a partnership is much stronger but still not conclusive. Ultimately, it is a question of fact in each case.

EXAMPLE: In *Keith Spicer Ltd*. v. *Mansell* (1970), the formation of a company was planned. In preparation for this, goods were ordered, a bank account opened and a number of other acts undertaken. One of the two persons involved was made bankrupt and the other was sued on an outstanding contract on the grounds that before incorporation the two persons involved were trading in partnership. HELD: (C.A.): the acts performed were not sufficient to establish a partnership, particularly as the objective was the formation of a company. Consequently, the solvent party was not liable for the bankrupt's business debts.

In practice a bank should rarely be involved in a dispute as to the existence of a partnership. Enquiries will always be made before an account is opened or transactions entered into if there is any possible doubt in the matter.

3. Formation of a partnership.

    (*a*) *By contract*. A partnership is the result of an express or implied agreement. While the 1890 Act does not require the contract to be in a specific form, written *Articles of Partnership* or a *Deed of Partnership* are often drawn up for they enable the members to lay down rules relating to the firm's management, the sharing of the profits and losses and other rights and duties amongst them: *see* **10** below. The 1890 Act applies to such matters in the absence of express provisions in the agreement.

(b) *Capacity*.

(i) *Minors*. A contract of partnership may be entered into by a minor but avoided by him before his majority (his eighteenth birthday) or within a reasonable time after attaining it.

A minor is never liable for the firm's debts incurred during his minority: Infants' Relief Act 1874. However, he becomes liable for debts incurred after his majority unless he repudiates the contract in time: *Goode* v. *Harrison* (1821).

(ii) *Limited companies*. It is possible for a limited company to become a member of a partnership but the liability of its shareholders for the firm's debts is limited to the value of their share in the company.

(iii) *Aliens*. The Treaty of Rome (to which the UK acceded by the European Communities Act 1972) prohibits discrimination on the grounds of nationality and gives an alien the right to establish or join a partnership on the same terms and conditions as a British subject.

(iv) *Mental patients*. While rather unlikely to be encountered in practice, a mental patient can become a partner in a firm but he can avoid the contract if he can show that he did not understand its nature and consequences of membership when he entered into it and that the other party was aware of this.

More significantly, on the mental disorder of a partner the court may order the firm's dissolution following an application by the "patient" or other partner: (*see* **14** below).

(c) *Maximum numbers*. The Companies Act 1985 limits the number of partners in a firm to a maximum of twenty but allows certain professional partnerships, e.g. solicitors, to exceed twenty members.

Before the Banking Act 1979, a banking partnership was limited to a maximum of ten members unless the Board of Trade's approval was obtained for a membership of up to twenty.

NOTE: The Sex Discrimination 1975, s.11, prohibits sexual discrimination in relation to potential membership of a firm which consists of six or more members.

(d) *The firm name*. The firm name is the partnership's "business name". While it confers no separate legal identity on the firm, it may sue and be sued in this name.

Under the Business Names Act 1985, s.4 the names of persons using a business name (a name other than their true names) must be legibly stated on all business letters, written orders, invoices and receipts and written demands for payment. These must give an address where any documents relating to the business can be served and accepted. In addition, a notice giving the names and addresses of the persons or partners using the business name must be displayed prominently in any place where business is carried on and to which customers have access.

(*e*) *Illegality*. An association is illegal if:

(*i*) its objects are illegal;

(*ii*) its membership exceeds the statutory maximum numbers (*see* above); or,

(*iii*) it is an association forbidden by law, e.g. a professional partnership between a solicitor and an unqualified person.

The effects of illegality are that (*a*) rights and obligations among the partners are unenforceable, (*b*) contracts cannot be enforced against innocent third parties, and (*c*) the partners cannot raise the illegality of their association as a defence in any action brought against them by an innocent outsider.

4. Types of partners.

(*a*) *A general partner*. A partner who takes an active part in the firm's management. He is fully liable for its debts.

(*b*) *A sleeping or dormant partner*. One who takes no part in the firm's management but who nevertheless contributes capital and shares profits and losses in the same way as a general partner.

(*c*) *A quasi or nominal partner*. A person who, although not actually a member of the firm, incurs liability for its debts because he has held himself out to be a partner. He is estopped (prevented) from denying his apparent membership to any person who relied on his representation and gave credit to the firm in consequence: Partnership Act 1890, s.14. Since he is not an actual partner, he does not take part in the firm's management nor share in its profits.

(*d*) *A limited partner*. A partner whose liability for the firm's debts is limited to the amount of his capital contribution. He shares in the firm's profits but he may not participate in its management. He is not an agent of the firm and his death, bankruptcy or mental disorder does not dissolve it.

The *limited partnership*, in which one or more limited partners will be found, is the creation of the Limited Partnership Act 1907. The essence of such a business organisation is that it must have at least one of each of two kinds of partner:

(*i*) a *limited* partner (*see* above);

(*ii*) a *general* partner, who manages the firm's activities and who has unlimited liability for the firm's debts.

In order for a limited partner not to be treated as a general partner, a limited partnership must be registered with the Registrar of Companies.

Limited partnerships are uncommon and of little practical importance. Corporate status as a private limited company is usually more attractive (*see* 4:**4**).

Relations between partners and outsiders

5. Partners as agents. Agency is the foundation of partnership law relating to a firm's dealings with outsiders. Each general partner has *actual authority* and *implied* or *usual authority* (authority as it appears to outsiders) to bind his fellow partners when acting in the usual course of the firm's business, unless the outsider either knew that the partner had no authority in the matter, or knew or believed that he was not a partner: Partnership Act 1890, s.5.

Thus, an outsider dealing with a general partner is not affected by any secret limitation on his authority. This is a basic principle of agency (*see* 2:**2**).

EXAMPLES: (1) In *Mercantile Credit Ltd*. v. *Garrod* (1962), A and B had entered into partnership to let garages and to repair motor cars. The partnership deed expressly excluded the buying and selling of cars. A, without B's knowledge, "sold" a car, to which he had no title, to the plaintiff. The proceeds were paid into the partnership bank account. HELD: B was accountable for the proceeds since the buying and selling of cars *appeared* to be within the firm's normal course of business. The limitation in the partnership deed was no defence. (2) In *Higgins* v. *Beauchamp* (1914), however, it was held that it was not within the usual course of a firm's business for a partner to accept a "bill of exchange" which lacked the drawer's name.

6. A partner's implied authority. A partner in any type of partnership has implied authority to bind the firm by:

(a) *buying and selling* goods in the course of the firm's business;

(b) *receiving payment* of debts due to the firm and *giving receipts* for such payment;

(c) *engaging* employees for the firm;

(d) *drawing* cheques.

In a *trading partnership* (one whose business consists mainly of buying and selling) a partner's implied authority also includes:

(a) *borrowing money* on the firm's credit;

(b) *pledging* the firm's goods or *giving an equitable mortgage* over the firm's premises by deposit of title deeds or land certificate to secure such borrowing;

(c) *signing of bills of exchange* on behalf of the firm.

NOTES: (1) No partner has implied authority to (i) execute deeds on behalf of the firm, (ii) give a guarantee in the firm's name, unless the firm gives guarantees in the ordinary course of its business, (iii) submit disputes involving the firm to arbitration, or (iv) accept property other than money in satisfaction for a debt owed to the firm. (2) A partner who exceeds his authority is personally liable to an outsider for any loss caused to him by the misrepresentation: *Collen* v. *Wright* (1856) (*see* 4:**10**). (3) In the absence of ratification (*see* 2:**3**(b)) by the other partners, the firm is not bound by a contract made by one partner which is clearly outside the firm's usual course of business.

7. The liability of the partners. The liability of the partners for the debts and other obligations of the firm is *joint*: Partnership Act 1890, s.9. The liability for wrongs (torts) authorised by the firm or committed in the ordinary course of the firm's business is *joint and several*: Partnership Act 1890, s.12.

Until the Civil Liability (Contribution) Act 1978 there existed an important difference in the consequences of the two different types of liability.

Before the 1978 Act, *joint* liability gave a creditor of the firm one right of action only and this he could exercise by suing one partner, a combination of the partners, or the firm jointly. Once judgment was obtained, however, he had no further right of action against any of the remaining partners: *Kendall* v. *Hamilton* (1879). This rule applied whether or not the judgment debt was satisfied.

Conversely, where liability is *joint and several*, judgment against one partner does not prevent subsequent actions being brought against other partners should the original judgment debt remain unsatisfied. Thus, the claim may be cumulatively satisfied.

The Civil Liability (Contribution) Act 1978, s.3, abolished the rule in *Kendall* v. *Hamilton* (1879). A creditor who obtains judgment against one or some parties is now able to bring subsequent actions against others if the original judgment debt remains unsatisfied.

NOTES: (1) The estate of a deceased or bankrupt partner has always been severally liable for partnership debts incurred prior to his death, subject to the prior payment of his separate debts: Partnership Act 1890, s.9. (2) The Rules of the Supreme Court largely avoided possible complications with joint liability by allowing an action to be brought against the partnership in its firm name. In this case, judgment operated against the firm and there-fore each partner individually. (3) As between the partners them-selves, whether liability was joint or joint and several, each was liable to contribute fairly to the damages paid.

To avoid possible complications with joint liability, it has always been standard banking practice to insist on joint and several liability being accepted by each partner in dealings between a bank and a partnership. Thus, the rule in *Kendall* v. *Hamilton* (1879) was always excluded.

8. Changes in membership.

(*a*) *Retirement.* A retiring partner continues to be liable for debts incurred by the firm before his retirement: Partnership Act 1890, s.17(2).

A retiring partner may be released from his existing liabilities by *novation*, an agreement to that effect between himself and the members of the firm as newly constituted, and the creditors. The agreement may be express or inferred from the course of dealings between the creditors and the firm as newly constituted: Partnership Act 1890, s.17(3).

In short, novation means that the liability of the new firm is substituted for that of the old, that of the old being discharged. (Novation is not uncommon where a new partner joins a firm on the retirement of an existing partner.)

A retiring partner is not liable for the firm's debts incurred after his retirement unless he has allowed creditors to believe that he is still a partner: Partnership Act 1890, s.36, for example, by knowingly allowing his name to continue to appear on the firm's stationery. This is an example of "holding out" under s.14 of that Act: *see* **4**(*c*) above.

To avoid such liability, a retiring partner must *publish* his retirement in the "London Gazette" and *give actual notice* of his retirement to previous clients of the firm.

NOTES: (1) In *Tower Cabinet Co.* v. *Ingram* (1949), where the firm's old notepaper bearing the name of the retiring partner was accidently used after his retirement, it was held that negligence or carelessness was insufficient to raise liability on the basis of "holding out". To incur such liability, a retiring partner must *knowingly* allow himself to be held out as still being a partner of the firm. (2) Under the principle in *Scarf* v. *Jardine* (1882), a creditor cannot take advantage of a "holding out" situation by taking action against the firm both as it is actually constituted and as he thought it was constituted. For example, if X retires from partnership with Y and is replaced by Z, a previous client who deals with the firm in ignorance of X's retirement may bring an action for debt against X and Y, or Y and Z. He cannot, however, take action against X, Y and Z.

(*b*) *Death or bankruptcy*. A deceased or bankrupt partner's estate is not liable for the firm's debts incurred *after* death or bankruptcy. The estate remains liable, however, for debts incurred *before* death or bankruptcy.

(*c*) *Incoming partners*. An incoming partner is not liable for debts incurred before he joined the firm: Partnership Act 1890, s.17(1). An agreement (novation) to the contrary can, however, be made (*see* above).

Relations between partners

9. Introduction. Where formal articles or a deed of partnership exist, these will usually govern the relations between the partners. Where such a formal arrangement does not exist, the Partnership Act 1890, ss. 19–31, applies. Section 24, in particular, provides a code of rights and duties amongst partners.

NOTE: Any of the arrangements may be varied subsequently by an express agreement or course of dealing among the partners.

10. Rights and duties.

(a) *Good faith*. The principle of *uberrima fides* is reflected in three specific duties owed by each partner.

(i) To render true accounts and full information on partnership matters to fellow partners: Partnership Act 1890, s.28.

(ii) To account for any benefit derived from the partnership business without the consent of the other partners, i.e. a "secret profit" must not be made (*see* 2:5): Partnership Act 1890, s.29.

EXAMPLE: In *Bentley* v. *Craven* (1853), one of two partners was responsible for buying goods for his firm. Without informing his fellow partner, he sold his own goods to the firm, thereby making a large profit for himself. HELD: he had to account to the firm for the profit that he had made.

(iii) To account for any profit made by competing with the firm without the consent of the other partners: Partnership Act 1890, s.30.

NOTE: In *Thompson's Trustee in Bankruptcy* v. *Heaton* (1974), it was HELD that the duty of good faith can survive the dissolution of the firm.

(b) *Membership*. All partners must consent to the admission of a new member.

A partner can only be *expelled* from a firm if power to do so is contained in the articles or deed of partnership. There is no implied power allowing one partner to be expelled by the others.

The *retirement* of partners is usually covered by express provisions in the articles or deed of partnership, e.g. as to notice and the continuation of the firm after a retirement.

(c) *Management.* Every *general partner* is entitled to take part in the management of the firm, although the right of "junior" partners to do so may be restricted by the partnership agreement.

Day-to-day decision making is by majority vote, but unanimity among the partners is required before any changes in the nature of the firm's business can take place.

Partnership books must be kept at the firm's principle place of business and every partner may inspect and copy them whenever he wishes.

(d) *Equal shares.* Under the 1890 Act, partners are entitled to share equally in the firm's capital and profits, and they must contribute equally to its losses.

(e) *Interest on advances.* No partner is entitled to interest on his capital before profits have been determined. A partner is entitled to interest at 5 per cent on money (other than his agreed capital contribution) advanced for the use of the firm.

(f) *Remuneration.* Unless, otherwise agreed, a partner is not entitled to any payment for his services to the firm's business. In a partnership with one or more sleeping partners, however, it is common to find that the partnership agreement entitles the active or managing partner(s) to a salary in addition to a share of the profits.

(g) *Indemnity.* A partner is entitled to an indemnity from the firm for expenditure and liability incurred by him (i) in the ordinary course of the firm's business, and (ii) in preserving the business or property of the firm.

11. Assignment of a partner's share. A partner's share in the firm's business is that proportion of the proceeds of the notional sale of its assets to which he would be entitled after the firm's debts have been paid.

A partner may *assign* his share to another person either absolutely (by sale or gift), or by mortgage. The assignee does *not* become a partner in the firm and, unless the other partners agree, has no right to take an active part in management or to inspect the books. He is entitled, however, to the assignor's share of the profits, and to his share of the assets in the event of the firm's dissolution.

The assignor remains liable for the firm's debts, although he can claim an indemnity from the assignee unless otherwise agreed.

NOTE: A bank may possibly accept an assignment of a partnership share as security for a loan to provide working capital. The bank would have to make its position as assignee as secure as possible by insisting that the other partners join in the agreement. In particular, the arrangement must prevent the remaining partners taking decisions which would reduce or prejudice the bank's share of the firm's profits, e.g. by a *bona fide* agreement between the partners to pay themselves salaries for their services to the firm: *Re Garwood's Trust, Garwood* v. *Paynter* (1903).

12. Partnership property. This includes:

(*a*) property brought into the partnership stock: Partnership Act 1890, s.20(1);

(*b*) property acquired for the firm in the course of the firm's business: s.20(1);

(*c*) property purchased with the firm's money, unless otherwise agreed: s.21.

It is important to distinguish between partnership property and property owned by an individual partner, but used in the firm's business, for the following reasons.

(*a*) The firm takes the benefit of any increase in the value of partnership property.

(*b*) Partnership property must be used exclusively for partnership business.

(*c*) On the firm's dissolution, partnership property must be sold and the proceeds applied in satisfaction of the firm's debts and liabilities: Partnership Act 1890, s.39.

(*d*) In the event of the firm's bankruptcy, the claims of the partner's separate creditors against the partnership property are postponed to the claims of the firm's joint creditors (*see* **19** below).

NOTE: Partnership land is treated among the partners as personal property and not as real property: Partnership Act 1890, s.22. It is usual to convey the land to the partners (or to four of them in a large firm) on *trust for sale*, thereby facilitating dealings in relation to it. Section 22 means that a partner's share of the partnership land is the specified portion of the proceeds which would be left after its notional sale, the firm's debts having been paid. It is not a specific piece of land or property.

Dissolution of a partnership

13. Introduction. In common with any other contract, a partnership agreement can be terminated by agreement between the parties to it. Similarly, contract law enables the agreement to be rescinded by the other partner(s) where one partner has been guilty of duress, fraud or misrepresentation.

14. Dissolution under the Partnership Act 1890.

The Act specifically provides that certain events will dissolve a partnership, and empowers the court to order dissolution in certain other cases:

(*a*) when the partnership was entered into for a fixed term, by the ending of that term: s.32;

(*b*) if entered into for a single venture, by the completion of that venture: s.32;

(*c*) where the partnership was entered into for an undefined time, or where a fixed term of partnership has expired and the business is continued without an express agreement (a partnership at will), by any partner giving notice to the others: s.32;

(*d*) unless otherwise agreed, by the death or bankruptcy of any partner: s.33(1) (dissolution operates from the date of death or the commencement of bankruptcy);

(*e*) at the option of the others, if a partner's share is charged by the court to secure payment of his judgment debts: s.33(2);

(*f*) where an event occurs which makes the firm's business unlawful: s.34.

15. Dissolution by court order. Following an application by a partner, s.95 of the Partnership Act 1890 gives the court power to dissolve a partnership on any of the following grounds.

(*a*) Where a partner has become mentally incapable of managing and administering his property and affairs (the Mental Health Act 1983 is now the relevant Act in this situation).

(*b*) Where any partner, other than the applicant, becomes permanently incapable of performing his duties within the firm.

(*c*) Where any partner, other than the applicant, is guilty of conduct prejudicial to the firm's business. (This may relate directly to the firm's business, e.g. a solicitor-partner misusing clients' money, or may indirectly affect the firm, e.g. conviction for a serious criminal offence: *Carmichael* v. *Evans* (1904). Each application must, however, be judged on its own facts.)

(*d*) Where any partner, other than the applicant, wilfully or persistently breaks the partnership agreement, or otherwise acts in a way which makes it impracticable for the other partners to continue in partnership with him, e.g. keeping erroneous accounts: *Cheeseman* v. *Price* (1865).

(*e*) Where the business can only be carried on at a loss.

(*f*) Where in the court's opinion, it is just and equitable that the firm should be dissolved, e.g. where there is personal deadlock between the partners.

NOTE: Where a formal partnership agreement was drawn up, it is usual for it to include specific terms governing the dissolution/ continuation of the firm, particularly on the death or retirement of a partner.

16. The effects of dissolution.

(*a*) The partnership agreement is terminated.

(*b*) The authority of the partners to bind the firm ceases, except for the purposes of winding up the business.

EXAMPLE: In *Re Bourne* (1906), one partner died and, in order to secure the firm's overdraft while winding up the partnership business, the surviving partner gave the firm's bank an equitable mortgage over the partnership land by deposit of the title deeds. HELD (C.A.): the personal representatives of the deceased partner were bound by the equitable mortgage.

NOTE: In no circumstances is the firm bound by the acts of a partner who has been made bankrupt.

(*c*) Each partner is entitled to have the partnership property, including the firm's goodwill, sold and the proceeds applied in payment of the firm's debts and liabilities and for any surplus to be used in payment of what may be due to the partners.

(*d*) Where the firm is dissolved through fraud or misrepresentation, the innocent partner(s) who rescinds the partnership agreement has the following rights:

(*i*) a lien on the firm's assets, after its liabilities have been discharged, for his share of the partnership;

(*ii*) to be subrogated to the firm's creditors that he has discharged (subrogation is taking the place and assuming the rights of a creditor against his debtor);

(*iii*) to be indemnified by the fraudulent partner against all the firm's liabilities.

NOTE: Dissolution generally takes effect from the date of the court order.

17. Settling accounts. By the Partnership Act 1890, s.44(b), the firm must settle its liabilities in the following order:

(*a*) repayment to outside creditors,

(*b*) repayment of loans to the firm made by the partners,

(*c*) repayment of each partner's capital contribution.

The ultimate residue, if any, is divided among the partners according to their respective rights to share in the firm's profits.

Should there be losses, including losses of capital, these must be met in the following order: Partnership Act 1890, s.44(a):

(*a*) from undrawn profits,

(*b*) from the firm's capital,

(*c*) by the partners individually in the proportions in which they were entitled to share profits.

EXAMPLE: X, Y and Z contributed capital of £5,000, £3,000 and £1,000 respectively, but shared profits and losses equally. Creditors are paid, resulting in a loss of capital of £6,000. This must be shared equally by the partners, and gives the following settlement.

	X	Y	Z	Total
Capital	£5,000	3,000	1,000	9,000
Loss of Capital	£2,000	2,000	2,000	6,000
Balance	£3,000	1,000	(–1,000)	3,000

X is left with £3,000 of his original £5,000 capital and Y with £1,000 of his original £3,000. Z, however, must contribute £1,000 to the dissolution.

Partnership and banking

18. The firm account.

(a) *Opening of the account.* Rarely, if ever, will a bank have to verify the existence of the firm, but it must ensure that the names of all partners are known.

Prior to 1981 the Register of Business Names could be searched to discover the composition of a partnership. Now a banker can rely on the requirements of the Business Names Act 1985 (*see* 3 above) unless there are circumstances which a reasonable banker would consider to warrant further investigation.

NOTE: Making such enquiries can be important where a collecting banker seeks to rely on his statutory protection under the Cheques Act 1957, s.4: *Smith and Baldwin* v. *Barclays Bank Ltd.* (1944) (*see* 12:**19**).

References must be taken to ensure the firm's suitability as a customer. References may be waived where one or more of the partners is already known to the bank.

The account must be opened in the names of *all* the partners. One partner has no implied authority to open an account for the firm in his name only and, if he is allowed to do so, the firm is not bound by his action and not liable, therefore, for any overdraft: *Alliance Bank* v. *Kearsley* (1871). Express authority to open such an account is needed from the other partners.

NOTE: By opening an account in the firm name, the bank is able to take action against all partners, both known and unknown, should it need to (*see* 7 above).

The formal *articles or deed of partnership* may not be inspected by the bank because the bank is taken to know their contents if it does so and would have to operate the account and conduct any other business with the firm in strict accordance with them. Without an inspection, the bank may be able to rely on a partner's implied authority to bind the firm if he ever exceeded his actual authority (*see* 5–6 above).

NOTE: In contrast a bank will *always* inspect the Memorandum and Articles of Association of a company when opening an account for the company (*see* 4:**23**).

The bank's *mandate* form, showing how and by whom the account is to be operated, must be signed by all the partners.

Despite the Civil Liability (Contribution) Act 1978, the partners will still specifically assume *joint and several* liability in the mandate, thereby excluding s.9 of the Partnership Act 1890 (*see* **7** above). Joint and several liability is necessary for four reasons:

(*i*) a credit balance on a partner's private account may be set-off against a debit balance on the firm account;

(*ii*) the bank will rank equally with his separate creditors should a partner die or become bankrupt;

(*iii*) should the partnership itself become bankrupt, the bank has a double right of proof, i.e. it may prove against both the joint estate of the firm and the separate estate of each partner (*see* **19** below).

(*iv*) Security deposited by a partner for all personal liabilities may be appropriated by the bank against either his personal debt or the partnership debt (*see* **19** below).

(*b*) *Operating the account.* While the mandate must be signed by all partners, it may be cancelled by any one partner. Similarly, any one partner may countermand ("stop") payment of a cheque, irrespective of whether or not he himself signed it.

A banker would be put on enquiry when a partner pays into his personal account cheques payable to the partnership indorsed by that partner in his own favour, or where cheques are drawn by the partnership payable to third parties and indorsed to the partner. (Payment and collection of cheques is considered generally in 12:**10–21**.)

NOTE: In *Central Motors (Birmingham) Ltd.* v. *P.A. and S.N. Wadsworth* (1982), one of two brothers in partnership signed a cheque as payment for a car in his name only and without his brother's authority; the mandate requiring both signatures on the cheque. The cheque had the names of the brothers printed on it and below these the firm's name. The cheque was dishonoured and an action was brought against both brothers. The second brother claimed he was not liable on the cheque since he had not signed it. HELD (C.A.): He was liable. Under the Bills of Exhange Act 1882, s.23(2), the signature of the name of the firm is equivalent to the signature by the person so signing of the names of all persons liable as partners in that firm. The word "signature" was not limited to the manuscript writing of a name and a printed name accompanied by the manuscript signature of one of the persons authorised to sign on the account was sufficient to render the firm, and therefore both the partners, liable on the cheque.

(*c*) *Borrowing.* A partner in a trading partnership has implied authority to borrow money for use in the firm's business, and to give security to cover such borrowing. However, the mandate usually contains the partners' express undertaking to be liable for any overdraft.

Express power must be given to a partner in a non-trading partnership to borrow money or to give securities on behalf of the firm (*see* **6** above).

NOTE: (1) A partner who is a minor is not liable for the firm's borrowing. (2) Rather than rely on implied authority, it is usual for a bank to insist on the partners executing the necessary documents where the firm's property is pledged or mortgaged as security for an advance.

(*d*) *Events affecting the account.*

(i) *Retirement.* If a partner retires and the firm continues in business, new mandate forms must be signed by the remaining partners and any incoming partner. New security forms must also be completed unless those held remain effective despite changes in the constitution of the firm.

If the firm's account is in *credit*, it may be continued unbroken, although cheques drawn by the retiring partner should be confirmed by the remaining partners.

A retiring partner remains liable for the firm's debts as at the date of his retirement (Partnership Act 1890, s.17(2)), but the firm's account must be broken and future entries passed through a new account, in order to preserve his liability and to establish the bank's right over any security deposited by him to secure the account.

This procedure results from the Rule in *Clayton's Case* (1816)—a decision of great importance to bankers. The Rule states that in a current account payments-in are appropriated to the debit items in chronological order, unless the customer or bank has taken steps to appropriate particular credits against particular debits.

EXAMPLE: X, Y and Z were in partnership. At the date of X's retirement the firm's overdraft was £5,000, for which he was, of course, liable. If the account had been continued unbroken and credits of £5,000 had been paid in and payments of £5,000 had been made, the debit balance for which X was liable would have been completely extinguished, through the operation of the Rule in *Clayton's Case* (1816), although the overdraft itself would have remained at £5,000. However, only Y and Z would now be liable on it.

The doctrine of *holding-out* would apply to a partner who retires without informing the firm's bank (*see* **8** above).

(*ii*) *Death.* If a firm is dissolved on a partner's death, the surviving partner(s) may continue the account in order to wind up the firm's business. For this purpose a mortgage may be granted to the firm's bank in order to secure the firm's overdraft: *Re Bourne* (1906) (*see* **16** above).

If the firm continues in business, new mandate forms must be signed. The completion of new security forms may also be necessary.

Should the firm's account be overdrawn, it must be broken and a new account opened in order to preserve the liability of the deceased partner for the overdrawn balance as at the date of his death: *Clayton's Case* (1816).

Cheques previously drawn by the deceased partner and presented after his death should be confirmed by the survivors.

(*iii*) *Mental disorder.* Cheques previously drawn by a partner who becomes mentally disordered should be confirmed by the others.

An overdrawn account must be broken to preserve his liability for the overdraft: *Clayton's Case* (1816).

New mandate forms are necessary and new security forms may also have to be completed.

(*iv*) *Bankruptcy of a partner.* If the firm is continued, new mandate forms must be signed and new security forms may have to be completed.

Confirmation of cheques drawn by the partner before his bankruptcy *should* be sought, confirmation of cheques drawn by him afterwards *must* be sought, since his bankruptcy terminates his authority as an agent of the firm.

Should the bank wish to enter a proof against his estate, the firm's account must be broken to avoid the Rule in *Clayton's Case* (1816) operating to the bank's detriment.

(*v*) *Bankruptcy of the firm.* This involves the bankruptcy of all the partners and not merely of individuals within the firm.

A bankruptcy order against the firm operates against each partner named in the order. Alterntively, an order can be made against each partner individually.

Whether in credit or overdrawn, the firm's account and the accounts of each partner must be stopped immediately. Any credit balances must be held available for the trustee in bankruptcy.

NOTE: The protection afforded by the Insolvency Act 1985, s.131(4), only applies to transactions entered into before the date of the bankruptcy order and without knowledge that a petition has been presented against the debtor. This is discussed fully in 5:**4**.

19. Distribution of assets on a firm's bankruptcy. The bankruptcy process is designed to ensure that the debtor's available assets are distributed fairly among his creditors.

(*a*) *General rights of proof.* At the time of writing, the Bankruptcy Act 1914 was still in force. Section 33(6) of the 1914 Act contains the general rights of proof until it is replaced by statutory instrument under the Insolvency Act 1985, s.227. It is understood, however, that there will be no change in the present rules, *viz*:

(*i*) the *joint estate* of the firm is used first to pay joint (the firm's) creditors;

(*ii*) the *separate estate* of each partner is used first to pay each partner's separate creditors;

(*iii*) a *surplus on any separate estate* is dealt with as joint estate;

(*iv*) any *surplus on the joint estate* is divided among the separate estates of the partners in proportion to the right and interest of each partner in the partnership estate.

NOTE: Since a partnership has no legal existence distinct from its members, no segregation of the joint and separate creditors on dissolution is necessary where the partners are *solvent*: all will be paid.

(*b*) *Exceptional rights of proof.* It follows from the general rule laid down in s.33(6) that the private creditors and the partnership creditors cannot prove in competition with each other, the private creditors cannot prove against the firm's estate and firm's creditors against each partner's separate estate. To this there are the following exceptions.

(*i*) Joint creditors may prove against the separate estates in competition with the separate creditors where there is *no joint estate*.

(*ii*) A joint creditor who submits a petition in the *separate bankruptcy* of one of the partners is allowed to prove for his joint debt in competition with the separate creditors.

(*iii*) A creditor may prove against both the joint and separate estates where he can establish *joint and several liability*. This could arise:

(1) under the terms of a bank mandate (*see* **18** above);

(2) where one or more partners defrauded the creditor (he must, however, elect to prove against the firm or the partners concerned);

(3) where the creditor has separate rights of action against the firm and one or more partners individually, e.g. where a bill of exchange accepted by the firm was indorsed in a personal capacity by one or more of its members: *ex parte Honey, Re Jeffery* (1871).

(*c*) *Proof by partners in competition with creditors.* A partner *may not* prove against the joint estate of his firm or the separate estates of his fellow partners until the firm's creditors have been paid in full.

To this rule there are certain exceptions:

(*i*) where he has *personally* paid the firm's creditors;

(*ii*) where the separate estate concerned is *insufficient* to pay the separate creditors (no surplus would be available to augment the joint estate).

A partner *may* prove against the joint estate of the firm and/or the separate estates of the partners where:

(*i*) debts have arisen in the *ordinary course of business* between the firm and the partner's own separate business (a similar rule applies where the position is reversed);

(*ii*) where a partner's separate property has been *fraudulently converted* to the firm's use, or the firm's property fraudulently converted to the separate use of a partner without the consent of the partners not involved.

(*d*) *The bank as a secured creditor.* A bank may take a charge over a partner's separate property as security when it makes a loan to the firm (or over the partnership property to secure a loan to an individual partner). Should the firm be made bankrupt, the security is *collateral* security since it need not be given up when a proof is entered against the joint estate. This is because the release of the charge over the separate property would not augment the joint estate.

Thus, a bank can enter a proof against the joint estate for the full amount owed and make up any deficiency from the security deposited.

Progress test 3

1. Define a partnership. (**1**)

2. What is the principle legal distinction between a partnership and a registered company? (**1**)

3. What is the maximum number of possible members in a banking partnership? (**3**)

4. What information about the firm must be disclosed under the Business Names Act 1985? (**3**)

5. Explain the terms: (*a*) "quasi or nominal partner", (*b*) "limited partner". (**4**)

6. What is meant by a partner's implied authority? (**5–6**)

7. Explain the nature of a partner's liability for the debts and other obligations of the firm, and the effect of the Civil Liability (Contribution) Act 1978 upon that liability. (**7**)

8. What is meant by novation? (**8**)

9. Why is the assignee of a partner's share in a potentially vulnerable position? (**11**)

10. What is partnership property? (**12**)

11. Explain briefly the circumstances in which a partnership may be dissolved. What is the effect of dissolution? (**14–16**)

12. On the dissolution of a partnership how, in the absence of a contrary agreement, should the accounts be settled? (**17**)

13. Why should a bank always open an account for a partnership in its firm name? (**18**)

14. Why is joint and several liability specifically assumed by the partners in a bank mandate form? (**18**)

15. State and explain the importance of the Rule in *Clayton's Case* (1816). (**18**)

16. Why must cheques drawn by a partner after the commencement of his bankruptcy be confirmed by the other partners? (**18**)

17. State the general rights of proof on the bankruptcy of a firm. (**19**)

18. In what circumstances will a creditor be able to prove against both joint and separate estates? (**19**)

19. In what circumstances may a partner prove in competition with the firm's creditors? (**19**)

20. Why is a charge over a partner's separate property, which was taken as security for a loan to the firm, collateral security? (**19**)

4
Companies

The nature of a company

1. Definition. A company may be defined as an organisation of individuals who contribute finance to a common stock which is to be used for business activities and who share the profit or loss arising. The common stock is the company's *financial capital*, and the contributories of it are its members, the *shareholders*.

A company is a *corporation*, i.e. an artificial legal person recognised by the law as having an existence, rights and duties quite separate and distinct from the individuals who are its members.

EXAMPLE: In the leading case of *Salomon* v. *Salomon & Co.* (1897), Salomon had incorporated his business as a limited company in which he held 20,000 shares, his wife and five children one share each. Salomon made a loan to his company which it secured by a charge (*see* **36** below) on its assets. The company went into liquidation with debts exceeding its assets. HELD (H.L.): Salomon and his company had quite separate legal identities and, as the only secured creditor, Salomon was entitled to the available assets in preference to the company's unsecured trade creditors.

2. Methods of incorporation.

(*a*) *By Royal Charter.* Chartered corporations are sometimes referred to as *common law* corporations. A few very old companies were incorporated in this way, e.g. the Hudson Bay Co., but today this method is not used for trading companies.

(*b*) *By Act of Parliament.* Public utility companies and the controlling corporations of some nationalised industries were formed by special Acts of Parliament. Trading companies are not formed by this method.

(*c*) *By registration under the Companies Act 1985*. Such companies are incorporated by registering certain documents with the Registrar of Companies in accordance with the Companies Act 1985 (*see* **5–10** below). The vast majority of trading companies are incorporated in this way.

NOTE: The corporate status of a company is fundamental to both the law and practice of its operation. It is also the essential legal distinction between the company and the partnership: *see* **4** below.

3. Classifying registered companies. Two main classifications are possible: (*a*) according to the limit, if any, of the shareholders' liability to contribute towards payment of the company's debts; (*b*) according to whether the company is a public company or a private company.

(*a*) *Companies limited by shares, by guarantee and unlimited companies.*

(*i*) *Limited by shares*. The liability of the company's members to contribute towards payment of its debts is limited to their investment in the company, i.e. to the value of their shareholding. Most registered companies are limited by shares.

(*ii*) *Limited by guarantee*. The liability of its members is limited to the amount that they have undertaken to contribute should the company be wound up through insolvency.

Registered companies limited by guarantee are usually non-profit making organisations, e.g. the Business and Technician Education Council.

(*iii*) *Unlimited companies*. In the event of its insolvency there is no limit on the liability of the members of an unlimited company to contribute towards the payment of its debts. Thus, their private property can be seized in order to pay the company's creditors.

Unlimited companies tend to provide services rather than trade; alternatively they are often involved in non-profit making activities.

There has been an increase in the number of unlimited companies since the Companies Act 1967 exempted them from the duty to file annual accounts with the Registrar of Companies. (The advantage of financial secrecy must be weighed against the disadvantage of unlimited liability.)

Such a company can only be a private company: Companies Act 1985, s. 1.

(*b*) *Public and private companies.*

(*i*) *Public.* A public company is a company limited by shares or guarantee, having a share capital, with a memorandum which states that it is to be a public company and which has been registered or re-registered as a public company under the Companies Act 1985, s. 1 or previous Acts. It has two or more members and can invite the general public to subscribe for its shares or debentures. It must have a minimum authorised and allotted share capital of (at present) £50,000. (No new company limited by guarantee can have a share capital and therefore must be a private company: Companies Act 1985, s. 1.)

(*ii*) *Private.* A private company is any company which does not satisfy the requirements for a public company. In common with a public company, it has two or more members.

(*iii*) *Distinctions.* The main distinctions between a public and a private company are as follows.

(1) A public company can offer its shares or debentures to the public, a private company cannot. It is a criminal offence to invite the general public to subscribe for shares or debentures in a private company.

(2) A public company must have at least two directors. A private company need have only one but a sole director cannot also be the secretary.

(3) A public company requires a "business certificate" (*see* **5** below) before it can commence business.

NOTE: Restrictions on share transfers and the size of membership no longer constitute an essential part of private company status but a private company can retain such restrictions in its articles if it wishes.

4. Registered companies and partnerships compared.

(*a*) *Formation.* A partnership is formed by an express or implied agreement between its members. A registered company is formed by registration in accordance with the Companies Acts (*see* **5–10** below).

NOTE: Limited partnerships also require registration with the Registrar of Companies.

(*b*) *Legal status*. A company is a *corporation* and possesses a separate legal identity from its members: *Salomon* v. *Salomon & Co.* (1897) (*see* **1** above). A partnership has no separate legal personality; at law it is merely a collection of individuals who find it an advantage to combine together to pursue their business ventures.

It follows that company property belongs to the company and not to its members as individuals, while partnership property is owned jointly by the partners (*see* **3:12**).

(*c*) *Succession*. It follows from its corporate status that a company has perpetual legal existence until wound up under the Companies Act 1985; a partnership has not.

(*d*) *Membership*. Both public and private companies must have at least two members but there is no upper limit. Private companies, however, will often limit their membership. A partnership must also have at least two members but, with certain exceptions, it must not exceed twenty (*see* **3:3**).

(*e*) *Transfer of shares*. Shares in a public company are freely transferable, but restriction on transfers are often imposed in a private company. A partner, however, may assign his share in the firm but may not transfer it without his fellow partners' consent (*see* **3:11**).

(*f*) *Powers*. A registered company's powers are fixed by its *memorandum of association*; these cannot be exceeded. Its *articles of association* govern its internal affairs (*see* **7–8** below). The members of a partnership decide both its commercial objects and the internal organisation of the firm.

While statutory formalities and procedures apply to any alteration of a company's memorandum or articles (*see* **7–8** below), the objects and internal organisation of a partnership, even if contained in a deed or articles of partnership, can be altered by simple agreement among the partners.

(*g*) *Publicity of affairs*. A company's *memorandum of association* and *articles of association* are public documents which, along with the various company registers, are open to public inspection. In contrast, partnership affairs are private and the contents of any deed or articles of partnership may only be known to its members.

(*h*) *Agency.* Every general partner is his firm's agent with power to bind the firm by contracts he makes in the usual course of its business (*see* 3:**6–7**). The members of a company—its shareholders—are not its agents unless expressly appointed as such, e.g. its directors.

(*i*) *Management.* Every general partner can take part in the management of his firm unless the partnership agreement states otherwise. A shareholder can take no part in company management unless he is also a director.

(*j*) *Liability.* Except in a limited partnership, there is *no limit* on a partner's liability for his firm's debts and wrongs, and he may be sued personally for the moneys owing. In the case of a limited liability company, legal action can only be taken against the company and the liability of the members to contribute to payment of its debts is *limited* to the amount of their investment or guarantees.

(*k*) *Raising loan capital.* Only a registered company can create a *floating charge* over its assets to secure a loan made to it (*see* **36** below). A partnership can only offer to mortgage partnership property or the separate property of the partners as security for a loan.

The formation of a registered company

5. Incorporation. A registered company is formed by its promoters obtaining the necessary minimum number of members, registering certain documents with the Registrar of Companies and paying certain fees and stamp duties. When satisfied that the statutory requirements have been met, the Registrar issues a *Certificate of Incorporation.* This brings the company into existence as a separate legal person (*see* **1** above).

NOTE: A private company may commence business as soon as the Certificate of Incorporation is granted. A public company, however, may not do business or exercise any borrowing powers until the registrar has issued it with a certificate ("business certificate") under the Companies Act 1985, s.117 that it has complied with the requirements as to share capital. Alternatively, the company must re-register as a private company.

6. Documents to be filed.

(*a*) Memorandum of association (*see* **7** below).

(*b*) Articles of association (*see* **8** below).

(*c*) A statement of the names of the intended first director(s) and the first secretary, together with their written consents to act as such. The statement must also contain the intended address of the company's registered office.

(*d*) A statutory declaration of compliance with the Companies Act 1985 regarding registration.

(*e*) A statement of the company's capital, unless it is to have no share capital.

Of these documents, the memorandum of association and the articles of association are the most important.

7. Memorandum of association.

This governs the external activities of a company. A registered company can only act within the objects and powers contained in its memorandum—the *ultra vires* rule (*see* below).

The memorandum is a public document and it can be inspected by any individual or organisation intending to deal with the company.

The memorandum must be signed by the first members (subscribers) of the company. The memorandum must contain the following things:

(*a*) *Name.* If a private limited company, the name must end with the word "limited" (or ltd.); if a public limited company, the words "public limited company" (or p.l.c.), or the Welsh equivalent for a company with its registered office in Wales, must be used.

General restrictions exist preventing a name being registered which suggests, for example, a royal connection, or which might tend to mislead the public, for example, a name which closely resembles that of an existing company.

A company may change its name by special resolution with the written approval of the Department of Trade and Industry.

NOTE: The provisions of the Business Names Act 1985 regarding the use of business names apply to any business organisations. Thus, a company trading under a name other than its registered name must comply with the disclosure and display requirements of the 1985 Act (*see* 3:**3**).

(*b*) *Registered office.* The memorandum does not state the actual address, only whether it is to be situated in England, Scotland or Wales. The actual address must, however, be filed with the Registrar on application for registration.

By the Companies Act 1985, s.351 all business letters and order forms of a registered company must state its registered number and place of registration.

(*c*) *Objects clause.* The memorandum of association must clearly state the purposes for which the company was formed. It is usual to list a comprehensive range of objects which the company may need to pursue in the course of its activities, stipulating that each is a separate main object which can be pursued independently of the others. Widely drafted objects clauses lessen the constraining effect of the *ultra vires* rule.

(*i*) *The Ultra Vires Rule.* This provides that any transaction entered into by a company incorporated and registered under the Companies Acts which is not authorised by its objects clause, or which is not reasonably incidental to its objects, is *ultra vires* (beyond the powers of) the company and void. Furthermore, an *ultra vires* act cannot be ratified by the members of the company: *Ashbury Railway Carriage & Iron Co.* v. *Riche* (1875): *see* 2:**3**.

The rule was originally developed to protect shareholders and persons dealing with the company. However, widely drafted objects clauses and the increased ease with which they can be changed (*see* below) lessened the protection of the former, while unwary third parties were sometimes caused loss through its workings, e.g. *Introductions Ltd.* v. *National Provincial Bank Ltd.* (1970) (*see* below).

The rule was eventually modified by the European Communities Act 1972, s.9(1)—now the Companies Act 1985, s.35. This provides that a person dealing with a company can enforce an *ultra vires* contract against it *provided* (*a*) he dealt in good faith and (*b*) that the transaction was decided on by the directors. (This probably means approved by the board of directors.)

Under s.35 the third party may assume that the powers of the directors to bind the company are free of any limitation under the memorandum of association or articles of association; he need not inquire as to the capacity of the company to enter into the transaction or as to any such limitation on the powers of the directors. Furthermore, he is presumed to have acted in good faith unless the contrary is proved.

NOTE: (1) Section 35 does not protect a person dealing with the company who has actual knowledge of its objects and in *International Sales and Agencies Ltd. and Another* v. *Marcus and Another* (1982), it was held that a person would not be acting in good faith where in all the circumstances of the case he could not reasonably have been unaware of the *ultra vires* nature of the transaction. Since a bank will receive or inspect a copy of the memorandum and articles before opening an account for a company, it is highly unlikely that a bank could ever rely on s.35. (2) The position of the company remains unaltered, e.g. it cannot enforce an *ultra vires* contract against the third party and a shareholder can seek an injunction to restrain the company from *ultra vires* actions.

(*ii*) *Powers*. In addition to the objects of the company, the memorandum will normally list a number of powers which are reasonably incidental to its objects. Such powers would be implied if they were not listed, e.g. the power to acquire similar businesses and the power to issue bills of exchange.

The power to borrow money for the purposes of the business is implied in the case of a trading company but it must be expressly given to a non-trading company. Borrowing money is *not* an independent activity, even if the memorandum states that it is an independent object of the company. Thus, a company's borrowing must only be for purposes consistent with its objects clause.

EXAMPLE: In *Introductions Ltd.* v. *National Provincial Bank Ltd.* (1970), the company's main object was to provide entertainment and services for overseas visitors but the objects clause also gave the company power to raise money as it saw fit. It provided that each of its objects was an independent object. The company changed to the sole activity of pig-breeding and the bank, who had been given a copy of the memorandum of association, lent money to the company for this purpose and took debentures as security. On the company's liquidation both the loan and the debentures were held by the Court of Appeal to be void. (N.B. On similar facts the Companies Act 1985, s.35, would now probably protect, for example, the company's suppliers but almost certainly not the bank.)

(*iii*) *Alteration of the objects.* A company may alter its objects by special resolution for one of *seven* purposes specified in the Companies Act 1985, s.4. For example, to increase economy and efficiency, to enlarge the area of its operations, or to include a convenient side-line business. However, this list is largely nullified by s.5 which provides that an alteration cannot be challenged on the grounds that it is outside s.4 more than twenty-one days after the date of the resolution.

If 15 per cent by value of the shareholders object to any alteration within twenty-one days of the resolution on the grounds that it is unfair or inequitable, the alteration requires the court's confirmation. This procedure is designed to protect "minority shareholders".

NOTE: The objects clause *cannot* be altered retrospectively.

(*d*) *Limitation of liability.* The memorandum of association must state that the liability of the members is limited.

(*e*) *The share capital.* The memorandum of association must state the amount of the company's authorised capital and its division into shares of a fixed amount. (A company's share capital is discussed in **15–21** below.)

8. Articles of association. These regulate the internal administration of the company, the relationship between the company and its members, and the relationship between the members themselves. They also govern the issue and transfer of shares, the rights of shareholders, the conduct of meetings, the appointment and powers of directors, and accounts. Many companies adopt the model set of articles, modified to their requirements, contained in Table A as prescribed by regulations made by the Secretary of State under the Companies Act 1985, s.8.

The articles must be printed and signed by each subscriber to the memorandum of association in the presence of a witness.

The articles can be altered by special resolution at a general meeting. Any alteration must, however:

(*a*) be consistent with the memorandum of association,

(*b*) not amount to a fraud on a minority of members, and

(c) not increase the liability of a member to the company in any way without his written consent.

NOTE: The articles of association *can* be altered retrospectively.

9. Filing the documents. The memorandum of association and articles of association are filed with the Registrar of Companies and are available for inspection on payment of a small fee.

At one time, constructive notice of the contents of the documents was presumed and a person wishing to deal with the company had to ensure that a proposed transaction was *intra vires* the company. The Rule in *Turquand's Case* (1856) afforded protection where he had done this but there had been administrative or procedural irregularities within the company affecting the transaction. The Companies Act 1985 s.35 however, now protects a third party who enters into an *ultra vires* transaction in good faith provided that the transaction was decided upon by the directors (*see* **27** below).

10. Preliminary contracts. Should a person purport to make a contract on behalf of a company as its agent before its incorporation, the contract will not bind the company when it is formed and the agent will, subject to any agreement to the contrary, incur personal liability on it: Companies Act 1985, s.36: *Phonogram Ltd*. v. *Lane* (1981). After incorporation, however, the company and the third party can make a new contract adopting the terms of the pre-incorporation contract.

NOTE: Contracts entered into by a public company after incorporation but before it is entitled to commence business are provisional only: *see* **5** above.

The operation of a company

11. Directors. A company acts through its directors; they are both its executive controllers and its principal agents.

As agents they are subject to the general rules of agency (*see* II), e.g. they must not make a secret profit in any transaction they enter into on their company's behalf, and they incur personal liability when they exceed their authority unless the company ratifies their action.

In addition, directors are regarded as *quasi-trustees* of their company's money and property, and of the powers given to them, e.g. the power to approve transfers of shares. As such, they owe *fiduciary duties* to the company and they must exercise their powers in good faith and for the benefit of the company.

The first directors are often named in the articles of association. One is normally appointed managing director under the articles with powers exercisable without reference to the board of directors. The board can usually vary his powers, or delegate additional powers to him.

12. The secretary. Every company must have a secretary. A director may also be the secretary except where he is the sole director, i.e. of a private company. One company can be the secretary of another.

Today, a company secretary is the chief administrative officer of his organisation and he has extensive duties and responsibilities. He can no longer be regarded, as he was in the nineteenth century, as a mere servant of the company. Consequently, he has been held to have the authority to enter into contracts within the administrative side of the day-to-day running of the company's business.

EXAMPLE: In *Panorama Developments (Guildford) Ltd.* v. *Fidelis Furnishing Fabrics Ltd.* (1971), the defendant company was held liable to pay outstanding hire charges on cars which its secretary had hired, ostensibly on the company's business, but which he had fraudulently used for his own purposes.

In practice the secretary's importance varies with the size of his company and the functions entrusted to him.

13. Quorums. A quorum is the number of directors which must be present at a board meeting to make the proceedings valid. The quorum is usually fixed by the articles of association but it is also usual for the articles to provide that the directors present may act where the quorum is not reached.

The board quorum will particularly concern a banker when he lends money to and takes security from a company. It is normal practice for him to require a certified copy of the board resolution authorising the transaction and, if the quorum is fixed by the articles, he could not rely on any security created at a meeting which was clearly inquorate. He would be deemed to have had notice of the non-compliance with the articles and the company's other directors or its liquidator, should the company go into liquidation, could repudiate the security at a later date.

If, however, the articles allow the directors to fix the quorum, he could probably rely on the Rule in *Turquand's Case* (1856), if the meeting subsequently proves to have been inquorate or otherwise irregularly held, provided he received a duly certified copy of the resolution (*see* 27 below).

Particular care must be exercised where one or more directors has a personal interest in the resolution being passed. Under the Companies Act 1985, s.317 a director who is in any way directly or indirectly interested in a proposed transaction of the company owes a duty to disclose the fact. If the articles of association allow an interested director to vote, the certified copy of the board's resolution need only record the disclosure of the interest. Where this is not so, the resolution must be passed by a quorum of independent directors or by a general meeting of the company if this in turn is not possible.

The possibility of directors with personal interest in a transaction is especially important to a banker when a company gives security, since the effect of the transaction could be to relieve one or more of the directors from existing personal liabilities. In such a situation, a banker's knowledge of the circumstances would probably be sufficient to prevent him from relying on the Rule in *Turquand's Case* (1856), and he must ensure that the relevant resolution is passed by a quorum of independent directors.

EXAMPLE: In *Victors Ltd*. v. *Lingard* (1927), an overdrawn account of the company was secured by the personal guarantees of all its directors. At a later date the directors passed a resolution authorising the issue of debentures to the bank to replace their personal guarantees, even though the articles of the company prohibited a director from voting on a matter in which he had a personal interest. The bank had notice of the articles. Although on the facts the company was estopped from denying the validity of the debentures, the resolution of the directors was held to be a nullity and the bank had sufficient knowledge of the circumstances to prevent it from relying upon the Rule in *Turquand's Case* (1856). The bank had argued, nevertheless, that when it received the debentures under the company's seal it was entitled to assume that the seal had been properly affixed.

14. Making loans and giving guarantees. A company's memorandum of association may give it power to make loans and to give guarantees. However, the Companies Act 1985, s.330(2) prohibits, with exceptions (ss.332–8), a company from making loans to its directors or to a director of its holding company, and from giving guarantees or providing security for loans to directors from other persons.

EXCEPTIONS: (1) Where the loan is by a subsidiary company and the director is its holding company. (2) Where the company's ordinary course of business includes lending money and giving guarantees and the arrangement made is within the ordinary course of its business. (A bank may, therefore, allow its directors ordinary overdrafts.) (3) Where the loan is made to provide a director with funds to meet expenses incurred by him for the company's purposes, or to enable him to perform his duties properly. (4) Where the aggregate amount of the loan does not exceed £2,500.

Section 151 of the Companies Act 1985 further prohibits, again with exceptions (s.153), a company from providing financial assistance to any person to purchase or subscribe for its own shares or the shares of its holding company. This would include a subsidiary company transferring assets to its new parent company at less than their true value, and possibly a transfer at their true value if it could be shown that the transfer was not in the commercial interests of the subsidiary: *Belmont Finance Corporation Limited* v. *William Furniture Ltd.* (1979).

EXCEPTIONS: (1) A loan by a company whose normal business includes the lending of money. (Thus, a bank may lend money to a customer so that he may purchase shares in the bank.) (2) A loan made to a trust for the benefit of the company's employees, including a director holding a salaried employment or office in the company. (3) A loan made to enable employees, other than directors, to acquire fully paid shares in the company or its holding company.

NOTE: The restrictions imposed by s.151 of the 1985 Act are relaxed by s.155 in favour of a private company in order to provide a means by which its managers can obtain assistance from the company in acquiring its shares, thereby facilitating a smooth transfer of control, e.g. from retiring shareholders.

The capital of a company

15. Definitions of capital. The term capital is used in two senses:

(a) to describe *capital items*, or

(b) to describe *financial resources* (in this sense a further distinction can be made between *invested finance* (share capital) and *loaned finance* (loan capital secured by debentures)).

A banker will be primarily concerned with capital used in the sense of a company's *financial resources*.

16. Types of capital.

(a) *Authorised or nominal capital*. This is the total face value of shares which a company's memorandum of association authorises it to issue.

(b) *Issued capital*. This is the face value of the shares actually issued and may be only a part of the authorised capital.

(c) *Paid-up capital*. This is the amount of the issued capital which has been paid-up by the shareholders.

(d) *Uncalled capital*. This is the remaining part of the issued capital which can be called up by the company from the shareholders at any time in accordance with the articles of association, i.e. their shares are only *partly paid-up*.

NOTE: For commercial reasons, it is now unusual for a company to issue partly paid-up shares.

(e) *Reserve capital*. This is a part of the uncalled capital which can only be called up for use in the event of the company's liquidation. Since partly paid-up shares are unusual, it follows that reserve capital is also rare.

(f) *Loan or debenture capital*. This is money lent to the company on the security of debentures. It is not true capital because it is a *debt* and not an asset.

17. Shares and debentures. Companies raise finance by issuing shares and debentures. While both produce money which the company can use to pursue its economic activities, there are three main differences between them.

(*a*) *Debentures* are loan capital which acknowledge and secure loans to the company while *shares* are evidence of part ownership of the company and investment in it. Thus, debenture holders are a company's creditors while shareholders are its members.

(*b*) Debentures normally provide for repayment and they are usually secured by a mortgage over the property of the company. A shareholder's investment is only completely repaid if and when the company is wound up while solvent. Thus, shareholders take a much greater *risk* than debenture holders.

(*c*) Dividends on shares can only be paid out of profits, and therefore presuppose a profitable year's trading but the interest on debentures can be paid out of capital. Hence, a debenture-holder receives payment for the loan he makes irrespective of whether the company makes a profit or a loss. (Debentures are discussed more fully in **32–40** below.)

18. The issue of shares and debentures. A public company wishing to issue shares or debentures will invite the public to subscribe for them through a document known as a *prospectus*. This will set out the objectives and past performance of the company and give other information designed to prevent investors from being misled.

A copy of the prospectus must be delivered to the Registrar of Companies by the company or issuing house before the prospectus is issued.

19. Types of shares.
(*a*) *Preference shares.* These have the following characteristics.
(*i*) Their holders have priority over all other shareholders in the payment of dividends.
(*ii*) The dividend paid is fixed. (Thus, the holders of preference shares receive a secure if somewhat moderate return on their investment.)
(*iii*) The shares are presumed to be cumulative, i.e. any deficiency in the payment of the fixed dividend is carried forward to the following year.

(*iv*) They normally carry very restricted voting rights.

(*v*) They carry no right to share in the surplus assets on winding up unless they are participating preference shares.

(*b*) *Ordinary shares.* Ordinary shareholders are entitled to the following.

(*i*) To attend and vote at meetings of the company.

(*ii*) To receive such dividends as the company decides to pay from time to time.

(*iii*) To share in the surplus assets after payment of all debts on winding up. (This right is called the *equity* of ordinary shareholders, hence the term *equity shares*.)

NOTE: The precise rights of ordinary shareholders vary widely from company to company according to their own articles of association. Ordinary shares are the *risk-bearing* shares because they have the greatest potential for either profit or loss.

(*c*) *Deferred shares.* These are now rare but they may still be issued to the promoters or employees of a company. Their holders are only entitled to a dividend after full payment has been made to the preference and ordinary shareholders. However, they are then entitled to distribution of the whole available surplus as dividend. (Such shares are usually held to show confidence in the enterprise and to provide a personal interest in its success.)

20. Stock and debenture stock. Fully paid-up shares may be converted into *stock*. There is, however, no advantage in doing this today and the holder's investment in the company remains the same, merely being expressed in different terms. For example, 1,000 £1 shares can be converted into £1,000's worth of stock.

The essential difference between stock and shares is that the former is expressed in terms of money and can be transferred in fractional amounts, e.g. £51.25's worth (although the articles of the company usually provide that stock can only be transferred in round sums), while the latter are units, e.g. 10, 50 or 100 shares, and can only be transferred as such.

Debenture or *loan stock* is borrowed finance consolidated into one debt in the same way as shares may be consolidated and converted into stock. It is usually issued for short periods and it avoids the expense and formality involved in a public issue. Debenture stock differs from debentures in the same way that stock differs from shares, i.e. it may be transferred in fractional amounts.

NOTE: Debenture stock may be convertible into ordinary shares. This gives the investor a choice between fixed but secure interest on the loan stock and the possibly better but less certain return (dividend) paid to shareholders.

21. Alteration of share capital. A company may, if so authorised by its articles, *increase* or *alter* (Companies Act 1985, s.121), or *reduce* (s.135) its share capital.

(*a*) *Increase.* This is done by issuing new shares and requires, according to the articles, an ordinary or special resolution of the company in general meeting. Notice of the increase must be filed with the Registrar of Companies within 15 days of the resolution. When existing shareholders are given the right to apply for new shares in proportion to their existing shareholding, the issue is known as a *rights issue*.

(*b*) *Alteration.* This is achieved by:

(*i*) consolidating shares, e.g. by converting every ten 10p shares into one £1 share;

(*ii*) converting shares into stock (*see* **20** above);

(*iii*) subdividing shares into shares of smaller amounts, e.g. by dividing one £1 share into five 20p shares;

(*iv*) cancelling unissued shares.

Alteration of share capital requires an ordinary or special resolution of the company, depending on its articles, and the alteration must be filed with the Registrar within one month of the resolution.

(*c*) *Reduction.* A company might reduce its share capital in order to relieve shareholders of their liability to pay any uncalled up capital in respect of their shares, e.g. by reducing 50,000 £1 shares on which 50p per share has been paid to 50,000 50p shares fully paid; or to return paid-up capital in excess of its needs, e.g. where a company has issued 50,000 £1 shares fully paid-up and reduces its capital to 50,000 50p shares fully paid-up by repaying 50p per share.

A reduction in a company's share capital is only possible where (*i*) authority to do so is contained in the company's articles, (*ii*) the reduction is approved by a special resolution of the company in a general meeting, and (*iii*) the court sanctions the reduction.

The court's sanction is necessary because a reduction in share capital may adversely affect the company's creditors, i.e. they will be deprived of funds which would otherwise have been available to them in winding up. A banker, who has made a loan on the security of a company's shares, would be particularly affected by a reduction in the company's share capital because his security would be automatically reduced.

The court must settle a list of the company's creditors and ensure that if they object to the reduction they will be paid off or given adequate security to protect their interests should their claim be disputed by the company.

In addition, the reduction must be fair and equitable between different classes of shareholders and it must not prejudice members of the public who may deal with or invest in the company.

Company bank accounts

22. Introduction. A company can pursue its business activities in much the same way as a sole trader or partnership; this includes using a bank account. Nevertheless, as a consequence of a company's corporate status, three matters concerning a company's account require a banker's particular attention. These are: (*i*) opening the account; (*ii*) its operation; (*iii*) borrowing by the company (*see* 25–7 below).

23. Opening a company account. Before opening an account for a company, a banker must be certain of the following.

(*a*) That the company has been properly incorporated. Sight of the Certificate of Incorporation is required.

(*b*) In the case of a public company, that a certificate under s. 117 of the Companies Act 1985 has been issued by the Registrar.

NOTE: A banker can open an account *solely* for the receipt of subscriptions from the public before a certificate has been issued.

(*c*) That he obtains or inspects a copy of the company's memorandum and articles of association and makes sure that they are up to date, if need be by making a search at Companies House. (He must subsequently ensure that he receives copies of any resolutions amending them.)

NOTE: The account must be conducted in strict accordance with the memorandum and articles of association and a banker should check that the company's activities in general are within its stated objects because he cannot rely on the protection of s.35 of the Companies Act 1985 (*see* **7** above).

(*d*) That he receives a certified copy of the resolution appointing the first directors, if they are not named in the articles (and afterwards that he is notified when a director retires or a new director joins the board).

(*e*) That the bank's mandate form is signed by the chairman and secretary of the company after the resolutions that they contain have been passed by a meeting of the board of directors.

The mandate must cover all the banking operations relating to the account and incorporate the names, number and positions of persons authorised to:

(*i*) draw, indorse and accept bills of exchange, promissory notes and cheques;

(*ii*) deposit and withdraw security and safe custody items;

(*iii*) overdraw the account.

Specimen signatures of the directors and all authorised signatories are required.

24. Operating a company account. A company bank account must be operated in strict accordance with the bank mandate form, e.g. each cheque must bear the required signature(s).

NOTE: The authority to draw cheques should be expressly conferred on certain directors and the secretary by the mandate.

A person drawing, accepting or indorsing a bill of exchange or promissory note on behalf of a company must clearly indicate that he signs as agent for the company. He can do this by using words such as "per pro", "for" or "for and on behalf of", followed by the full name of the company (*see* below), his signature and his capacity within the company, e.g. director or secretary. If he does not make his representative capacity quite clear, he incurs personal liability on the instrument.

By s.349 of the Companies Act 1985 a person who signs a cheque, bill of exchange or promissory note on behalf of a company, without stating the name of the company accurately and in full, incurs personal liability on it if the instrument is not paid by the company. Failure to include the word "limited" in the name of a limited company can be quite sufficient to infringe s.349: *British Airways Board* v. *Parish* (1979).

EXAMPLE: In *Maxform SPA* v. *B. Mariani & Goodville Ltd.* (1979), the sole director of G. Ltd. accepted a bill of exchange drawn on "Italdesign", the registered business name of G. Ltd. The bill was not paid by G. Ltd. and the plaintiff sought payment from the director. HELD: the director was liable on the bill; use of the registered business name was insufficient to comply with the requirements of (now) s.349. The director should have accepted in the way the company's cheques were signed—"Goodville Ltd. trading as Italdesign".

In operating a company's account a banker must always be aware of the possibility that one or more of the directors could be using the account for their own purposes. This is most likely to occur, perhaps innocently through ignorance of a director's duties and the requirements of company legislation, in the case of small companies and "one-man" companies in particular. If such misuse occurs and a reasonably aware businessman would have realised that it was happening, a banker can be sued by the company for the loss incurred.

Borrowing by companies

25. Power to borrow. A banker must always refer to a registered company's memorandum of association to see whether the objects clause specifically deals with the borrowing of money.

A trading company, however, has implied power both to borrow and to give security for its debts, e.g. by mortgage of its assets. A non-trading company does not have implied power to borrow: it must be expressly given in its memorandum.

It is usual for borrowing powers to be vested in the directors, but occasionally borrowing must be sanctioned by the company in a general meeting.

The borrowing powers of a company are seldom limited by its memorandum of association, but a company's articles of association frequently limit those of its directors.

26. Directors' borrowing powers. In addition to any specific limit contained in a company's articles, the power of directors to borrow money is limited in two other ways.

(*a*) The rules of the stock exchange require that there be a reasonable limit (often liberally interpreted) on the borrowing powers of directors of quoted public companies.

(*b*) Table A, Article 79 of the Companies Act 1948, which continues to apply to companies registered under that Act, if adopted, limited the borrowing powers of the directors to the amount of the company's *issued share capital* unless the consent of the company in a general meeting was obtained. The Article *included* securities given by a company to cover its liabilities (not necessarily debts) or the debts or liabilities of third parties, e.g. guarantees but excluded loans from its bankers in the ordinary course of business. (Table A to the Companies Act 1985 does not contain a similar limitation.)

NOTE: No certain meaning can be given to the words "temporary loans", and a banker must therefore not rely on the exception unless the temporary nature of a particular loan is very clear indeed. It would, for example, almost certainly include an over-draft facility granted to accommodate variations in cash flow.

Should the addition of a proposed loan to existing borrowing exceed a company's issued share capital, its banker will require a certified copy of the resolution of the company in a general meeting authorising the borrowing or altering the articles to increase its directors' borrowing powers.

Article 79 further provided, however, that a lender of money to a company need not enquire whether the limit on the directors' borrowing powers is observed, although the debt and any security given for it will be invalidated where he has express notice that it is exceeded.

NOTE: In practice bankers do make such enquiries. They will also enquire into the purpose of the loan because an *ultra vires* loan is void and cannot be recovered.

The borrowing powers of the directors of a company registered under the Companies Act 1929 are similarly limited to its issued share capital, unless the relevant Article was excluded by the company's own articles. However, under this Act *temporary loans* from its bankers are included in the calculations of the company's total borrowing.

27. "Ultra vires" borrowing.

(a) *"Ultra vires" the company.* Any advance which is *ultra vires* the company is void, as is any security given to cover the advance, e.g. *Introductions Ltd.* v. *National Provincial Bank Ltd.* (1970) (*see* **7** above). Ratification is not possible.

This position was modified by s.9(1) of the European Communities Act 1972 (now s.35 of the Companies Act 1985) to the extent that any loan sanctioned by the directors and entered into in good faith by the lender will bind the company even though the company's powers have been exceeded.

NOTE: It is highly unlikely that a banker could ever rely on s.35 where he has made an *ultra vires* loan to a company (*see* **7** above).

A banker has, however, four possible remedies where the loan he has made is *ultra vires* the company.

(*i*) He ranks as a creditor of the company to the extent to which the loan has been applied in paying off the legitimate debts of the company. A banker is thereby *subrogated* to the rights of (i.e. stands in the shoes of) the company's creditors who have been paid off but he is *not* entitled, however, to any securities or priorities held by the creditors.

(*ii*) He can sue for an injunction to restrain the company from parting with the money.

(*iii*) He can obtain a *tracing order* to recover any identifiable property purchased with the money.

(*iv*) He can sue the directors for *damages* for *breach of warranty of authority* (*see* **2**:**11**). An action for breach of warranty of authority is not possible where the lender is aware that the company has exceeded its borrowing powers.

NOTE: Any security taken from a *third party*, such as a director of the company, is enforceable if, as is usual, the charge agreement or guarantee includes an *indemnity clause* (*see* **10**:**9**), for this enables the security to be enforced even if the loan is void. In other words, the enforceability of the security is quite independent of the validity of the loan.

(*b*) *"Ultra vires" the directors.* Section 35 of the Companies Act 1985 provides in favour of a person dealing with a company in good faith that "the power of the directors to bind the company shall be deemed to be free of any limitation under the memorandum or articles of association." It further provides that no enquiry need be made into possible limits on the directors' powers, and that a third party is deemed to have acted in good faith unless the contrary is proved.

NOTE: Once again, it is very improbable that a banker could rely on the protection of s.35.

A loan which is merely *ultra vires* a company's directors does not present such a serious problem to a banker as a loan which is *ultra vires* the company itself. In addition to the four remedies above, the company can be asked to:

(*i*) ratify the transaction at a general meeting; or

(*ii*) alter the articles retrospectively at a general meeting to increase or to abolish the limit on its directors' borrowing powers.

Should the company refuse to do so, a banker may be able to rely on the decision in *Royal British Bank* v. *Turquand* (1856) (the Rule in *Turquand's Case*). The Rule states that a person dealing with a company is taken to know the contents of its memorandum and articles of association and he *must ensure* that the proposed transaction is consistent with them. However, he *may assume* that the company has properly completed any internal formalities which may be required before the transaction can be entered into by the company.

FACTS: The plaintiff bank had lent money to a company of which the defendant was the manager. The company had power to borrow provided that the borrowing was authorised by a resolution passed by a general meeting of the company. No such resolution had been passed. HELD: the company was bound by the loan. The loan was consistent with the company's powers and the bank were entitled to assume that the required resolution had been pased.

NOTE: The Rule is not restricted to transactions involving loans of money to a company.

The Rule in *Turquand's Case* (1856), cannot be relied on:

(*i*) by a third party who knows that the transaction is inconsistent with the memorandum or articles of association;

(*ii*) by a director of the company;

(*iii*) where the required signatures were forged;

(*iv*) where the transaction was outside the actual or implied authority of the company's servant who entered into it, even though power to do so could have been delegated to him under the articles, i.e. the transaction was sufficiently unusual to put a third party on enquiry.

EXAMPLE: In *A. L. Underwood Ltd.* v. *Bank of Liverpool and Martins* (1924), the sole director of the plaintiff company, who had authority to endorse cheques for the company as "sole director", paid cheques drawn in favour of the company into his private account. HELD (C.A.): the director could not be considered as acting within the scope of his implied authority and the Rule could not be relied on.

Section 35 of the Companies Act 1985 considerably reduces the general importance of the Rule, but it continues to be important to bankers because they are very unlikely to receive protection under that section of the Act. It still applies, for example, to a transaction which is not sanctioned by the directors, or which is sanctioned by an improperly conducted board meeting.

Securities given by companies

28. Introduction. Subject to any express restriction in its memorandum of association, a company may charge any of its property as security for a loan.

29. Registrable charges. Section 395 of the Companies Act 1985 requires the following charges to be registered with the Registrar of Companies.

(*a*) A charge to *secure any issue of debentures*.

(*b*) A charge on *uncalled share capital*.

(*c*) A charge created or evidenced by an instrument which would require registration as a *bill of sale* if created by an individual.

(*d*) A charge on *land or any interest therein*.

Even the most informal charge on land must be registered, e.g. a letter undertaking to deposit title deeds as security or even a charge created orally.

NOTE: In *Re Molton Finance Ltd.* (1968), the finance company had made a loan and had been given equitable charges on properties and had taken deposits of supporting documents as security. The charges were void for non-registration under s.95. The finance company argued, however, that they had a *common law lien* on the documents deposited with them. HELD (C.A.): the deposits were ancillary to the equitable charges and when these were avoided the lien too was lost.

A charge over *unregistered land* given by a company which is not supported by a deposit of title deeds must, unless it is a *floating charge*, also be registered under the Land Charges Act 1972 as either a *puisne mortgage* or a *general equitable charge* (*see* 6:5).

A charge created over *registered land* by a company must, in addition to registration under s.395, be protected by an entry on the land register under the Land Registration Act 1925 (*see* 7:7).

Thus, when a company offers land as security, searches are necessary in the land charges register or land register (as appropriate), as well as in the register at Companies House.

(*e*) A charge on *book debts*. These include deposits of hire purchase agreements entered into by the company for the disposal of its products.

NOTE: In *Paul and Frank Ltd.* v. *Discount Bank (Overseas) Ltd.* (1966), it was held that (now) s.395 of the 1985 Act did not apply to a charge on a bad-debt policy issued by the ECGD. Until a valid claim arose under the policy, the debt was hypothetical.

(*f*) *Floating charges* on the undertaking or property of the company (*see* **36** below).

(*g*) A charge on *calls made but not paid*.

(*h*) A charge on a *ship, or any share in a ship*. The Mortgaging of Aircraft Order 1972 brings charges on *aircraft* within s.395.

(*i*) A charge on *goodwill*, on a *patent* or a licence under a patent, on a *trademark* or on a *copyright* or a licence under a copyright.

30. Non-registrable charges. Only specific charges created by a company on life policies, produce, stocks and shares, negotiable instruments and ECGD policies do not require registration.

31. Registration of charges. Registration is effected by lodging the actual instrument of charge, accompanied by Companies Form 395 giving the prescribed details of the charge, with the Registrar of Companies. It is usual for the bank taking the charge to effect the registration on behalf of the company and claim back from the company the expenses involved.

NOTE: Where a registrable charge is not registered, the company and each of its officers who is aware of the failure to register is liable to a fine of £50 a day.

A charge within the Companies Act 1985, s.395 must be registered within twenty-one days of its creation, i.e. the date it was actually signed or sealed, not necessarily the date it bears.

EXAMPLE: In *Esberger and Son Ltd*. v. *Capital and Counties Bank* (1913), the bank's charge was set aside because its manager had held a completed but undated memorandum of deposit of title deeds for nine months before dating it and then registering a charge within 21 days of having done so.

An unregistered charge is void against a liquidator or a subsequent registered mortgagee, even though the subsequent mortgagee has actual notice of the prior unregistered charge. The loan, however, is not affected and it becomes immediately repayable. Thus, the holder of an unregistered charge becomes an *unsecured creditor*.

NOTE: A banker must bear this in mind if he is asked to hold unregistered a charge from a company.

By the Companies Act 1985, s.404 the twenty-one day period for registration may be extended by the court when it is satisfied that the failure to register was accidental; or due to inadvertence or some other sufficient cause; or will not prejudice the creditors or shareholders; or on other grounds where it is just and equitable to grant relief.

EXAMPLE: In *Re Kris Cruisers Ltd*. (1949), registration out of time under (now) s.404 of the 1985 Act was permitted where the secretary and the solicitor of the company each thought that the other had effected the registration.

If the court applies s.404, it will do so without prejudice to the rights acquired by other parties before the late registration, i.e. secured creditors holding registered charges against the company's property which were created and registered in the extension of time will not lose priority. This is because a registration under s.404 renders the charge valid from the date of its creation.

NOTE: Second charges created and registered *within* the twenty-one day period allowed by s.395 for registration of the first charge *do not gain priority* over the first charge: *Watson* v. *Duff, Morgan and Vermont (Holdings) Ltd.* (1974).

Section 404 also empowers the court to rectify the register on the same grounds and conditions upon which it can allow an extension of time for registration.

The Registrar's certificate of registration of the charge is con-clusive evidence of compliance with the statutory requirements: Companies Act 1985, s.401.

EXAMPLE: In *Re C. L. Nye Ltd.* (1971), it was HELD (C.A.) that the Registrar's certificate defeated the liquidator of the company's claim that a charge given by it to its bankers should be set aside. The undated charge had inadvertently been registered out of time and the date of its creation had been wrongly stated to the Registrar.

The decision in *Re C. L. Nye Ltd.* (1971), affords a way of avoiding the requirements of s.395 as illustrated by *Esberger and Son Ltd.* v. *Capital and Counties Bank* (1913). Although it can be argued that the decision could facilitate fraud, the principle has been affirmed by the Court of Appeal in *R.* v. *Registrar of Companies, ex parte Esal (Commodities) Ltd.* (1985).

A creditor personally damaged by a fraudulent registration can of course take action against those responsible.

NOTE: Following the decision in *R.* v. *Registrar of Companies, ex parte Esal (Commodities) Ltd.* (1985), where inaccurate or in-adequate documents are filed within the 21 day period, the Registrar cannot issue a certificate of registration for corrected documents filed outside the statutory period. An application under s.404 must be made in such cases (*see* above). Since numerous Forms 395 are returned for inaccuracy or incomplete-ness each day, this decision is of concern to bankers.

When the secured debt is satisfied in whole or in part, the Registrar may enter a *memorandum of satisfaction* on the register. He will enter a release when some or all of the property is released from the charge, or ceases to belong to the company. Registration of any discharge or release of security is only *permissive*, whereas registration of the charge itself is *obligatory*.

Every company must keep at its registered office a copy of every instrument creating a registrable charge: Companies Act 1985, s.406; and a register of *all* charges, registered and unregistered created by the company: s.407. This must be open for inspection by any creditor or member of the company.

Debentures

32. Definition. Debentures are documents issued by a company acknowledging a loan and any charge securing it. It is by the issue of debentures that companies usually borrow money.

33. Types of debentures.

(*a*) *Secured and unsecured.* An unsecured debenture is given without security; it merely acknowledges the debt. A secured debenture grants a mortgage or charge over property of the company.

(*b*) *Single or series.* A single debenture is issued to cover a single debt, e.g. to a bank to secure an overdraft. More usually, however, debentures are issued in series to several holders. These debentures will rank *pari passu* (equally) among themselves.

(*c*) *Registered or bearer.* Most debentures are registered in the names of the various holders in the same way as shares; their transfer is similarly registered (*see* 9:**8**). However, bearer debentures may be issued. These are *negotiable instruments* transferable by delivery (*see* 11:**1**). They are not registered and Treasury consent is required for their issue.

(*d*) *Perpetual or redeemable.* The former are only repaid when the company is wound up, the latter are repayable on or before a specified date.

34. Debentures issued to the public. These are usually *fixed sum* debentures. They provide for repayment at or before a specific date and they are issued in series ranking *pari passu* (equally) with each other. Interest is paid on them at a specified rate. They are normally registered and frequently quoted on a stock exchange.

Large companies now frequently issue *debenture stock* to the public. This takes the form of a single loan in which each lender has a specified holding (*see* **20** above).

A large public issue of debentures or debenture stock often involves the execution of a *trust deed* under which the assets charged are transferred by the company to *trustees* to hold on behalf of the debenture or debenture stock holders.

35. Debentures issued to a banker. A banker will almost invariably take an *all-moneys* debenture on his standard terms. This is because such a debenture will secure all moneys owing on any account at any time, and it will always keep pace with the overdrawn balance(s).

Should a *fixed-sum* debenture be accepted, a special *memorandum of deposit* (a "Buckley agreement") must be taken in order to link the debenture with the advance and to secure a fluctuating debit balance.

The following provisions are usually found in a banker's standard debenture form:

(*a*) an all-moneys clause;

(*b*) an undertaking to repay on demand;

(*c*) a clause making the debenture a continuing security;

(*d*) a clause dealing with the payment of interest;

(*e*) conditions upon which the moneys secured by the debenture become payable;

(*f*) a combination of fixed and floating charges over the company's assets;

(*g*) restrictions on the company's power to give any mortgage or charge which ranks in priority to, or equally with, the debenture;

(*h*) conditions for the appointment of a receiver if the company does not make repayment;

(*i*) an undertaking to supply the banker with regular copies of the company's balance sheet, profit and loss and trading accounts duly certified by the company's auditors;

(*j*) an undertaking to keep its property and assets repaired and insured;

(*k*) an undertaking to deposit with the bank all deeds and

documents of title to the company's freehold and leasehold property while the debenture is being relied upon.

The normal form of a bank debenture involves a fixed charge on the goodwill of the business and any uncalled capital; a fixed first charge by way of legal mortgage on any freehold or leasehold properties, including all fixtures and fixed plant and machinery from time to time therein; and a first floating charge on all the other assets of the company.

NOTE: A fixed charge over present and future book debts can be created in a bank debenture insofar as the debenture requires the company to pay into its account with the bank all moneys received in respect of book and other debts. It can also prohibit the company from charging such debts elsewhere without the bank's consent: *Siebe Gorman & Co. Ltd.* v. *Barclays Bank Ltd.* (1979).

36. Fixed and floating charges.

(*a*) *Fixed charge*. This is a legal or equitable mortgage of specific property (*see* 7:2).

A fixed charge is to a banker's advantage in that specific property is always available as security for the advance, but to his disadvantage in that the property charged may depreciate in value.

To a company, the disadvantage of a fixed charge is that it cannot dispose of the property charged without the consent of the holder of the charge.

(*b*) *Floating charge*. This is an equitable charge which floats over the fluctuating assets of a company, e.g. its stock, without attaching to specific assets until *crystallisation*, i.e. until it becomes fixed.

Crystallisation occurs:

(*i*) whenever the company commits any breach of the charge agreement such as failure to pay interest or failure to repay the capital sum, and the lender takes steps to crystallise the charge, e.g. by appointing an administrative receiver;

(*ii*) automatically when the company is wound up or ceases business.

Until crystallisation, a company can freely dispose of assets covered by a floating charge. This is an important advantage to a company.

A banker obtains the benefit of a range of assets as security, but the disadvantages (*see* **37** below) of a floating charge are such that a banker will not wish to take such a charge by itself unless no other security can be offered.

37. Defects of a floating charge.

(*a*) *Running down of assets*. The value of a floating charge depends on the value of the assets when it crystallises. Since a company can freely dispose of the assets charged, a banker's position depends to a certain extent upon the conduct of the company. It could, for example, realise the assets to repay other creditors.

A banker will wish to see, therefore, that the assets charged are maintained at a satisfactory level, but this is still no protection against a sudden depletion of the assets or a sudden fall in their value.

(*b*) *Fixed charges have priority*. A subsequent *fixed charge* on a company's assets will take priority over existing floating charges, *provided* the fixed charge was taken for value and without notice of any prohibition or restriction in the original debenture on the company's power to create such a charge.

While the mere registration of a floating charge is not notice that the charge contains a restriction on the future power of the company to mortgage its assets, a banker can protect himself by including the restriction in Form 395 when registering the debenture at Companies House (*see* **31** above).

NOTE: Unless the terms of the charge permit, a company cannot create another floating charge over its assets to rank in priority to, or equally with, the original charge.

(*c*) *Other postponements*. The rights of a holder of a floating charge are also postponed to:

(*i*) a landlord's right to distress for rent before crystallisation (*see* 5:**11**);

(*ii*) a judgment creditor if before crystallisation the goods are seized and sold by the sheriff, or if he obtains a garnishee order absolute;

(*iii*) the rights of preferential creditors after crystallisation: *see* **51** below;

(*iv*) the rights of a third party who has retained ownership of the goods covered by the charge. This may arise where goods have been sold to the company under a hire-purchase agreement, but also and more importantly where goods have been supplied to the company under a contract containing a *Romalpa Clause*.

The name given to such a clause is taken from the Court of Appeal's decision in *Aluminium Industrie Vassen BV* v. *Romalpa Aluminium Ltd.* (1976), where the plaintiff company successfully claimed from the receiver appointed by the defendant company's bankers under their debenture:

(*a*) redelivery of aluminium foil which they had supplied to the defendant company (a claim admitted by the receiver); and

(*b*) the proceeds of the re-sale of the foil by the defendant company.

The essence of the decision was that the plaintiff company (the suppliers), in their contract with the defendants, had expressly reserved the title to the foil supplied (ownership under the Sale of Goods Act 1979) to themselves until they had been paid in full. This entitled them to trace the proceeds of the re-sale of the goods in priority to the bankers secured by their floating charge.

In short, if title to stock is reserved to the supplier until he is paid, then it will not be part of the company's assets and not subject to another creditor's floating charge.

The *Romalpa* decision is of great importance in the general law on the sale of goods, and it has considerable significance to bankers because the "security" created by the decision, a "security" which is neither registered nor open to public inspection, to some extent undermines the value of a floating charge. Even preferential claims, e.g. to pay wages, are postponed to a supplier protected by a *Romalpa Clause*. A banker must bear this in mind before accepting a floating charge as security for an advance.

NOTE: The present law can be summarised as follows. (1) Provided the goods remain *identifiable in their original state*, the seller can reserve title in them: *Romalpa Case* (1976). (2) If the goods are *changed into* or *become part of another object*, hence losing their separate identity, the seller cannot retain his title to them: *Borden (UK) Ltd.* v. *Scottish Timber Products Ltd. and another* (1979). (3) Where separate identity has been lost, a Romalpa clause giving the seller equitable and beneficial ownership of the new product creates a *floating charge* over that product in favour of the seller.

This charge requires registration under the Companies Act 1985, s.395: *Re Bond Worth Ltd.* (1979). (4) If the seller knew that the goods were to be *on-sold* by the buyer, the seller's rights (whether by title retention or by charge) pass to the proceeds of the sale: *Romalpa Case* (1976).

(*d*) *Invalidation by the Insolvency Act 1985, s.104.* Unless consideration is received by the company at the same time as or after the charge is created, a floating charge is invalidated on the application of the liquidator or administrator if it was created within the following periods before the commencement of a liquidation or the application for an administration order:

(*i*) *two* years—in favour of a connected person;

(*ii*) *one* year—in favour of any other person, *provided*, in this latter case, at the time the charge was created the company was unable to pay its debts or became unable to pay its debts as a result of the transaction under which the charge was created.

A charge is also invalidated if made in the period between the petition for and the making of an administration order.

Consideration includes money paid, goods or services supplied and the discharge of debts and interest due.

NOTE: The charge is merely invalidated; the creditor remains an unsecured creditor. Thus, the liquidator cannot recover repayments to the creditors made before liquidation commences merely because their floating charge is invalidated by s.104.

Section 104 prevents insolvent companies from creating floating charges to secure past debts to the prejudice of their other unsecured creditors.

The Rule in *Clayton's Case* (1816) (*see* 3:**18**) may assist a banker in this situation because subsequent payments in will reduce and perhaps eventually extinguish the past (unsecured) advances made by him, and any fresh advance will be covered by the floating charge in accordance with s.104.

EXAMPLE: In *Re Yeovil Glove Co. Ltd.* (1965), all the company's accounts were overdrawn and the bank, who held a floating charge from the company, had been making drawings from the No. 1 account and crediting these to two others for the payment of wages and salaries, thereby allowing the bank to monitor its preferential rights (*see* **50** below). HELD (C.A.): the drawings made after the charge was taken were advances made in consideration of it, and subsequent payments into the No. 1 account were set against drawings made before the charge was taken. It made no difference that payments in and payments out were more or less equal.

(*e*) *Invalidation by the Insolvency Act 1985, s. 101.* If created within six months, or two years in the case of a connected person, of a company going into liquidation or an administration order being made against it, a floating charge may be invalidated as a *preference* under s. 101 (*see* **47** below).

38. Transfer of debentures. Fixed-sum debentures quoted on a stock exchange are readily transferable by an ordinary instrument of transfer. A *bearer* debenture can be transferred by mere delivery.

Bankers' debentures are usually transferable, but one banker who accepts a transfer of a debenture from another or from a non-banker will seldom rely on the wording of the original debenture. This is because each banker drafts his own standard debenture to cover all foreseeable contingencies in conformity with his own practices and procedures. He will normally insist, therefore, on taking his own debenture and having the original discharged.

39. Discharge of bank debentures. A bank's debenture form usually includes a form of receipt. When the bank is repaid, it will impress its seal on the receipt as evidence of the discharge.

A *memorandum of satisfaction* should then be filed by the company with the Registrar of Companies.

40. Remedies of a debenture holder. A banker's debenture will specify in detail the circumstances in which he can intervene to enforce his security. In a quoted public issue of debentures the associated trust deed will also provide for intervention.

The intervention crystallises (*see* **36** above) any floating charge contained in the debenture.

(*a*) *Unsecured debenture holders* may:
    (*i*) sue for the principal and interest due;
    (*ii*) petition for the windingup of the company on the ground that it is unable to pay its debts.

(*b*) *Secured debenture holders* may in addition:

(*i*) exercise any of the powers conferred by the debenture or the trust deed, e.g. appoint a receiver or an administrative receiver (*see* below); sell the assets charged; or take possession of the assets and carry on the business (a bank's debenture will confer such powers);

(*ii*) if such powers are not conferred by the debenture or trust deed, apply to the court for the appointment of a receiver or a receiver and manager, or an order for sale or for foreclosure (*see* 7:**15**).

A bank's debenture form will contain the power to appoint a receiver on the company's failure to repay. This is the remedy usually chosen by banks. The debenture form will specifically provide that the receiver is the agent of the company in order that the company and not the bank is liable for his acts and remuneration. By s.50 of the Insolvency Act 1985, an *administrative receiver* is the agent of the company. He is personally liable on any contract he enters into while carrying out his functions and on any contract of employment adopted by him in carrying out those functions, although he is entitled to an indemnity out of the company's assets for liabilities properly incurred.

NOTE: In *Standard Chartered Bank Ltd* v. *Walker and Another* (1982), it was held (C.A.) that:

(1) A debenture holder, e.g. a bank, would be liable for a receiver's actions to the extent that he gives him directions or interferes with his conduct, e.g. giving specific instructions regarding a sale;

(2) a receiver acting under a debenture owes a duty to obtain the best possible price for the assets not only to the company but also to a guarantor of the company's liability under the debenture.

A receiver appointed by the court incurs personal liability for his acts, although he is entitled to an indemnity paid from the company's assets in priority to the debenture holders.

(*c*) *Receivers, liquidators and managers.* A *receiver* is distinct from a *liquidator* (*see* 42 below). The former is appointed when the creditors believe that they can recover their money without necessarily closing down the company. The latter is appointed to wind up the company. Liquidation does, however, often eventually follow the appointment of a receiver. A *manager* is appointed (usually the same person is

appointed both receiver and manager) when it appears possible to
sell the company as a going concern. With the court's permission, he
may borrow money in order to do so and charge the company's
property as security, the charge taking priority over the rights of the
debenture holders.

(*d*) *The role of the receiver.* The receiver's task is to take possession
of the assets charged by the debenture and to realise them for the
benefit of the debenture holder(s).

He must, however, pay out *preferential creditors* (*see* **51** below)
before debenture holders secured by a floating charge: Companies
Act 1985, s.196 but holders of *fixed charges* are not subject to the
payment of the preferential debts.

He must then apply any surplus in the following order of priority:

    (*i*) in payment of the costs of the receivership;

    (*ii*) in full or partial discharge of the debt owing to the deben-
ture holder(s);

    (*iii*) to the company where there are any assets left.

Once the receiver has completed his task, the company can
recommence normal business if it financially viable. Usually, however, this is not so and a creditor will present a winding up petition.
The receiver may petition where it is necessary to protect the
company's assets: *Re Emmadart* (1979). The liquidator appointed
takes over any surplus from the receiver.

Notice of the appointment of a receiver or manager must be given
to the Registrar of Companies within seven days. The appointment
will be entered on his register of charges. Invoices, orders and letters
must all contain notice of the appointment while he is acting.

NOTE: Where an *administration order* has been made, any receiver
of part of the company's property, i.e. a receiver appointed under
a fixed charge, must vacate office if asked to do so by the
administrator: Insolvency Act 1985, s.30(2) (*see* **45** below).

(*e*) *The administrative receiver.* The administrative receiver was
introduced by the Insolvency Act 1985, s.45. He is a receiver or
manager of *the whole or substantially the whole* of the company's
property appointed by the holders of any debentures secured either
by a *floating charge* or by such a charge and one or more other
securities. The term reflects the wider functions that he has in
comparison to receivers appointed under fixed charges. Bank

debentures secured by floating (and other) charges contain the right to appoint an administrative receiver.

Any right in a floating charge to appoint an administrative receiver cannot be exercised after an *administration order* has been made. An application for an order does not prevent an appointment (*see* **45** below). Once appointed, an administrative receiver can *only be removed by the court.*

Within 28 days he must inform all creditors of his appointment. Within a further 21 days a statement of affairs of the company must be submitted to him. He must then submit a report to the Registrar of Companies and send it to all creditors, usually within three months, and present it to a meeting of the company's creditors. The meeting may appoint a *committee of creditors* which can request information from the administrative receiver. It has, however, no power to supervise or direct him.

An administrative receiver has the *powers* given by the floating charge under which he was appointed. These are deemed to include those set out in Schedule 3 of the Insolvency Act 1985 unless they are inconsistent with the charge. He has, therefore, powers similar to an *administrator* and, as with an administrator, a person dealing with him in good faith and for value need not enquire whether he is acting within those powers. His powers include:

(*i*) carrying on the business of the company as its agent;

(*ii*) selling the business;

(*iii*) borrowing money and granting security for it over the company's property;

(*iv*) making an arrangement or compromise with creditors;

(*v*) drawing, accepting, making or endorsing any bill of exchange or promissory note in the name of or on behalf of the company.

With the consent of the court, he also has the power to dispose of certain other charged property. This power does not cover, for example, property that is subject to any other security held by the person, e.g. a bank, by or on whose behalf he was appointed. The net proceeds of the sale must be applied in discharge of the sums secured by the charge. If the proceeds are, in the court's opinion, less than the market value of the assets concerned, the administrative receiver must make up the difference.

Winding up and dissolution of a company

41. Introduction. A registered company is an artificial legal person created by legal process. Its existence is similarly ended by legal process—*winding up* or *liquidation* (the terms are interchangeable) under the Companies Act 1985 and the Insolvency Act 1985.

There are important similarities between the process of winding up companies and the process of bankruptcy of individuals and partnerships. For example, the rights of *preferential creditors* are the same and the concepts of *transactions at an undervalue* and *preferences* apply to both. However, in bankruptcy the debtor is always insolvent while the process of liquidation applies whether the company is solvent or insolvent.

The Companies Act 1985, as amended by the Insolvency Act 1985, provides two methods of winding up: (*a*) compulsorily by the court; (*b*) voluntarily.

42. Compulsory winding up by the court.

(*a*) *Grounds for winding up.* A company can be wound up by the court following a petition to it if one of the following situations arises (Companies Act 1985, s.517).

(*i*) The company resolves by special resolution that it should be wound up by the court. (This is unusual because the company is in a position to wind up voluntarily. This is a cheaper and more convenient procedure.)

(*ii*) If a public company registered as such in its original incorporation has not been issued with a certificate under the Companies Act 1985, s.117 and more than a year has expired since it was so registered.

(*iii*) The company has not commenced business within a year after its incorporation or suspends business for a whole year.

(*iv*) Its members fall below the statutory minimum.

(*v*) The company is unable to pay its debts. Winding-up petitions are most frequently presented on this ground.

By the Companies Act 1985, s.518 inability to pay its debts occurs where:

(1) a creditor to whom at least £750 is owed has made a proper demand for payment and has remained unpaid for three weeks;

(2) execution issued on a judgment of the court in favour of a creditor is returned unsatisfied in whole or in part;

(3) the court is satisfied that the company is unable to pay its debts.

NOTE: In *Re Capital Annuities Ltd.* (1978), it was held that the mere fact that a company has insufficient *liquid assets* to pay its immediate debts does not necessarily satisfy (now) ss.517 and 518 of the 1985 Act. It might have, for example, other assets which could be readily realised in a few days to do so.

(*vi*) The court is of the opinion that it is just and equitable that the company should be wound up.

This residual power of the court is seldom invoked, but it could, for example, be used where personal deadlock exists between the only two directors of a company: *Re Yenidje Tobacco Co. Ltd.* (1916).

NOTE: In *Ebrahimi* v. *Westbourne Galleries Ltd.* (1973), the House of Lords recognised for the purposes of winding up the existence of the *incorporated partnership*, i.e. a business organisation to which, in practice, some important partnership principles apply although at law it is a registered company. In this case the plaintiff, one of the company's three directors, had been quite legally removed from office and prevented from participating in the management of the company by the other two directors. On the facts, however, the company had always been run along the lines of a partnership and this made their action inequitable. Consequently, the House found that it was just and equitable that the company be wound up on the plaintiff's petition.

(*b*) *Who may petition.* It is nearly always a *creditor* who petitions for a compulsory winding-up order.

A *contributory* (*see* **46** below) may petition under (*iv*) above, and in any other of the situations provided he has held shares for at least six months out of the eighteen months preceding his petition. A petition by a contributory is unusual.

The *Department of Trade and Industry* has power to present a petition against a company under the Companies Act 1985, s.440 if it appears to be in the public interest, after investigations by the Department's inspectors, that the company should be wound up.

The *Bank of England* is empowered by the Banking Act 1979,

s. 18(1), to present a petition for the winding up of a *recognised bank* or *licensed institution* (*see* 1:**1**) under the Companies Act 1985 if:

(*i*) the institution is unable to pay sums due and payable to its depositors or is able to pay such sums only by defaulting in its obligations to other creditors; or if

(*ii*) the value of the institution's assets is less than the amount of its liabilities.

When any petition is presented, the court may make a winding-up order, dismiss the petition, or postpone the petition while further enquiries are made. The court may refuse to make a winding-up order if the majority of creditors oppose it.

(*c*) *Commencement of the winding up.* The effect of the winding-up order dates back to the commencement of the winding up. By the Companies Act 1985, s.524 this occurs:

(*i*) at the time of the presentation of the petition to the court; or

(*ii*) at the time of the passing of the resolution for voluntary winding up (*see* **43** below) where the company was in voluntary liquidation before the petition was presented.

(*d*) *Consequences of the winding-up order.* The main consequences are as follows.

(*i*) Any disposition of property made after the commencement of the winding up is void unless sanctioned by the court: Companies Act 1985, s.522. This applies, for example, to the transfer of shares, credits to the company's account and the payment of third party cheques.

EXAMPLE: In *Re Gray's Inn Construction Company Ltd.* (1980), a winding-up petition was presented against the company and advertised. The company's account was overdrawn but, in accordance with standing instructions from head office, the bank continued to operate the account until the winding-up order was made, expecting the court to validate transactions in the ordinary course of the company's business if a winding-up order was made. HELD (C.A.): (1) Credits, as well as debits, during the relevant period are "dispositions" within the meaning of (now) s.522. (2) The bank was liable to the liquidator for the trading loss that resulted from the company's continuation in business.

NOTE: A bank has always taken a risk if it continued such an account without the court's sanction. As a result of this decision there seems to be no good reason why a bank should continue to take this unnecessary risk. If the company wishes to withdraw funds the proper course of action is for the company or the bank to seek a court order regarding the operation of the account and for it to be exhibited to the bank. The bank must then, of course, ensure that it complies with the order.

(*ii*) Any attachment, sequestration, distress or execution put in force against the estate or effects of the company after the commencement of the winding-up is void: s.523; and *no action* can be proceeded with or commenced against the company except by leave of the court: s.525.

(*iii*) Floating charges are void in certain circumstances: Insolvency Act 1985, ss.101 and 104 (*see* **37** above); and any lien or other right to retain possession of any books, papers or other records of the company is unenforceable against the liquidator: Insolvency Act 1985, s.105.

NOTE: This does not apply to liens on documents which give a title to property and are held as such. Thus, a bank's general lien over cheques, bills of exchange, promissory notes, share certificates and bills of lading, or particular lien over title deeds and insurance policies, is protected.

(*iv*) The liquidator assumes most of the powers of the directors.

(*v*) The employees are dismissed.

(*vi*) Following a complaint to him by a liquidator, an administrator, an administrative receiver or the official receiver about the conduct of a present or past director of the company, the Secretary of State can apply to the court for an order disqualifying that person from acting as a director of a company for a minimum period of two years: Insolvency Act 1985, s.12. Under the Companies Act 1985, s.300, a person can be disqualified from acting as a director of a company, or in any way being concerned with its promotion, formation or management, when he has been involved, e.g. as a director, with two companies that have gone into insolvent liquidation in a five-year period. The disqualification period can be up to fifteen years.

NOTE: The winding-up order terminates the banker-customer relationship: *National Westminster Bank Ltd.* v. *Halesowen Presswork and Assemblies Ltd.* (1972) (*see* **49** below).

(*e*) *The role of the official receiver.*

(*i*) He may require the directors of the company to submit to him a *statement of affairs*. This must contain particulars of the assets, debts and liabilities of the company, particulars of the creditors and any securities that they hold and such other information as he may ask for. The statement must be submitted within twenty-one days of the winding up order or appointment of a provisional liquidator.

(*ii*) He must *investigate* the company's failure and generally the promotion, formation, business, dealings and affairs of the company. He may *submit a report* to the court if he considers it to be necessary.

(*iii*) At any time before the company's dissolution, he may apply to the court for a *public examination* of any person who is or has been an officer of the company, or who has acted as its liquidator or administrator, or who has been concerned with or taken part in its promotion, formation or management. He must apply if he is asked to do so by one-half in value of the company's creditors or three-quarters in value of the company's contributories.

(*iv*) The official receiver becomes the liquidator by virtue of his office when a winding up order is made. He remains in office until replaced. Within twelve weeks he must decide whether or not to *summons meetings of creditors and contributories* to choose another person to act as liquidator. If he does not, he must give notice of his decision to them and to the court. He must summon meetings if requested to do so by one-quarter in value of the creditors. The meetings can also appoint a *committee of inspection* to act with a liquidator other than the official receiver.

(*f*) *The role of the liquidator.* After the winding-up order is made, his major duties are:

(*i*) to take the company's property into his custody:

NOTE: A liquidator can disclaim *onerous property*. Under the Insolvency Act 1985, s.91, this is any unprofitable contract and property which is unsaleable or not easily saleable, or property which might give rise to a liability to pay money or perform any other onerous act, e.g. a lease containing obligations to repair or to insure.

(*ii*) to settle a list of contributories (*see* **46** below);
(*iii*) to collect the company's assets; and

(*iv*) to apply them in discharge of its liabilities;

(*v*) to distribute any surplus among the members of the company according to the rights attaching to their share of the company's capital.

(*g*) *Appointment of a special manager.* Where a company is in liquidation or a provisional liquidator has been appointed, an application can be made by the liquidator or provisional liquidator for the appointment of a special manager where he considers it to be in the interests of the creditors, contributories or members that someone should be appointed to manage the company's affairs. He has whatever powers the court gives him: Insolvency Act 1985, s.90.

(*h*) *Insolvency practitioner.* An insolvency practitioner is a person who acts:

(*i*) in relation to companies: as a liquidator, administrator, administrative receiver, or as supervisor of a voluntary arrangement;

(*ii*) in relation to individuals or partnerships: as a trustee in bankruptcy or interim receiver, trustee under a deed of arrangement, or administrator of an insolvent estate of a deceased individual.

Under the Insolvency Act 1985, all insolvency practitioners must be *licensed* and it is a criminal offence to act in such a capacity without a licence. Authorisation will be available either from certain professional bodies, e.g. the leading accountancy bodies, or direct from the Secretary of State in the case of individuals experienced in insolvency practice who are not members of such professional bodies. The Official Receiver can also act in any of the capacities of an insolvency practitioner.

(*i*) *Banking considerations.* The period of time between a petition being presented and a winding-up order being made poses a problem to a banker because any disposition of property is void unless sanctioned by the court, and a banker has no special legal protection if he pays the company's cheques during this period.

NOTE: No such period of uncertainty arises in a *voluntary* winding up because this commences when the resolution to wind up is passed and because the liquidator is usually appointed on the same day. When he receives notice of the resolution a banker should simply pay no further cheques drawn by the company and act only on the liquidator's instructions.

After a banker receives notice that a petition has been presented to the court, only cheques presented for cash over the counter, e.g. for wages, can be paid; other cheques should be returned marked "Winding-up petition presented". However, some bankers are prepared to anticipate the court's sanction and pay third party cheques drawn in the ordinary course of business to enable the company to continue trading.

EXAMPLE: In *Re Operator Control Cabs Ltd.* (1970), the court sanctioned, on the company's application, dispositions of its property and payments from its account in the ordinary course of business after its bankers had stopped its account. On the facts, it was in the interests of the company and its creditors that the company should continue trading.

A banker must stop a company's account completely when a winding-up order is made against it. The liquidator will claim any credit balance and the banker can take steps to enforce any security that he holds from the company should the company be indebted to him.

43. Voluntary winding up. The great majority of liquidations are voluntary.

(a) *How initiated.* Section 572 of the Companies Act 1985 provides that a company may be wound up voluntarily:

(i) by *ordinary resolution* at the end of the period, if any, fixed for its duration by the articles or, if the articles provide that the company is to be dissolved on the occurrence of a certain event, when that event occurs;

(ii) by *special resolution* (no particular reason is required);

(iii) by *extraordinary resolution* where, by reason of its liabilities, it cannot continue its business and it is therefore advisable to wind up.

Copies of the resolution must be filed within fifteen days and advertised in the *Gazette* within fourteen days.

(b) *Effect of the resolution.* A voluntary winding up commences from the passing of the resolution. Its effects are that:

(i) the company ceases business, except for business necessary to its beneficial winding up;

(ii) transfers of shares are void unless made with the consent of the liquidator;

(iii) the powers of the directors cease on the appointment of the liquidator unless sanctioned by him or by the company in a general meeting in a members' voluntary winding up (*see* below);

(*iv*) floating charges made within the previous two years are void in certain circumstances (*see* **37** above);

(*v*) if the company is insolvent, its employees are dismissed.

Proceedings against the company are not stayed unless the court so orders.

(*c*) *Types of voluntary winding up.*

(*i*) A members' voluntary winding up. This can only take place when the company is solvent, for example, where the directors and principle shareholders of a solvent company wish to retire but no buyer for the company can be found. The company's creditors are paid in full and therefore its members control the liquidation, appointing a liquidator of their choice.

A members' voluntary winding up requires the directors to file a *declaration of solvency* to the effect that after having made a full enquiry into the company's affairs they are of the opinion that the company will be able to pay its debts in full within a specified period not exceeding twelve months from the commencement of the winding up.

To be effective, the declaration must be made within the five weeks immediately preceding the date on which the resolution to wind up was passed and filed with the Registrar of Companies before that date. It must embody a statement of the company's assets as at the last practicable date before it is made.

(*ii*) A creditors' voluntary winding up. If no declaration of solvency can be made and filed, the creditors control a voluntary winding up and can appoint a liquidator of their choice.

A meeting of the creditors must be called and at least seven days' notice of the meeting must be sent by post to creditors and advertised in the *Gazette* and in two local newspapers.

44. Voluntary arrangements. These can be made under either the Companies Act 1985 or the Insolvency Act 1985. Such arrangements do *not* involve the liquidation of the company.

(*a*) *Companies Act 1985, s.425.* Under s.425 a company can enter into a compromise or arrangement with its creditors (or members), or any class thereof, *without* going into liquidation. It can do this by asking the court to summons a meeting of the creditors (or members), or a class thereof, at which the compromise or arrangement must be agreed to by a majority in number representing three quarters in value of those present and voting. It must be subsequently sanctioned by the court. An arrangement under s.425 can also be used for total reconstruction of a company, e.g. where the court orders dissolution and transfer of its undertaking to a new company, in which members and creditors shall have such rights as are agreed and sanctioned by the court. This process does not involve winding up the existing company.

(b) *Insolvency Act 1985, ss.20–6*. These sections provide an alternative procedure by which a company may come to terms with its creditors (by agreeing and implementing a scheme or composition) with the minimum of formality and court involvement. A proposal for a composition in satisfaction of debts or a scheme of arrangement of the company's affairs can be put to the company and its creditors by (i) the *liquidator*, if the company is in liquidation; (ii) by the *administrator*, if an administration order (*see* **45** below) is in force; and (iii) by the *directors* in any other case. An insolvency practitioner must act in relation to the arrangement. He is referred to as the *nominee*. A liquidator or administrator acting as nominee may summons meetings of the company and its creditors as he thinks fit; any other nominee must report to the court within 28 days of his appointment and act on its directions.

The meetings must approve the proposal. However, no proposal or modification of it can be approved which affects the rights of *secured* or *preferential creditors*, e.g. banks, unless the creditors affected agree. Every person who had notice of and was entitled to vote at the meetings, whether or not he did so, is bound by the composition or scheme as though he were a party to it.

If the company is being wound up or is subject to an administration order when the proposal is approved, the court may stay the winding up or discharge the administration order and give such directions as it thinks will help implement the approved composition or scheme.

The decision of the meetings may be challenged by a member or creditor of the company (a bank for example), the nominee and (if applicable) the liquidator or administrator on the grounds that the approved composition or scheme unfairly prejudices the interests of a creditor, member or contributory of the company and/or that there had been some material irregularity at or in relation to either of the meetings. An application challenging the meetings' decision must be made within 28 days of the reports of the meetings being made to the court.

When the proposal is approved and not subject to a challenge, the nominee becomes known as the *supervisor* of the composition or scheme. He acts under the supervision of the court to whom he may apply for directions. He can also apply to the court to have the company wound up or made subject to an administration order.

45. Administration orders. These are made under the Insolvency Act 1985, s.28. The procedure is intended to provide an alternative to liquidation where a company is in serious financial difficulties and a receiver cannot be appointed because no floating charges exist. The mechanism is similar to that of a receiver appointed under a floating charge and the protection of the court is gained while schemes of reconstruction are arranged.

(*a*) *Grounds for an administration order.* The court may make an administration order following a petition by a company, its directors or creditors where it considers that doing so:

(*i*) would promote the *survival of the company* as a going concern;

(*ii*) lead to a *voluntary arrangement* being agreed (*see* **44** above);

(*iii*) secure a more advantageous *realisation* (sale) of its assets than a winding up would produce.

The court must be satisfied that the company is, or is likely to become, unable to pay its debts. An administration order cannot be made where a company has gone into liquidation, or where it is an insurance company, or a recognised bank or licensed institution within the meaning of the Banking Act 1979.

Under s.28(2), notice of the application for an administration order must be given to any person who has appointed, or is or may be entitled to appoint, an administrative receiver of the company, i.e. the holder of a debenture secured by a floating charge. If there is already an administrative receiver of the company, an order will not be made *unless* either the person, e.g. a bank, on whose behalf the receiver was appointed consents or the floating charge is liable to be set aside (s.28(3)).

NOTE: The application does not prevent the holder of a floating charge, e.g. a bank, appointing an administrative receiver and, providing the charge is not liable to be set aside, he can prevent an order being made by appointing one before the court reaches its decision on the application. Banks may therefore be tempted to step in earlier than they might otherwise have done, and before another creditor does so, in order to retain control of the situation and protect their interest. It also puts in jeopardy any informal rescheduling of debts. The adverse publicity this formal and more public intervention could cause at such a critical time might very well prejudice any chance of survival the company might have. Clearly, professional judgment in the use of the law is going to be very important.

(b) *The effect of the order*. An administration order restricts the rights of existing creditors, secured or unsecured. Specifically, it:

(i) prevents the company from being wound up;

(ii) prevents any security given by the company being enforced without the consent of the administrator or leave of the court;

(iii) prevents goods subject to hire purchase, leasing or retention of title agreements (*Romalpa clauses*) being repossessed;

(iv) prevents an administrative receiver being appointed and removes from office an existing administrative receiver or receiver appointed under a fixed charge;

(v) requires all documents issued by or on behalf of the company or the administrator to state the fact that an administration order is in force and give the name of the administrator.

The *application* for an administration order prevents the company from being wound up or action taken to enforce securities which it has given. On *appointment* an administrator must inform the company and advertise details of it, file a copy of the order with the Registrar of Companies and inform all creditors within 28 days.

(c) *The administrator's powers*. These are detailed in Schedule 3 of the Act. Essentially, the administrator can do anything which may be necessary for the management of the affairs, business and property of the company; he has in effect the full powers of the directors of the company. For example, he can:

(ii) carry on the business of the company as its agent;

(ii) sell the business of the company;

(iii) borrow money and grant security for it over the company's property;

(iv) make an arrangement or compromise with creditors;

(*v*) draw, accept, make or endorse any bill of exchange or promissory note in the name of or on behalf of the company;

(*vi*) dispose of property which is the subject of a floating charge, the proceeds of the disposal becoming the subject of the floating charge;

(*vii*) with the court's consent, dispose of any other charged property, or any goods in the company's possession under a hire-purchase, conditional sale, lease or retention of title agreement. The net proceeds of the sale must be applied in discharge of the debts owed to the chargeholder or the owner of the goods. If the proceeds are, in the court's opinion, less than the market value of the assets concerned, the administrator must make up the difference.

These powers enable an administrator to reorganise the affairs of the company. As in dealings with an administrative receiver, a person who deals with an administrator in good faith and for value need not inquire whether he is acting within his authority. He also has powers similar to those of a liquidator to deal with voidable preferences, the collection of assets, the acquisition of information and the making of an application for a disqualification order against a director.

(*c*) *The administrator's proposals.* Within three months of the administration order being made, the administrator must send to all creditors his proposals for achieving the purposes stated in the order and present them to a creditors' meeting. This meeting must approve them and may establish a *committee of creditors*. A creditor or member may petition the court if he believes that the administrator is not acting in the best interests of the creditors or members. If the proposal, or an amended version of it, fails, the company can be put into liquidation.

At the end of the administration, the administrator must account to the company or to a liquidator who may then be appointed.

46. Contributories. A contributory is any person liable to contribute to the assets of the company in the event of its being wound up: Companies Act 1985, s.507. Both present and certain past members of the company are contributories, including the holders of fully paid-up shares.

(*a*) *Unlimited companies.* By definition there is no limit on the members' liability to contribute.

(b) *Companies limited by guarantee*. Members are liable to contribute to the extent of their guarantee. Past members may be liable as "B List" contributories (*see* below).

(c) *Companies limited by shares*. Members holding fully paid-up shares are under no further liability to contribute but members holding partly paid-up shares must (if called) contribute the amounts unpaid on their shares.

A list of contributories is drawn up by the liquidator. It is in two parts:

(i) the "A List", containing present members of the company;

(ii) the "B List", which includes all persons who were members during the preceding twelve months.

In the case of shares which are not fully paid-up, the liquidator first makes calls on their holders on the "A List". If they cannot pay, he has recourse against the ex-holders of the shares on the "B List", but only for contributions towards the debts and liabilities of the company contracted while they were members.

47. Transactions at an undervalue and preferences. These principles are common to both liquidation of companies and bankruptcy.

(a) *Transactions at an undervalue*. A company enters into such a transaction with a person if it:

(i) makes a *gift* to that person;

(ii) is to receive *no consideration* from that person under the transaction;

(iii) is to receive a consideration which is worth *significantly less* than the consideration provided by the company: Insolvency Act 1985, s. 101(2).

To be actionable, the liquidator must show that:

(i) the company was *unable to pay its debts* at the time of the transaction, or became unable to pay its debts as a result of the transaction; and that

(ii) the transaction was entered into in the *two years* before the company goes into liquidation or a petition for an administration order is presented.

NOTE: (1) No intention to benefit the other party is required; liability arises from the fact that the transaction was entered into.

(2) Where a transaction at an undervalue is entered into with a person *connected with the company* (*see* below), the company is *presumed to be insolvent* unless the contrary is proved: Insolvency Act 1985, s. 101(9). (3) A transaction at an undervalue can also be challenged if entered into in the time between the petition for and the making of an administration order.

(*b*) *Preferences.* A company gives a preference if it does anything which has the effect of putting a creditor or a guarantor for any of its debts or liabilities in a *better position* in the event of the company going into insolvent liquidation than he would have been in had that thing not been done: Insolvency Act 1985, s. 101(4).

To be actionable, the liquidator must show:

(*i*) The company was *unable to pay its debts* at the time the preference was made or became unable to pay its debts as a result of the preference;

(*ii*) the company was *influenced by a desire* to put the person in a better position than he would have been in had nothing been done: Insolvency Act 1985, s. 101(5).

NOTE: This is *presumed* to be the case where the person was connected with the company. A *connected person* is defined by s. 108(5) as a director or shadow director, an associate of either, or an *associate* of the company. Being employed by the company is not by itself sufficient for a person to be "connected" with a company for this purpose. (By s. 223, an *associate* of a company is, for example, a director or other officer, another company under the same control or controlling shareholders.)

(*iii*) the preference took place within *certain periods* before either the company goes into liquidation or a petition for an administration order is presented, *viz*:

(1) *six months*: where the person preferred was *not* connected with the company;

(2) *two years*: where the person preferred was connected with the company.

NOTE: A preference can also be challenged if made in the time between the petition for and the making of an administration order.

In the context of (*ii*) above, it may be that the liquidator or administrator's claim will be defeated if the company's payment followed pressure by the creditor preferred, unless the creditor knew that the debtor was about to file his own petition. An instance would be where a bank presses for the reduction of an overdraft and receives payment in preference to other creditors. Much depends on the meaning of the phrase *influenced by a desire*. It has no history in insolvency law and judicial interpretation is required.

However, as under the previous law, the mere fact that a creditor *is* preferred is insufficient.

EXAMPLE: In *Re William Hall (Contractors) Ltd.* (1967), the company's bank had held, for some thirteen years, memoranda of deposit of title deeds. These contained the company's undertaking to execute a legal mortgage when requested to do so. The company did so at their bank's request shortly before going into liquidation. HELD: The mortgage could not be avoided by the liquidator. The company was merely carrying out its pre-existing obligation and *no intention to prefer* (as the law then required) could be proved.

(c) *Powers of the court.* Under the Insolvency Act 1985, s.101(1), the court, on the application of the liquidator or administrator, has wide powers to restore the position to what it would have been if the company had not entered into the transaction or made the preference. For example, it can order that the property or benefits received be returned to the company, this could include the setting aside of mortgages or charges which are part of the transaction, or reviving the obligations of a surety released by a bank.

However, a purchaser for value of property which was the subject of a preference or a transaction at an undervalue who buys in good faith and without notice of the relevant circumstances, acquires a good title to it even though the vendor's title was voidable. The court cannot make any order which upsets his interest. Nor can the court order a person who received a benefit from the transaction or preference in the same circumstances to make any payment to the liquidator or administrator unless the person was a party to the transaction or the payment is in respect of a preference given to the person at the time he was a creditor of the company: Insolvency Act 1985, s.102(2). (For a bank's position, *see* below.)

Furthermore, in the case of a transaction at an undervalue, the court will not make an order if it is satisfied that the company entered into the transaction in good faith and for the purpose of carrying on the business and that at the time there were reasonable grounds for believing that the transaction would benefit the company: Insolvency Act 1985, s. 101(3).

(*d*) *Preferences and banking.* A bank may find itself unwittingly involved in a preference where the company's payments to the bank are intended to reduce or extinguish the liability of a *surety or guarantor* of its overdraft.

Although the payments in are (usually) designed to benefit the surety or guarantor, the bank receives a preference within the meaning of the Act.

EXAMPLE: In *Re M. Kushler Ltd.* (1943), K, one of two co-directors of the company, had guaranteed its overdraft. He was advised that his company was insolvent and two weeks later a resolution to wind up voluntarily was passed. In the meantime, however, the company's overdraft was completely repaid while only two trade bills were satisfied, even though an important trade creditor had been pressing for payment. HELD (C.A.): on the facts, K's action and the pressure from trade creditors taken together established a voidable preference. The liquidator could recover payments from the bank.

A similar situation could arise in relation to a *bill of exchange* accepted for an insolvent debtor's accommodation and discounted by his bank. Should the debtor pay funds into his bank to meet the bill with the intention of preferring the *acceptor*, his trustee or liquidator could recover the payments from the bank if a bankruptcy or winding up order is subsequently made against the debtor. The acceptor is in effect a surety for the party accommodated, i.e. the debtor (*see* 11:**16**).

By analogy with the Bankruptcy Act 1914, a person who deposits securities to secure another's indebtedness is a surety or guarantor within the meaning of the Insolvency Act 1985, s. 101, even though he makes no *personal undertaking* to the creditor, e.g. a bank: *Re Conley* (1938).

Although the bank will have to make repayment, under s. 102 (companies) and s. 175 (individuals), the court has power to revive the obligations of, or impose new obligations on, a surety released by the bank. It can order and specify security to be provided for any obligation imposed.

48. Transactions defrauding creditors. Such transactions are those:

(*a*) entered into by a company with another person *at an undervalue*; and

(*b*) entered into for the purpose of *putting assets beyond the reach of* actual or potential claimants against the person, or with the intention to otherwise prejudice the interests of such claimants: Insolvency Act 1985, s.212(1).

If it is satisfied that such was the purpose of the transaction, the court can make such an order as it thinks fit to restore the position to what it would have been if the transaction had not been entered into and/or to protect the interests of such claimants. An application under this section can be made by the liquidator or administrator, as appropriate.

NOTE: *Undervalue* has the same meaning as in s.101(2) (*see* **47** above) and the court has the same powers.

However, a purchaser for value of property which was the subject of a fraudulent transaction within s.212 who buys in good faith and without notice of the relevant circumstances acquires a good title to it even though the vendor's title was voidable. The court cannot make any order which upsets his interest. Nor can the court order any person who received a benefit from the transaction in the same circumstances to make any payment to the liquidator or administrator unless he was a party to the transaction.

49. Extortionate credit transactions. A credit transaction is extortionate under the Insolvency Act 1985, s.103(3), if, having regard to the risk accepted by the person providing the credit, it requires grossly exorbitant payments to be made or otherwise grossly contravenes ordinary principles of fair dealing. The transaction is presumed to be extortionate unless the contrary is proved.

If the company has been a party to such a transaction within the *three year* period before the company went into liquidation or an administration order was made, the court, on the application of the liquidator or administrator, may make an order setting aside or otherwise varying the terms of the transaction or the terms on which security is held.

It is clearly possible for a credit transaction with a bank to be challenged by the liquidator under s.103(3).

50. Fraudulent and wrongful trading. *Fraudulent trading* is a criminal offence committed where in the course of a liquidation of a company its business has been carried on with intent to defraud its creditors or for any fraudulent purpose: Companies Act 1985, s.630.

The court may declare any person who is a party to the fraudulent trading to be personally responsible without limitation of liability for all or any of the company's debts and liabilities. Criminal penalties may also be incurred and a company director can be disqualified from acting as director of another company for up to 15 years.

NOTE: The expression "party to" involves some positive step being taken in order to carry on the company's business. For example, in *Re Maidstone Buildings Provisions Ltd.* (1971), it was held that the failure of the company's secretary to advise that the company was insolvent and should cease trading did not make him a "party to" carrying on the business of the company in a fraudulent manner.

Wrongful trading occurs where a company has gone into insolvent liquidation and at some time before this commenced a director knew or ought to have known that there was no reasonable prospect that this could be avoided and did not take the steps that ought to have been taken to minimise the potential loss to the company's creditors: Insolvency Act 1985, s.15.

On the application of the liquidator, the court may order the director to make whatever contribution it thinks proper to the company's assets. Proof of an intention to defraud a creditor is *not* necessary to incur this *civil liability* under s.15. The court can also make a disqualification order against the director.

51. Creditors. The position of creditors is similar to that of creditors in a bankruptcy.

(*a*) *Provable debts.* These include all claims against the company, present or future, certain or contingent, except:

(*i*) unliquidated damages not arising out of breach of contract or trust, for example, claims in tort for personal injuries;

(*ii*) Debts contracted with knowledge of a petition for compulsory winding up;

(*iii*) statute-barred debts.

Mutual dealings are taken into account in assessing what is payable, e.g. set-offs available at the date of commencement of winding up.

NOTE: The Insolvency Act 1985, s.164, gives a right of *set-off* in bankruptcy where there are mutual dealings between a bankrupt and a third party, e.g. his bank. This right of set-off *cannot be excluded* by agreement. At the time of writing, it is thought that this mandatory right of set-off will continue to apply in the winding up of companies.

In *National Westminster Bank Ltd.* v. *Halesowen Presswork and Assemblies Ltd.* (1972), the company's No. 1 account was frozen by agreement with a large overdrawn balance, and the No. 2 account was in operation with a substantial credit balance when the winding-up resolution was passed. The agreement purported to prevent the accounts being combined. HELD (H.L.): when the winding-up order terminated the banker-customer relationship, it also ended this ancillary agreement and the bank was entitled to set-off the credit balance on the No. 2 account against the overdrawn balance on the No. 1 account.

(*b*) *Secured creditors.* Secured creditors hold a mortgage, charge or lien on property *belonging to the debtor* as security for a debt due to them from the debtor. They can:

(*i*) rely on their securities and not prove for their debts;

(*ii*) realise their securities and prove as unsecured creditors for any deficiency;

(*iii*) surrender their securities and prove for the whole debts;

(*iv*) value their securities and prove as unsecured creditors for the balance.

If a secured creditor chooses to value his security, the liquidator (or the trustee in the bankruptcy process) may (*a*) redeem the security at that value, or (*b*) if he disagrees with the valuation, require that the security be sold.

A secured creditor cannot both enter a proof and retain his security.

NOTE: Guarantees and third party mortgages, charges or liens can be ignored when submitting a proof since these, if given up, would not increase the amount available for distribution to creditors: *Turner, ex parte West Riding Union Banking Co.* (1881).

(*c*) *Proof of debts.* Proof is by affidavit plus statement of account. Proof may be dispensed with by the liquidator in a voluntary winding up, but must always be made in a compulsory winding-up.

(*d*) *Preferential creditors.* These receive preference over certain other creditors (*see* below) in the winding up of a company. Under the Insolvency Act 1985, s.89, the following are preferential debts.

(*i*) *Corporation/income tax* due for the twelve month period before the relevant date.

(*ii*) *VAT* due for the six month period before the relevant date.

(*iii*) *Social security contributions*: for Class 1 and 2 contributions, those owing for the twelve month period before the relevant date; for Class 4 contributions, those owing for any twelve month period.

(*iv*) State and occupational *pension scheme* contributions.

(*v*) *Wages and salaries* of employees of the company for the four months before the relevant date, subject to a limit of (at present) £800 per employee (a director is not, as such, an employee of his company). This includes the current statutory payments in respect of sick pay, protective awards, payments during medical suspensions and time off work, e.g. on trade union duties.

(*vi*) Accrued *holiday pay*.

(*vii*) *Advances* made to make payments under (*v*) and (*vi*) above, to the extent to which the advance is actually used to satisfy these preferential claims. Typically, such advances would be made by a bank on a wages account. (Advances to make payments under "labour only" contracts between an employer and a sub-contractor do not have preferential status: *Re C.W. & A.L. Hughes Ltd.* (1966).)

For the purposes of determining the periods of time specified in s.89, the *relevant date* is the date the:

(*i*) *administration order was made*—for a compulsory liquidation where the winding up order was made immediately upon the discharge of an administration order;

(*ii*) *provisional liquidator was appointed*, if there is one, or the date the *winding up order* was made—for a compulsory liquidation where no administration order was made and where the company was not already in voluntary liquidation;

(*iii*) *resolution for the company's winding up was passed*—for a voluntary liquidation;

(*iv*) *receiver was appointed*—where the company is in receivership.

As between themselves preferential creditors rank equally (*pari passu*) but as a class they have priority over unsecured creditors and creditors secured by floating charges. They do not have priority over creditors secured by fixed charges nor over the costs of the winding up. Bank debentures normally give both fixed and floating charges and preferential creditors therefore only have priority over the assets covered by the floating charge (*see* **35** above).

NOTE: Where a banker has both a preferential claim against and holds security from his customer, he may realise the security and apply the proceeds in satisfaction of any non-preferential debt and claim as preferential creditor for the preferential debt: *Re William Hall (Contractors) Ltd.* (1967).

52. Distribution of assets in winding up. Debts and liabilities may be settled in any order if the company is solvent because every creditor will be paid in full. If the company is insolvent, the order of distribution of assets is as follows:

(*a*) to creditors secured by fixed charges—from the securities charged to them;

(*b*) to the costs of the liquidation;

(*c*) to the preferential creditors (*see* above);

(*d*) to debenture holders secured by floating charges;

(*e*) to unsecured creditors;

(*f*) any surplus assets are distributed proportionately among the company's members.

53. Wages accounts. The protection afforded by the Insolvency Act 1985, s.89, accounts for the practice of operating special wages accounts for company customers whose financial position is weak.

There is no necessity to open a wages account in order to rely on s.89: *Re Primrose (Builders) Ltd.* (1950), but in three ways it is to a banker's advantage to do so.

(*a*) It enables him to keep the position under review, the exact amount of the preferential claim being known at any time.

(*b*) It facilitates proving that the advance was made for the purpose of paying wages and salaries.

(*c*) It prevents the operation of the Rule in *Clayton's Case* (1816) to his detriment (*see* 3:**18**). Subsequent credits into a current account could easily cancel out the advances made to pay wages and salaries.

NOTE: In *Re Primrose (Builders) Ltd.* (1950), it was held that (now) s.614 still applies where cheques to pay salaries and wages are only paid on the receipt of covering credits. In the absence of a clear indication to the contrary, the Rule in *Clayton's Case* (1816) applies to such credits and they are appropriated to the earliest debit items on the account and not to the payment of the wages cheques. (Nevertheless, the Rule would eventually operate to the bank's detriment.)

A banker will usually still open a wages account when he holds a debenture secured by the usual fixed and floating charges, thereby enabling him to claim preference over his own floating charge. This is done because there may be other large preferential debts and, since these will rank equally with his own preferential claim, no assets may be left on which his floating charge can fasten.

54. Dissolution of a company. On completion of a winding up, a company must be dissolved. An order to this effect may be made by the court on the liquidator's application following a *compulsory liquidation*. The company will be dissolved from the date of the order.

It is usual, however, for the liquidator to prefer to apply to have the company struck off the register by the Registrar under the Companies Act 1985, s.652 on the grounds that the company is defunct (*see* below).

Following a *voluntary liquidation*, the liquidator must submit his accounts to a final general meeting of the company, and also to a final meeting of the creditors if the company was insolvent, and file a copy with the Registrar within one week. The company is automatically dissolved three months afterwards. The court may set aside the dissolution within two years on the application of the liquidator or any other interested party.

Under s.652, the Registrar may strike a company's name from the register, and thereby dissolve it, if he has reasonable cause to believe that the company is not carrying on business or otherwise not in operation, i.e. it is defunct. This does not affect the liability of any director or member, or the power of the court to wind up the company. Any member or creditor may within twenty years apply to the court for the name to be restored to the register.

Progress test 4

1. Define a corporation. (**1**)

2. State the distinctions between a public company and a private company. (**3**)

3. State the distinctions between a company and a partnership. (**4**)

4. What documents must be filed with the Registrar of Companies when registering a company? (**6**)

5. List the contents of a memorandum of association. (**7**)

6. Explain the *ultra vires* rule. (**7**)

7. Explain the effect of the Companies Act 1985, s.35 on the *ultra vires* rule. (**7**)

8. What do the articles of association regulate? (**8**)

9. What is the relationship of: (*a*) directors, and (*b*) a company secretary to their company? (**11–12**)

10. What does *Victors Ltd*. v. *Lingard* (1927) illustrate? (**13**)

11. In what circumstances can a company make a loan to one of its directors? (**14**)

12. Distinguish between: (*a*) authorised and issued capital; (*b*) shares and debentures. (**16–17**)

13. List the characteristics of preference shares. (**19**)

14. In what circumstances can a company reduce its share capital and how may this adversely affect a banker? (**21**)

15. Explain the importance of the Companies Act 1985, s.349. (**24**)

16. What limit does the Companies Act 1948, Table A, Article 79, impose on the borrowing powers of directors? (**26**)

17. List the remedies available to a banker who has made an *ultra vires* loan to a company. (**27**)

18. State the Rule in *Turquand's Case* (1856) and explain its importance to a banker. (**27**)

19. In relation to the Rule in *Turquand's Case*, what is the

importance of *A. L. Underwood Ltd.* v. *Bank of Liverpool and Martins* (1924)? (**27**)

20. List the charges created by a company which are registrable under the Companies Act 1985, s.395. (**29**)

21. In what circumstances may the 21 day period prescribed in s.395 be exceeded? (**31**)

22. Explain the importance of the decision in *Re C. L. Nye Ltd.* (1971). (**31**)

23. List the provisions usually to be found in a banker's debenture form. (**35**)

24. What advantage to a banker is an *all-moneys* debenture? (**35**)

25. Distinguish between a fixed charge and a floating charge. (**36**)

26. In what circumstances does a floating charge crystallise? (**36**)

27. List the defects of a floating charge. (**37**)

28. What is a *Romalpa Clause*, and what is the significance of such a clause to a banker? (**37**)

29. Explain the relevance of the Rule in *Clayton's Case* (1816) in relation to the Insolvency Act 1985, s.104. (**37**)

30. List the remedies available to a debenture holder. (**40**)

31. On what grounds can a petition be made to the court for a winding up order? (**42**)

32. When does a winding up commence? (**42**)

33. What are the consequences of a winding up order? (**42**)

34. List the duties of a liquidator. (**42**)

35. Distinguish between a members' voluntary winding up and a creditors' voluntary winding up. (**43**)

36. How is a bank's position protected in a voluntary arrangement under the Insolvency Act 1985, ss.20–6? (**44**)

37. What is the purpose of an administration order? (**45**)

38. Define transactions at an undervalue and preferences. (**47**)

39. List the categories of preferential creditors. (**51**)

40. In what order are assets distributed in a winding up? (**52**)

41. What are the advantages of operating a wages account? (**53**)

5
Individual insolvency

The legal framework

1. Background. The Insolvency Act 1985 rewrote, simplified and replaced the bankruptcy code contained in the Bankruptcy Act 1914 as amended. Wherever possible the new procedures parallel those used in winding up a company. (The parts of the Insolvency Act 1985 dealing with individual insolvency will not be fully in force until January 1987 and at the time of writing the detailed regulations required under some sections had not been made.)

There are three parts to the framework. Under the Insolvency Act 1985:

(*a*) the *bankruptcy process*;

(*b*) *voluntary arrangements*.

Under the Deeds of Arrangement Act 1914:

(*c*) *schemes of arrangement*.

The bankruptcy process

2. Introduction.

(*a*) *Definitions*. *Bankruptcy* is the legal process by which the estate (property) of an insolvent person is taken into the control of a trustee who uses it to pay off the debts owed to the creditors of that person. Bankruptcy does not apply to a company registered under one of the Companies Acts or to any other type of corporate body.

A *bankrupt* is a person against whom a *bankruptcy order* has been made by the court. Until the order is made he or she is referred to as a debtor.

(*b*) *The aims of the bankruptcy process.* The primary aim is to secure a fair distribution of a debtor's assets among his creditors, e.g. by preventing preference being shown to some at the expense of others.

The process also assists the honest and unfortunate debtor to free himself from a hopeless financial position, and imposes penalties upon the dishonest or reckless debtor, avoiding his fraudulent transactions so that he may not subsequently enjoy any profits from his dishonest or reckless behaviour.

To a lesser extent, the process enquires into the reasons for a person's insolvency.

(*c*) *Capacity in bankruptcy.* Any person with contractual capacity can be made bankrupt but the following require special consideration.

　(*i*) *Aliens* must fulfil the general residence or business activity qualification (*see* **3** below).

　(*ii*) *Minors* have only limited contractual capacity and they can only be made bankrupt in respect of debts incurred on contracts for necessaries (food, clothing, lodgings, etc.) or on judgment debts arising from proceedings in tort or for liability created by statute, e.g. for taxes.

　(*iii*) *Persons of unsound mind* can be made bankrupt, but the proceedings are subject to control by the court of protection.

　(*iv*) *Deceased persons* cannot be made bankrupt but their estates may be administered in bankruptcy. The administration order operates in a similar way to a bankruptcy order and overrides a grant of probate or letters of administration.

　(*v*) *Partnerships* can be made bankrupt and a bankruptcy order against a firm operates as a bankruptcy order against each named person who was a partner in the firm when the order was made (*see* 3: **19**).

3. The petition. Bankruptcy proceedings begin with a petition for a bankruptcy order.

(*a*) *Who may petition?* Under the Bankruptcy Act 1985, s.119(1), a petition can be presented by:

　(*i*) a creditor, or two or more creditors jointly;

　(*ii*) the debtor;

　(*iii*) the supervisor or any other person bound by a voluntary scheme or composition made as part of a voluntary arrangement under the Act;

(*iv*) where a criminal bankruptcy order has been made against the debtor, by the Director of Public Prosecutions under the Powers of Criminal Courts Act 1973.

(*b*) *Conditions of a valid petition.*

(*i*) The *debtor* must:

(1) be domiciled or personally present in England or Wales when the petition is presented; or

(2) have, at any time during the previous three years, been ordinarily resident or had a place of residence or carried on business in England or Wales: s. 119(2). This last condition includes carrying on a business by means of an agent or manager or as a member of a partnership.

(*ii*) The *debt or debts claimed* must be at least £750 and for a liquidated (certain) sum payable immediately or at some certain future time: s. 120(2).

(*iii*) The *debt must be unsecured*.

NOTE: A secured creditor, e.g. a bank holding a mortgage, charge or lien over the debtor's property, can petition provided that he states in the petition that he is willing to give up his security or that he can value it and petition on the unsecured balance: s. 120(5).

(*c*) *Creditor's petition.* The petition must allege that:

(*i*) the debtor appears *unable to pay* or has *no reasonable prospect of paying* the debt or debts specified in the petition; and

(*ii*) there is *no outstanding application* to have a *statutory demand* set aside: s. 120(2).

The petitioner can show apparent inability to pay by proving that he served on the debtor a *statutory demand* requiring him to pay, compound for (come to an arrangement on) or secure the debt and that the debtor did not comply with this within three weeks. (The three week period can be reduced if the petitioner establishes that there is a serious possibility of the debtor's property being significantly reduced or devalued if he waits the full period.) Alternatively, he can show that enforcement proceedings upon a judgment debt due to him have been returned wholly or partly unsatisfied.

The absence of reasonable prospects of being able to pay is shown by non-compliance within three weeks with a *statutory demand* requiring the debtor to establish such prospects. The three week period can similarly be reduced where the petitioner can establish that it could result in a serious decrease in the debtor's property or its value.

Once presented, a petition can only be withdrawn with the court's permission. The court *must* dismiss a petition if the statutory demand has been complied with. It *may* dismiss it if the debtor is able to pay all his debts or if the petitioner has unreasonably refused to accept the debtor's offer following a statutory demand to secure or compound for the debt. (The words "unreasonably refused" are likely to cause dispute.)

(*d*) *Petitions following a voluntary scheme*. A supervisor of, or other person bound by, a voluntary scheme (*see* **22** below) must allege that the debtor has *failed to comply* with the scheme or the supervisor's reasonable requests in connection with it, or supplied *false or misleading information* to obtain the scheme or approval of it at any creditors' meeting.

(*e*) *Petition based on a criminal bankruptcy order*. A bankruptcy order under the Insolvency Act 1985 must be made on the petition of the Director of Public Prosecutions on production of a criminal bankruptcy order made under the Powers of Criminal Courts Act 1973 where a person has been convicted of causing loss or damage to property exceeding (at present) £15,000, unless the order has been rescinded on appeal.

(*f*) *Debtor's petition*. A debtor may present his own petition only on the grounds of inability to pay his debts. The petition must be accompanied by a statement of affairs containing particulars of his creditors, his debts and other liabilities, and his assets.

4. Consequences of the petition.

(*a*) *Restrictions on dispositions of property*. Before a bankruptcy petition is presented, the debtor's affairs, including his bank account(s), are unaffected by the Insolvency Act 1985, although payments and transactions may subsequently be avoided on a bankruptcy order being made as being *preferences* or *transactions at an undervalue*, etc. (*see* **14** below). In addition, a bank may have already begun to take less formal steps against him.

(*i*) *Void transactions*. Any disposition of property or payment of money made in the period between the petition being presented and the trustee in bankruptcy being appointed is *void* unless sanctioned by the court beforehand or subsequently ratified. Without the court's approval, the person to whom the property was transferred or the payment made, e.g. a bank receiving repayment of a loan or a charge over the debtor's property, holds it as part of the debtor's estate: Insolvency Act 1985, s.131.

NOTE: It is thought that the court will allow bona fide transactions entered into to keep the debtor's business going to stand even though the other party knew that a petition had been presented. Knowledge of the petition loses the protection of s.131(4) (*see* below). Preferences and transactions at an undervalue will effect the court's discretion under s.131.

(*ii*) *Protected transactions.* No recourse is possible against a person who dealt with the debtor in good faith, for value and without notice of the presentation of the petition in the period between the presentation of the petition and the making of the bankruptcy order: s.131(4). Any person subsequently acquiring that property or an interest in it *from* a protected person, e.g. a bank taking a charge over it, is similarly protected, apparently whether or not he acts in good faith, for value and without notice of the presentation of the petition.

NOTE: This protection does not apply to dispositions or payments made *after the commencement* of bankruptcy, i.e. after the date of the bankruptcy order, *except* where the bankrupt has incurred a debt to a *banker* or other person by making a payment void under s.131, *provided* that the banker or other person did not have notice of the bankruptcy order and the money was paid to someone from whom it was reasonably practicable to recover the payment: s.131(5). The subsection could apply where a banker continues the debtor's account in ignorance of the bankruptcy and paying third party cheques causes the account to become overdrawn or increases an existing overdraft.

(*b*) *Proceedings against the debtor.* While bankruptcy proceedings are pending the court can stay any action, execution or legal process against the property or person of the debtor.

(*c*) *Interim receivers.* An interim receiver is appointed where it is necessary for the protection of the debtor's estate: Insolvency Act 1985, s.133. He has such powers as the court gives him, including the power to take all steps to protect the estate.

The Official Receiver will be the interim receiver unless the debtor presented the petition himself and an insolvency practitioner has been appointed to report on his affairs (*see* below). In this case the insolvency practitioner may be appointed interim receiver.

(*d*) *Special managers.* The court can appoint a special manager with such powers as the court thinks fit where the appointment is required by the nature of the debtor's estate, property or business or by the interests of the creditors: Insolvency Act 1985, s. 198.

(*e*) *Voluntary arrangements and summary administrations.* As an alternative to making a bankruptcy order on a *debtor's petition*, the court can appoint an *insolvency practitioner* under the Insolvency Act 1985, s. 123(2), to inquire into and report to the court on the debtor's affairs and willingness to propose a voluntary arrangement. This is done in an attempt to avoid the full effect of a bankruptcy. The report must state whether or not a meeting of creditors should be summoned to consider the debtor's proposals.

This procedure can only be followed where:

(*i*) unsecured debts are below the *small bankruptcies level* (probably £15,000);

(*ii*) the value of the assets is at least of a *minimum amount* (possibly £2,000);

(*iii*) the debtor has not been adjudged bankrupt nor made a composition or scheme with his creditors within the five years before the presentation of the petition;

(*iv*) it would be appropriate to obtain such a report: s. 123(1).

After receiving the report from the insolvency practitioner, the court may:

(*i*) make an interim order to assist the making of a *voluntary arrangement* (*see* **21** below); or, where it thinks that this would be inappropriate —

(*ii*) make a *bankruptcy order* and issue a certificate for a *summary administration* under s. 123(6).

In a *summary administration* an insolvency practitioner will usually act as trustee and the Official Receiver will therefore not be involved. The court can revoke the certificate at any time in favour of the full bankruptcy process.

5. Bankruptcy order. This makes the debtor an *undischarged bankrupt* and, subject to exceptions (*see* **12** below), *title* to the bankrupt's property vests in his trustee in bankruptcy on the date of his appointment: s.153. Unsecured creditors lose their rights of action against the debtor and they can only prove in his bankruptcy. The order must be published in the *London Gazette* and a local newspaper.

An undischarged bankrupt commits a *criminal offence* under the Insolvency Act 1985, s.189, if he obtains credit of (at present) £50 or more without disclosing his status or engages (directly or indirectly) in any business under a name different to the one in which he was adjudged bankrupt without disclosing that name to all persons with whom he enters into any business transaction.

The Companies Act 1985, s.302, makes it a criminal offence for an undischarged bankrupt to act as a director or take part in the management of a registered company without the court's consent.

6. Proceedings following the bankruptcy order.

(*a*) *Official receiver*. Subject to the exceptions below, the Official Receiver becomes the receiver and manager of the bankrupt's estate pending the appointment of a trustee in bankruptcy: Insolvency Act 1985, s.134.

Exceptions:

(*i*) in criminal bankruptcy proceedings or summary administrations (*see* **4** above), the Official Receiver becomes trustee immediately the order is made;

(*ii*) if an insolvency practitioner was appointed following the debtor's own petition, he can be appointed trustee at the time the bankruptcy order is made;

(*iii*) where the order follows non-compliance with the terms of a scheme or composition, the supervisor may be appointed trustee at the time the order is made.

By s.136 the Official Receiver must investigate the bankrupt's conduct and affairs, including matters which occurred before the bankruptcy order was made. At his discretion he may make a report to the court and summons a general meeting of the bankrupt's creditors; he must summons a meeting if the court directs: Insolvency Act 1985, s.134(5).

(*b*) *Statement of affairs*. Unless the Official Receiver directs otherwise, the bankrupt has 21 days to prepare and submit to the Official Receiver a statement of affairs. Failure to do so is a contempt of court. The statement must include details of debts, liabilities and assets: Insolvency Act 1985, s.135.

NOTE: A debtor who presented his own petition will have submitted a statement of affairs with his petition.

(c) *Public examination.* The Official Receiver, at his own instigation or that of half by value of the creditors, may apply to the court for a public examination of the bankrupt. An application can be made at any time after the making of the bankruptcy order and before the bankrupt's discharge: Insolvency Act 1985, s.137.

NOTE: It is unlikely that the court will order a public examination where the total sum owed is small, or where the bankruptcy does not affect a wide circle of trade creditors and is of little public interest.

(d) *Appointment of a special manager.* A special manager can be appointed by the court on the application of the Official Receiver or trustee in bankruptcy (*see* **4** above).

(e) *Appointment of a trustee in bankruptcy. See* **8** below.

(f) *Appointment of a committee of creditors.* Unless the trustee in bankruptcy is the Official Receiver, the creditors may appoint a committee of creditors. Certain of the trustee's powers can only be exercised with the committee's consent (*see* **9** below).

7. Duration and discharge of bankruptcy. Bankruptcy *commences* with the day upon which the bankruptcy order is made and *continues* until the bankrupt obtains his discharge: Insolvency Act 1985, s.126(1).

Discharge occurs in:

(a) *summary administrations*: two years from the making of the bankruptcy order;

(b) *criminal bankruptcy*: by court order on an application by the bankrupt which can be made when five years have elapsed since the making of the bankruptcy order;

(c) *repeated bankruptcy*: if the bankrupt has been an undischarged bankrupt in the fifteen years before his current bankruptcy commenced, he can apply for discharge to the court when five years have elapsed since the making of the order;

NOTE: In (*b*) and (*c*) above, the court may allow, refuse, or suspend the discharge and/or make it conditional.

(*d*) *other cases*: automatically after three years have elapsed since the making of the order.

NOTE: The Official Receiver can defeat this automatic right by satisfying the court that the bankrupt failed to comply with his obligations under the Act. A successful application stops time running under s.126.

Trustee in bankruptcy

8. Appointment.

(*a*) *By the creditors* at a general meeting of creditors: Insolvency Act 1985, s.139. Where the Official Receiver acts as receiver and manager after the bankruptcy order, he has 12 weeks in which to decide whether to call a meeting and notify creditors of it. He must call a meeting if one-quarter by value of the creditors demand it.

An appointment by the creditors operates from the time stated in the certificate of appointment.

(*b*) *By the court* under s.144. In a *summary administration*, the court may appoint someone other than the Official Receiver on making the order. On a *debtor's petition* the insolvency practitioner who reported on the debtor's affairs (*see* **4** above) can be appointed trustee by the court when the bankruptcy order is made.

Where the order results from the debtor not complying with a *scheme or composition* (*see* **20** below), the supervisor of the scheme may be appointed by the court when the bankruptcy order is made.

An appointment by the court takes effect at the time it states on making the bankruptcy order.

(*c*) *By the Secretary of State*. If the creditors fail to appoint a trustee at their meeting, the Official Receiver can ask the Secretary of State to appoint one. If no application is made by the Official Receiver, or the Secretary of State does not make an appointment, the Official Receiver continues as the trustee.

An appointment by the Secretary of State takes effect at the time stated by him.

(*d*) *By s. 144(1)*. The Official Receiver becomes the trustee in a bankruptcy which follows a criminal bankruptcy order. His appointment takes effect from the making of the order.

NOTE: The creditors *cannot remove* the Official Receiver as trustee under a criminal bankruptcy order or where he is appointed by the court under the summary administration procedure. In other cases, appointees of the court or Secretary of State can be removed at a meeting requested by one-quarter in value of the creditors. The Secretary of State and the court can always remove their appointees.

9. Function and duties.

(*a*) *Function*. By the Insolvency Act 1985, s. 152(2), the trustee's function is to get in, realise and distribute the bankrupt's estate in accordance with the Act.

(*b*) *Duties*. His main specific duties are:

(*i*) to get possession and control over the debtor's property, e.g. by collecting debts due to the bankrupt;

NOTE: A banker holding property to the account of or for the bankrupt, e.g. moneys in his accounts and items deposited for safe custody, must pay or deliver this property to the trustee if it forms part of his estate and if he has no right to retain it as against the trustee or bankrupt. Thus, property that is the subject of a lien or a mortgage to the bank does not have to be delivered.

(*ii*) to convert the bankrupt's assets into money as quickly and as effectively as possible;

(*iii*) to make proper distribution of the proceeds among the creditors;

(*iv*) to call a meeting of creditors when called upon to do so by one-tenth in value of them;

(*v*) to keep proper accounts;

(*vi*) to act in the utmost good faith;

(*vii*) to call a final meeting of creditors when the administration is complete.

10. Powers

(*a*) On his *own authority* under the Insolvency Act 1985, s. 160, his powers include:

(*i*) selling all or any of the bankrupt's property;

(*ii*) giving receipts for money paid to the estate;

(*iii*) exercising any powers reasonably incidental to his duties and executing any necessary document.

(*b*) With the *permission of the committee of creditors* his powers include (s. 160):

(*i*) carrying on the bankrupt's business in order beneficially to wind it up;

(*ii*) bringing or defending legal proceedings in respect of the bankrupt's property;

(*iii*) mortgaging or pledging assets in order to raise money for the estate;

(*iv*) making a compromise or other arrangement on any claim by or against the bankrupt;

(*v*) appointing the bankrupt to manage the business.

NOTE: Every bankruptcy is under the general control of the court. If the bankrupt, any creditor, e.g. a bank, or any other person is dissatisfied with the trustee's decisions or intentions he can apply to the court. The court can then make such an order as it thinks is appropriate. (The controlling powers of the committee of creditors have yet to be prescribed by delegated legislation under the Insolvency Act 1985.)

Assets in bankruptcy

11. Introduction.

(*a*) *Key dates*. The three dates which determine the position are:

(*i*) the date the *petition is presented*;

(*ii*) the date of the *bankruptcy order*;

(*iii*) the date the *trustee's appointment takes effect*, i.e. the date the bankrupt's estate vests in the trustee.

(*b*) *Key principles*.

(*i*) By the Insolvency Act 1985, s. 131, any *disposition of property or payment of money* made in the period between the petition being presented and the trustee in bankruptcy being appointed is *void* unless sanctioned by the court beforehand or subsequently ratified (*see* **4** above).

(*ii*) The bankrupt's estate, i.e. the *available assets*, consists of property belonging to or vested in the bankrupt when the bank-ruptcy order was made — the commencement of bankruptcy. However, the estate is subject to the rights of any person other than the bankrupt, e.g. a secured creditor: Insolvency Act 1985, s. 130(6). Thus, a bank is able to sell or otherwise deal with property which is the subject of a legal charge or a lien without reference to the trustee.

12. Trustee's title.

(a) *Commencement.* The trustee's title commences on the day the bankruptcy order is made (s. 126(1)) but the bankrupt's property vests in the trustee on the day his appointment takes effect (s. 153(1)). These dates may be some weeks apart.

(b) *Property acquired after the bankruptcy order.* This may be claimed by the trustee by serving written notice on the bankrupt: Insolvency Act 1985, s. 154.

The trustee's title to such property relates back to the date it was acquired by the bankrupt *unless* (i) it is transferred to a bona fide purchaser for value without notice of the bankruptcy; or (ii) a banker enters into a transaction concerning the property, e.g. taking a mortgage or making payments to the bankrupt's direction, without notice of the bankruptcy. The trustee has no remedy in either case, nor against any person deriving title to the property from that person or banker: Insolvency Act 1985, s. 154(4).

(c) *Disclaimer of onerous property.* Under s. 161, the trustee can disclaim the following onerous property:

(i) unprofitable contracts;

(ii) unsaleable or not readily saleable property;

(iii) property which may give rise to a liability to pay money or perform any other onerous act.

The disclaimer determines all rights, liabilities and interests of the bankrupt in the property and discharges the trustee from any personal liability.

If a lease is disclaimed, a copy of the disclaimer must be served upon every person, e.g. a bank, claiming under the bankrupt as a mortgagee or underlessee. Within fourteen days such persons can apply to the court for an order making any person in whom the disclaimed property is vested subject to the same liabilities and obligations as those to which the bankrupt was subject under the lease on the day the bankruptcy petition was presented.

13. Unavailable assets.

(*a*) *Trade and personal property.* Unavailable for distribution are such tools, books, vehicles and other items of equipment necessary to the bankrupt for personal use by him in his employment, business or vocation; and such clothing, bedding, furniture, household equipment and provisions as are necessary for satisfying the basic domestic needs of the bankrupt and his family: Insolvency Act 1985, s. 130(2).

Where the realisable value of any such asset appears to the trustee to exceed the cost of replacement, however, the trustee can claim it. If he does, he is under an obligation to replace it.

(*b*) *Property held by the bankrupt as trustee.*

(*c*) *Personal income* necessary to support himself and his family.

(*d*) *Rights of action* to recover damages for injuries to his person or reputation.

(*e*) *Family home.* Under the Matrimonial Homes Act 1983, a spouse who is not the legal owner of the matrimonial home has rights of occupation that can be registered as a charge on the home and which can only be defeated by court order.

Should the other spouse be made bankrupt, the charge binds the trustee in bankruptcy. If he wishes to realise the bankrupt's interest in the home, he must apply to the court: Insolvency Act 1985, s. 171(2).

Under s. 171(4), the court can make any order it thinks fit and just having regard to the interests of the creditors, the conduct of the spouse or former spouse with regard to the bankruptcy, to the needs and financial resources of the spouse or former spouse, to the needs of any children and to all the circumstances of the case other than the needs of the bankrupt. A trustee must also apply to the court to realise the bankrupt's share in a jointly owned matrimonial home and the same factors are considered. Similarly, a bankrupt cannot be evicted without a court order from a dwelling house in which he has children under 18 years of age living and in which he has a beneficial estate or interest: Insolvency Act 1985, s. 172.

14. Recoverable property.

(*a*) *Preferences.* An individual makes a preference if he does anything or suffers anything to be done which has the effect of putting a creditor or guarantor for any of his debts or liabilities in a *better position* in the event of his bankruptcy than he would have been in had that thing not been done: Insolvency Act 1985, s.174. (*See* also 4:**47**.)

To be actionable, the trustee must show that:

(*i*) the individual was *insolvent* when he made the preference;

(*ii*) the individual was *influenced by a desire* to put the creditor or guarantor in a better position *unless* the preference was made to an *associate* of the individual when the influence will be presumed; (By the Insolvency Act 1985, s.223, a person is an associate of an individual if that person is the individual's spouse, or is a relative, or the spouse of a relative, of the individual or the individual's spouse. A company controlled by the individual or an associate (as defined above) of the individual is an associate.)

(*iii*) the preference took place within certain periods before the presentation of the petition:

(1) *six months*: where the person preferred was *not* an associate;

(2) *two years*: where the person preferred was an associate.

(*b*) *Transactions at an undervalue.* An individual enters into such a transaction with a person if he:

(*i*) makes a *gift* to that person;

(*ii*) is to receive *no consideration* from that person under the transaction;

(*iii*) enters into the transaction in *consideration of marriage*;

(*iv*) is to receive a consideration that is worth *significantly less* than the consideration that he provides: Insolvency Act 1985, s.174(2).

To be actionable, the trustee must show that:

(*i*) the individual was *insolvent* when he entered into the transaction;

(*ii*) the transaction was entered into in the *five years* prior to the presentation of the petition.

NOTE: No intention to benefit the other party is required; liability arises from the fact that the transaction was entered into.

In the case of *both preferences and transactions at an undervalue*, the court can make orders to restore the position to what it would have been if the individual had not entered into the transaction or made the preference. For example, it can order that the property transferred be vested in the trustee in bankruptcy and benefits received be returned, including the setting aside of mortgages or charges that are part of the transaction, or revive the obligations of a surety released by a bank.

However, a purchaser for value of property which was the subject of a preference or a transaction at an undervalue who buys in good faith and without notice of the relevant circumstances, acquires a good title to it even though the vendor's title was voidable. The court cannot make an order which upsets his interest. Nor can the court order a person who received a benefit from the transaction or preference in the same circumstances to make any payment to the trustee unless the person was a party to the transaction or the payment is in respect of a preference given to the person at the time he was a creditor of the individual: Insolvency Act 1985, s. 175(2).

(c) *Transactions defrauding creditors.* Such transactions are those:

(i) entered into by a person with any other person *at an undervalue*; and

(ii) entered into for the purpose of *putting assets beyond the reach of* actual or potential claimants against the person, or with the intention to otherwise prejudice the interests of such claimants: Insolvency Act 1985, s.212(1).

If it is satisfied that such was the purpose of the transaction, the court can make such an order as it thinks fit to restore the position to what it would have been if the transaction had not been entered into and/or to protect the interests of such claimants. An application for an order under this section can be made by the Official Receiver or the trustee in bankruptcy, or the supervisor of a composition or scheme, as appropriate.

NOTE: *Undervalue* has the same meaning as in s. 174(2) (*see* above) and the court has the same powers.

However, a purchaser for value of property which was the subject of a fraudulent transaction within s.212 who buys in good faith and without notice of the relevant circumstances acquires a good title even though the vendor's title was voidable. The court cannot make an order which upsets his interest. Nor can the court order any person who received a benefit from the transaction in the same circumstances to make any payment to the trustee unless he was a party to the transaction: Insolvency Act 1985, s.212(5)

(*d*) *Extortionate credit transactions*. A credit transaction is extortionate under the Insolvency Act 1985, s.176, if, having regard to the risk accepted by the person providing the credit, it requires grossly exorbitant payments to be made or otherwise grossly contravenes ordinary principles of fair dealing. The transaction is presumed to be extortionate unless the contrary is proved.

If the bankrupt was a party to any such transaction within *three years* of the bankruptcy order, the trustee in bankruptcy can apply to the court for an order setting aside the transaction or otherwise varying the terms of the transaction or the terms on which security is held.

NOTE: It would seem that the trustee may also be able to attack such transactions as being transactions at an undervalue (*see* above), in which case the operative period is five not three years.

(*e*) *Assignment of book debts*. If the assignor is subsequently made bankrupt, an assignment of any debts which have not been paid at the time the bankruptcy is presented can be avoided by the trustee *unless* the assignment was registered under the Bills of Sale Act 1878 as though it were an absolute bill of sale. This could effect a bank involved in factoring debts.

15. Rights of distress and execution. The Insolvency Act 1985, s.180(9), allows a landlord to distrain upon the goods or effects of the bankrupt either before or after the bankruptcy order for rent due for up to six months before the order was made.

Under s.179, a creditor who has issued execution against the property of the debtor or who has attached any debt due to him can only retain the benefit of the execution or attachment against the trustee if it is completed before the bankruptcy order is made.

By s.179(5):

(*a*) an *execution against goods* is completed by seizure and sale or by the making of a charging order under the Charging Orders Act 1979;

(*b*) an *attachment of a debt* is completed by the receipt of the debt; and

(*c*) an *execution against land* is completed by seizure, by the appointment of a receiver, or by the making of a charging order.

Payment of creditors

16. Proof of debts. A creditor must prove his debt before he can be paid. This must be done as quickly as possible after the receiving order. Proof is, at present, by a statement, accompanied by an affidavit if the Official Receiver so requires, asserting the claim and stating any surrounding circumstances. Within twenty-eight days of the proof being submitted, the trustee must (a) admit liability, (b) reject it, or (c) require further evidence. (Delegated legislation will be made under the Act regarding proof of debts.)

17. Provable debts. These are all debts and liabilities, present and future, certain or contingent, to which the debtor is subject at the date of the bankruptcy order, or to which he may become subject before his discharge by reason of any obligation incurred before the date of the bankruptcy order: Insolvency Act 1985, s.211.

If the debt is *contingent* (i.e. dependent on the happening of some future event), the trustee must assess its value and make allowance for it. If the creditor disagrees with the assessment, he can appeal to the court.

If there have been dealings between the bankrupt and another party (*mutual dealings*), an account is taken and only the balance is brought to account in the bankruptcy: Insolvency Act 1985, s.146. It is not possible to contract out of this right of *set-off*.

No set-off is possible if the creditor knew of an act of bankruptcy when he gave credit to the debtor.

18. Non-provable debts.

(a) Unliquidated damages not arising out of a breach of contract or breach of trust, e.g. damages from an action in tort.

(b) Debts which in the opinion of the court are incapable of being fairly assessed.

(c) Debts due to any person who knew that a bankruptcy petition had been presented at the time the debt was incurred.

(d) Debts contracted after the date of the bankruptcy order, i.e. the commencement of bankruptcy. (For a bank's position, *see* **24** below.)

19. Rights of creditors.

(a) *Types of creditor.* Secured creditors and preferential creditors (s.166) have already been fully discussed in 4:51.

Unsecured creditors can only enter a proof for amounts due to them from the debtor and await whatever dividend is ultimately paid. They rank *pari passu* (equally) among themselves. A landlord may, however, distrain for rent owed to him (*see* 15 above).

If any surplus remains after the above claims are met, interest on proved contractual claims is then paid from the date of the bankruptcy order.

Deferred creditors are paid *after* all other creditors have been paid in full. Such deferred claims include:

(i) loans between spouses for business purposes: Insolvency Act 1985, s.166(6).

(ii) loans to a business at a rate of interest varying with profits: Partnership Act 1890, s.3.

(iii) a joint creditor's claim against the separate estate of a bankrupt partner (*see* 3:19).

NOTE: In the case of a claim for payment of foreign currency arising under a contract subject to the law of a foreign country, the date for converting the "foreign currency claim" into sterling is the date of the admission of the proof, and not the date of the breach: *Miliangos* v. *George Frank (Textiles) Ltd.* (1975).

(b) *Order of repayment.*

(i) Creditors secured by fixed charges—from the securities charged to them (*see* generally 4:51).

(ii) Administrative costs and charges incurred in the bankruptcy, e.g. the expenses of the the trustee and the trustee's remuneration (if any).

(iii) Pre-preferential debts, e.g. a proportion of any premium paid to the bankrupt by an apprentice or articled clerk.

(iv) Preferential creditors (*see* 4:51).

(v) Unsecured creditors.

(vi) Deferred creditors.

Voluntary arrangements

20. Introduction. The aim of a voluntary arrangement is to avoid

bankruptcy. The procedure can be used by an individual in financial difficulties in advance of any bankruptcy proceedings and, by applying for an *interim order*, he can obtain a short period of protection from creditors' actions while a proposal for a *composition* of his debts or a *scheme of arramgement* of his affairs is put together. The system of *deeds of arrangement* (*see* below) has the weakness that only those creditors who assent to the arrangement are bound by it. A voluntary arrangement under the Insolvency Act 1985 is binding on all the debtor's creditors.

The system is similar to the voluntary arrangement system for companies.

21. Interim order.

(*a*) *Application.* The application may be made by the debtor or, if he is an undischarged bankrupt, by his trustee in bankruptcy or the Official Receiver. No application may be made, however, if the debtor has presented his own bankruptcy petition and an insolvency practitioner has already been appointed by the court to prepare a report and supervise the implementation of the composition or scheme (*see* **4** above): Insolvency Act 1985, s. 111.

The court will make an interim order where the debtor intends to make a proposal to his creditors for a composition in satisfaction of his debts or a scheme of arrangement of his affairs and where it considers that it will assist its consideration and implementation. The proposal must provide for a *nominee* to act in relation to the composition or scheme.

(*b*) *Effect.* While it is in force:

(*i*) no bankruptcy petition relating to the debtor may be presented or proceeded with; and

(*ii*) no other proceedings and no execution or other legal process may be commenced or continued against the debtor or his property without the court's consent.

The interim order is effective for 14 days but the court may extend this period.

22. Subsequent procedure.

(*a*) *Nominee's report.* The debtor must give the nominee details of his proposed scheme and a statement of affairs with details of his creditors, debts, liabilities and assets. On the basis of this information, the nominee prepares and submits his own report to the court. It must include a recommendation as to whether or not a debtors' meeting should be summoned to consider the proposals: Insolvency Act 1985, s.113.

(*b*) *Creditors' meeting.* If a meeting is held, notice of it must be sent to all creditors. At the meeting the creditors can approve the scheme as it is or amend it. They may also replace the nominee with another insolvency practitioner.

The debtor must consent to any amendments.

By s.115, the meeting cannot approve any proposal or amendment which:

(*i*) restricts the right of any secured creditor to enforce his security, e.g. a bank holding a mortgage;

(*ii*) removes the priority of any preferential creditor;

(*iii*) would pay preferential creditors at unequal rates.

The result of the meeting must be reported to the court.

(*c*) *Approval of the proposal.* Where the meeting approves the proposal, it takes effect as if made by the debtor at the meeting. It:

(*i*) binds all creditors who had notice of the meeting, whether or not they attended and voted;

(*ii*) dismisses any pending bankruptcy petition; and

(*iii*) if the debtor was an undischarged bankrupt, the court can annul any bankruptcy order against him and/or give directions as to the conduct of the bankruptcy and administration of his estate in order to facilitate the implementation of the approved composition or scheme.

(*d*) *Challenge of the meeting's decision.* The decision can be challenged within 28 days of the report of the meeting to the court on the grounds that it prejudices the interests of a creditor or that there was some material irregularity at or in relation to the meeting. The challenge can be made by the debtor, a creditor, the nominee or, if the debtor is an undischarged bankrupt, by his trustee in bankruptcy or the Official Receiver.

(*e*) *Supervision of the arrangement.* On its approval, the nominee or his replacement becomes the *supervisor* of the scheme or composition. He can apply to the court for directions and, if dissatisfied with his actions, the debtor or any creditor can apply to the court to confirm, reverse or modify any of his acts or decisions. The court can also replace him and appoint others to work with him: Insolvency Act 1985, s.118.

NOTE: A voluntary procedure can be changed into a bankruptcy on the application of the supervisor or a creditor.

Deeds of arrangement

23. Definition. A deed of arrangement is any agreement (whether under seal or not) made (*a*) for the benefit of creditors generally, or (*b*) by an insolvent debtor for the benefit of three or more creditors.

Alternatively, such agreements may take the form of a *composition with creditors*, i.e. a contract by which the creditors agree to accept a portion of what they are owed in complete discharge of their claims. Such a composition is binding on the creditors because of the mutual interchange of promises not to sue for the whole debt.

The making of a deed of arrangement is a private arrangement outside the Insolvency Act 1985. It avoids the depletion of the bankrupt's assets through the high costs involved and the delay and publicity attendant on the bankruptcy process. However, the assets available for distribution will probably be less because the trustee is unable to set aside preferences, etc. (*see* **14** above). Deeds of arrangement have, however, been little used and this was a reason for the introduction of *voluntary arrangements* by the Insolvency Act 1985.

24. The Deeds of Arrangement Act 1914. If an arrangement or composition is embodied in a document (whether under seal or not), it is *void* unless:

(*a*) it is registered at the Department of Trade and Industry within seven days of execution and is properly stamped: s.2;

(*b*) if made for the benefit of creditors generally, it is assented to by a majority in number and value within twenty-one days of registration. Within twenty-eight days of registration, the trustee must file a statutory declaration that the required assent has been obtained: s.3.

NOTE: A deed affecting unregistered land must also be registered at the Land Charges Registry in the Register of Pending Actions:

Land Charges Act 1925. If not registered, the assignment will be void against a purchaser for value of the land.

Bankruptcy and banking

25. Preferences. A preference is made under the Insolvency Act 1985, s.174, if an individual does anything or suffers anything to be done which has the effect of putting a creditor or guarantor for any of his debts or liabilities in a *better position* in the event of his bankruptcy than he would have been in had that thing not been done.

A bank's position has been discussed at **14** above and at **4:47**. You should refer to those sections now. Remember:

(*a*) the possibility of a bank being innocently preferred: *Re M. Kushler Ltd.* (1943);

(*b*) that the mere fact that a creditor is preferred is insufficient to render a payment voidable; the individual's action must be *influenced by a desire* to prefer: *Re William Hall (Contractors) Ltd.* (1967);

(*c*) pressure to make repayment may prevent a payment being voidable as a preference.

26. A bank's protection.

(*a*) *Preferences.* Where the bank has had to repay a preference, the Insolvency Act 1985, s.175, enables the court to revive any obligation released, e.g. that of a guarantor, or impose new obligations, and require security to be provided for the discharge of any obligation imposed (*see* **14** above).

NOTE: A bank can also protect itself by including a clause in any guarantee entitling it to be retained for at least six months after repayment has been made. This would be useful if the court declined to revive the guarantor's obligation.

(*b*) *Fraudulent transactions.* A bank's interest, e.g. as a mortgagee, in property which was the subject of a fraudulent transaction is protected if it was acquired for value, in good faith and without notice of the relevant circumstances (*see* **14** above).

(*c*) *Void transactions.*

(*i*) In the period between the petition being presented and a bankruptcy order being made, a bank is protected if it deals with the debtor in good faith, for value and without notice that the petition had been presented: s.131(4). If it subsequently acquires an interest in property from a protected person, that interest is similarly projected.

(*ii*) While protection is generally lost after the bankruptcy order is made, a bank is protected if it makes a payment provided it did not have notice of the bankruptcy order and it is reasonably practicable to recover the payment from the payee (*see* **4** above).

(*d*) *Rights as a secured creditor*. These cannot be effected without the bank's consent in any bankruptcy process or voluntary arrangement.

(*e*) *Preferential creditor status* in respect of advances made to pay wages and accrued holiday pay. Operating a *wages account* will help a bank monitor its position (*see* 4:**49** and **51**).

27. A customer's bankruptcy.

(*a*) *Introduction*. Apart from restrictions on the operation of his account, good banking practice can often at least enable a banker to avoid serious loss in a customer's bankruptcy and quite possibly any involvement at all. Initially, a customer's account can be operated normally, even where a banker has indications of his insolvency. Restrictions first become necessary when he receives notice that a bankruptcy petition has been presented against his customer: Insolvency Act 1985, s.131.

(*b*) *Action after notice of a bankruptcy petition*. If the account is in *credit*, payments from the account and delivery of securities or safe custody items may be made only to the debtor or to a person claiming by assignment from him, e.g. the trustee named in a deed of arrangement. The account must be operated only according to the instructions given by an *interim receiver* or *special manager*, provided their authority covers the operation of the account, if appointed by the court when the petition is presented.

Cheques payable to *third parties* should *not* be paid.

If the account is *overdrawn*, no payments can be made because debts contracted after notice of a bankruptcy petition are not provable.

Payments into the account, whether it is in credit or overdrawn, must be held in a *suspense account*.

(c) *Action after notice of a bankruptcy petition.* The account must be *stopped entirely* on receiving notice of the making of a bankruptcy order. No securities or safe custody items may be released.

The balance (if any) in the account and any securities held are automatically transferred to the Official Receiver or the trustee in bankruptcy, when appointed, on the making of a bankruptcy order. A banker is then under a duty to make delivery of such funds and securities to the trustee: Insolvency Act 1985, s.158(3).

Where a banker has notice of only a petition and this is subsequently dismissed, the restrictions on the account can be lifted.

NOTE: When a banker has already incurred obligations on his customer's behalf, he may debit his account even after having received notice of a petition or a bankruptcy order against him, e.g. a payment on settlement day following the purchase of shares on his instructions. (The share certificate, however, must be held for the trustee when it is received.)

The making of a *bankruptcy order* against a customer terminates his contract with the bank. His banker's authority to pay cheques or to accept or pay bills of exchange on his behalf is terminated because all his property rights become automatically transferred to his trustee in bankruptcy. By s.164, a right of set-off exists between the bank and customer where there are mutual debts, mutual credits or other mutual dealings. It is not possible to exclude this right.

(d) *Joint accounts.* The same rules and practices apply to a joint account if bankruptcy proceedings are begun against one of the joint account holders.

The balance in the account (if any) must be divided between the solvent party and the trustee.

Cheques drawn on the account must be returned, but the credit of the solvent party must not be damaged when doing so.

Liability on the account will invariably be *joint and several* and a banker is therefore able to prove against the bankrupt's estate for any balance due without prejudicing its rights against the solvent party. (*See* also 3:**18**.)

NOTE: Stopping the account prevents the Rule in *Clayton's Case* (1816) operating to the banker's detriment (*see* 3:**18**).

(e) *Undischarged bankrupts.* In the rather unusual event of a banker discovering that a customer is an undischarged bankrupt, he must immediately inform the trustee in bankruptcy or the Department of Trade and Industry.

No payments may be made from the account except by order of the court or on the instructions of the trustee, or the Department of Trade and Industry if the trustee's name cannot be discovered. If no instructions are received from the trustee *within one month*, the account can again be operated normally.

NOTE: Failure to follow this procedure will render the bank liable to the trustee for all moneys paid out of the account.

The same procedure should be followed where it is clear that an account is being operated by the *nominee* of an undischarged bankrupt, as only a person dealing directly with the bankrupt is protected. (*See* **4** above.)

If a banker has any suspicions that one of his customers is an undischarged bankrupt, a search of the *Bankruptcy Register* can be made.

28. The bankruptcy of a guarantor. Immediately a banker receives notice that a bankruptcy order has been made against a person who has guaranteed or deposited securities to secure the overdraft of a customer, the customer's account must be stopped.

In order to prove in the guarantor's bankruptcy, a banker must make a demand for immediate repayment from his customer, thereby fixing the guarantor's liability.

A similar procedure should be adopted if notice of a bankruptcy petition against the guarantor comes to the banker's attention. Fresh security must be provided if subsequent borrowing is to be allowed on the account.

29. Bills of exchange. A banker will be affected in two circumstances by the bankruptcy of a customer who is a party to a bill of exchange: (*a*) where his customer is the *acceptor* (*see* 11:2) and the bill is payable at the bank, or (*b*) where the bank has *discounted* the bill for its customer.

(*a*) *Bill accepted by a customer payable at the bank.* The bill will be returned unpaid if it is presented for payment at the bank after notice of a bankruptcy petition against the acceptor, or notice of any subsequent step in bankruptcy proceedings against him, has been received.

(*b*) *Bill discounted by the bank*. A banker may invoke the Insolvency Act 1985, s.164 and set off the contingent liability of his customer on the bill against any credit balance on his customer's account, paying any surplus over to the trustee.

As a *holder* of the bill (*see* 11:**29**), however, a banker can enforce payment against other parties to it. This would normally be the course of action followed to recover any deficiency after a set-off against the customer's credit balance has been made. It is usually preferable to proving for an uncertain dividend in the customer's bankruptcy.

NOTE: If the *acceptor* of a bill discounted by the bank for its customer becomes bankrupt, s.31 does not apply. The customer's potential liability on the bill cannot be set off against his credit balance; nor can he be required to take up the bill. A banker can either prove in the acceptor's bankruptcy before the bill's maturity and recover the balance from the other parties at its maturity, or ignore the bankruptcy proceedings and wait until the bill matures to enforce payment against the other parties.

30. Cheques payable to a bankrupt. Rarely would a banker be in a position to know that the payee of an open cheque presented over the counter was an undischarged bankrupt, but if this is the case the cheque cannot be paid because it may belong to the trustee. Payment in such circumstances would not discharge the cheque (*see* 11:**46**), and its customer would still be liable on it.

Care must be taken when returning the cheque not to damage the credit of the drawer.

Payment of a cheque to a known undischarged bankrupt renders a bank liable to the trustee in conversion, unless the bank can show that the moneys were properly acquired after adjudication and the transaction was protected by the Insolvency Act 1985, s.154(4) (*see* **12** above).

NOTE: Where a banker pays such a cheque in good faith and in the ordinary course of business without knowledge that the payee had been made bankrupt, he is protected against an action by the trustee for conversion by s.60 of the Bills of Exchange Act 1882 (*see* 12:**13**).

Progress test 5

1. Explain the aims of the bankruptcy process. (**1**)

2. By whom and in what circumstances can a bankruptcy petition be presented? (**3**)

3. What restrictions are there on the disposition of the debtor's property (*a*) before, and (*b*) after the presentation of a bankruptcy petition against him? (**4**)

4. When can a certificate of summary administration be issued? (**4**)

5. What is the effect of a bankruptcy order? (**5**)

6. List the proceedings which follow a bankruptcy order. (**6**)

7. When is a bankruptcy order discharged? (**7**)

8. Who can appoint the trustee in bankruptcy? (**8**)

9. State the functions, duties and powers of the trustee in bankruptcy. (**9 & 10**)

10. When does the bankrupt's property vest in the trustee in bankruptcy and when does his title commence? (**12**)

11. What assets are unavailable for division among the creditors? (**13**)

12. Define a preference and a transaction at an undervalue. (**14**)

13. What must the trustee prove to avoid a preference? (**14**)

14. List the debts that can be proved in bankruptcy and those that cannot. (**17 & 18**)

15. Define a secured creditor. (**19**)

16. Give examples of deferred claims. (**19**)

17. What is the aim of a voluntary arrangement under the Insolvency Act 1985. (**20**)

18. State the purpose of an interim order. (**21**)

19. List the steps which follow an interim order in a voluntary arrangement under the Insolvency Act 1985. (**22**)

20. Define a deed of arrangement. (**23**)

21. In what ways does the Insolvency Act 1985 protect banks in their dealings with insolvent individuals. (**26**)

22. What action should a bank take regarding a customer's account when it receives notice of a bankruptcy petition against him? (**27**)

23. At what state in his bankruptcy must a customer's account be stopped entirely? (**27**)

24. What action is required if a bank discovers (*a*) that one of its customers is an undischarged bankrupt, or (*b*) that a bankruptcy order has been made against the guarantor of a customer's overdraft? (**27 & 28**)

25. What protection is afforded to a banker if he pays a cheque to an undischarged bankrupt? (**30**)

6
Land and land law

An introduction

1. Definitions.

(a) *Land*. At law the term "land" embraces not only the visible surface of the earth but also, in theory, everything above and below the surface and rights over land.

When the term is used in Acts of Parliament, the Interpretation Act 1978 defines it as including: "buildings and other structures, land covered with water, and any estate, interest, easement, servitude or right in or over land."

Hence, in addition to the visible surface of the earth, land can be said to include minerals, buildings, fixtures in buildings, reasonable rights in the airspace above the surface and rights over another person's land such as a right of way.

(b) *Fixtures*. Fixtures are things which at law have become part of the land or building to which they are attached.

In deciding whether an object is a fixture, the court looks at the degree to which it is attached to the building (the greater the degree of annexation, the more likely it is to be a fixture) and, more importantly, the purpose of the annexation. If the intention was to permanently improve the building, and not merely to enjoy the object itself, it is a fixture, e.g. fitted cupboards in a house and permanent installations in a factory are fixtures, while pictures hung on walls and moveable machinery are not.

Whether or not an object is a fixture may be a question of some nicety.

EXAMPLE: In *Berkely* v. *Poulett* (1976), HELD (C.A.): pictures fixed in the recesses of pannelling in rooms, a marble statue (weighing half a tonne and standing on a plinth) and a sundial resting on a stone baluster outside a house, were not fixtures which passed to the purchaser of the house. They were *chattels personal* (*see* below), and accordingly the seller of the house was entitled to remove them.

(*c*) *Real and personal property.* *Real* property consists only of freehold interests in land, while *personal* property is everything else, including leasehold interests in land. (*Freehold* and *leasehold* are discussed in **2** below.)

Freehold and leasehold interests in land are treated in much the same way by the law in fact, and it is usual to refer to leaseholds as *chattels real* to distinguish them from other forms of personal property—*chattels personal* (moveables, e.g. a cheque, this book, your pen).

The division of property into "real" and "personal" is a legacy of the very rigid procedural rules which the common law courts (the Royal Courts) developed in the distant past. If a man's freehold land was wrongfully taken from him, he could recover the actual land by bringing a *real action* in the common law courts. If, however, he was dispossessed of anything else, it was not possible for him to recover the actual property. He was only entitled to a *personal action* for money compensation against the person who had taken it.

The idea of the *leasehold* developed later than the *freehold*, by which time legal procedure had become so rigid that the real action available to a freeholder could not be adapted to a leaseholder's claim.

In time, however, a remedy was developed which enabled a leaseholder to recover his land if he had been wrongfully dispossessed.

2. Ownership of land: the historical background. Since the Norman Conquest in 1066, all land in England has been theoretically owned by the Crown, and the same has been true of the rest of Great Britain for many centuries. The most that anyone else can own is one of the two legal estates which now exist: a freehold estate or a leasehold estate, an *estate* being a measure of a person's interest in a particular piece of land in terms of time.

In the olden days, an estate was held on a certain *tenure*, originally the provision of goods and services of some kind, and later the payment of a sum of money.

Tenancies and rents are very much part of modern land law, but they are very different from the original feudal ideas of tenure. These have now almost entirely disappeared (*see* below).

NOTE: Leaseholds stood outside the feudal system of tenures as such.

This feudal system of land law based on estates and tenures survived long after the feudal system itself had disappeared and been replaced by an increasingly industrialised society.

As new demands from a rapidly changing society were made upon it, the system of land law was altered and added to. It was not reformulated. By the early twentieth century it had become completely archaic and extremely complicated as a result.

The Property Legislation of 1925, consisting of seven statutes, completely reformed the system of land law and *conveyancing* (the transfer of estates and interest in land).

The main aims of the 1925 Legislation were:

(*a*) to reduce all remaining feudal tenures to one common form— "common socage"—which may now be regarded as identical with the term "freehold"; (Today freehold and leasehold are the only two possible forms of tenure.)

(*b*) to remove outdated concepts, in particular feudal rights;

(*c*) to apply the principles of personal property law to real property wherever possible, e.g. in relation to the transfer and registration of title to land;

(*d*) to simplify conveyancing. This was achieved by reducing the number of possible *legal estates* to two and the number of *legal interests* to five, and by extending the principle of *registration* of title to land and interests in and rights over it.

Estates and interests

3. Legal estates. A legal estate is an abstract idea and it is quite separate from the land itself. It can be bought or sold, transferred by gift or by will without affecting the actual land itself or the possession of it. It is possible, for example, to buy the freehold of a block of flats without in any way affecting the rights of occupation of the tenants in the flats.

By the Law of Property Act 1925, the number of legal estates was reduced to *two*.

(*a*) *Fee simple absolute in possession (freehold)*. All land in this country is now held on freehold tenure. For all practical purposes this amounts to absolute ownership. A freeholder may, for example, dispose of his estate to anyone he pleases.

Nevertheless, there are important restrictions upon the rights of a freeholder to do as he pleases with his land. At *common law*, the law of torts prevents him from using his land in a way which would cause an actionable nuisance to his neighbours, and his right to develop land is restricted by the Town and Country Planning Acts.

Before 1925 there were a variety of freehold estates which the common law recognised, but since the Law of Property Act 1925, only the fee simple absolute in possession is recognised as a *legal* freehold estate.

All the former freehold estates can now only exist as *equitable interests* in land (*see* **4** below).

The words used in the term have the following meanings.

(*i*) *Fee:* an estate of inheritance, i.e. one that may be inherited or which may pass by will.

(*ii*) *Simple:* the inheritance is not limited to a particular class of the freeholder's heirs, e.g. males only, or the offspring from a particular marriage. (An estate where the inheritance was limited was known as a *fee tail*.)

(*iii*) *Absolute:* not subject to any conditions, as a *life estate* would be for example.

(*iv*) *In possession:* takes effect immediately. This includes not only the right to immediate possession but also the immediate right to rents and profits where the land is leased to a tenant.

(*b*) *Term of years absolute (leasehold)*. The owner of a freehold estate may create from it an estate of limited duration: a leasehold.

The words used in the term have the following meanings.

(*i*) *Term of years:* this includes not only leases for a specific number of years, but also those for less than a year or from year to year, although short leases are commonly referred to as tenancies.

(*ii*) *Absolute:* not subject to conditions.

The essential features of a leasehold estate are:

(*i*) it gives the right to exclusive possession;

(*ii*) it is for a definite term, i.e. the start of the term and its duration are fixed or can be determined; (This is the essential distinction between a lease and a freehold, for the latter is of unlimited duration.)

(*iii*) it creates the relationship of landlord and tenant.

At the end of the lease, the land reverts back to the freeholder.

NOTE: The Leasehold Reform Act 1967 gives a leaseholder of a house, originally let for twenty-one years or more (a long tenancy) at a low rent, and who has held it for at least five years, the right to buy the lessor's freehold estate or to demand a new lease of fifty years when the original expires. This is known as *leasehold enfranchisement*. However, the Act only applies to houses (not flats) of less than £200 rateable value (£400 in greater London) as at March 1965 (as amended by subsequent revaluations).

(*c*) *The creation of a lease.* A lease for more than *three* years must be granted by deed to create a *legal estate*: Law of Property Act 1925, s.52(I).

A legal estate for a term not exceeding three years may be created orally or in writing, however, provided it takes effect in possession (immediately) and at the best rent which can reasonably be obtained.

A deed is required to effect a *legal assignment* of a lease, no matter how short the term (*see* **8** below).

NOTE: A contract to grant a lease is only enforceable if it is evidenced by a memorandum in writing or a sufficient act of part performance. If the contract can be proved in this way, a tenant who holds under an agreement to grant a lease will be in the same position against his landlord as he would have been in had a deed been executed. Hence, provided specific performance of the contract can be granted, a written or even a verbal lease for a term exceeding three years confers an equitable term on the tenant.

4. Interests in land.

(*a*) *Definition.* An interest in land is a right to a claim against the land of another less than actual possession. An estate is a right to the land itself, i.e. possession.

Interests in land are either *legal* or *equitable*. The former must be created by deed.

(*b*) *Legal interests*. Legal interests are rights against the land itself (rights *in rem*) and are therefore enforceable against the "whole world". Thus, whoever acquires the land is bound by any legal interest which exists over it, whether or not he had knowledge of it.

NOTE: A legal interest must be held in fee simple absolute in possession or for a term of years absolute.

Under the Law of Property Act 1925 (as amended), there are five types of legal interests.

(*i*) An easement, right or privilege in or over land. Such an interest may be a bare right over the land of another (an *easement*), e.g. a right of way; or a right to take something from the land of another (a *profit à prendre*), e.g. fishing or shooting rights.

(*ii*) A rentcharge. This charges a piece of land, quite independently of any lease or mortgage, with the payment of a periodical sum of money to the owner of the rentcharge.

NOTE: Under the Rentcharges Act 1977, the creation of rentcharges is prohibited subject to certain exceptions. Any remaining rentcharges will be extinguished at the end of a sixty year period beginning in July 1977, or on the date on which the rentcharge first became payable, whichever is the later.

(*iii*) A charge by way of legal mortgage. (This is the interest of most practical importance to bankers: *see* 7:2.)

(*iv*) A charge on land which is not created by an instrument but imposed by law. (Such charges are of little practical importance today.)

(*v*) A right of entry in respect of a legal term of years absolute or annexed to a legal rentcharge. A landlord usually has a right to re-enter if the tenant fails to pay rent or comply with his obligations (*covenants*) in his lease.

(*c*) *Equitable interests*. An equitable interest was originally treated as a right against only the person who granted it (a right *in personam*), but was finally established as being enforceable against everyone except a *bona fide* purchaser of a legal estate for value without notice of the interest, or somebody claiming through such a person. (*See* (*d*) below.)

The Property Legislation of 1925 provided that all estates, interests and charges in or over land, both legal and equitable, other than the fee simple absolute in possession, the term of years absolute and the five legal interests listed above, would subsequently only take effect as *equitable interests*. For example, a life estate became a life interest, a fee tail became an entailed interest and a future fee simple absolute (i.e. not in possession) became a *future interest*. All such interests must be created behind a *trust* (an arrangement whereby property is held by one person—a *trustee*—who must use it for the benefit of another—a *beneficiary*).

There are four important equitable interests which may exist independently of any trust.

(*i*) *A restrictive covenant.* An agreement whereby one person promises to restrict the use of his land for the benefit of another's adjoining land, e.g. an agreement preventing the land being used for the purposes of trade.

(*ii*) *The Equity of Redemption.* The right of a mortgagor to redeem the mortgaged property upon payment of the outstanding principal and interest.

(*iii*) *An equitable charge.* An interest in land given as security for the payment of a sum of money. The chargee is entitled to take legal action for the sale of the land if payment is not made (*see* 7:**16**).

(*iv*) *An estate contract.* This arises where the estate owner contracts to convey the estate to the other contracting party, or to create a term of years in his favour from it. (The equitable interest arises at the time of the contract, but the legal interest does not pass until an actual conveyance or lease has been executed: *see* **8** below.)

(*d*) *Position before 1925.* Since there were many legal estates and interests before 1925, a purchaser of land took the risk of there being an estate or interest over his land of which he knew nothing at the time of purchase. The position of the person having an equitable estate or interest was even more perilous. His equity would be lost if the legal estate was purchased in good faith and for value without notice of the equity.

(*e*) *Registration of interests after 1925.* The reduction in the number of legal estates and interests after 1925 greatly improved the position of a purchaser of land. However, many more equitable interests now existed and the doctrine of *notice* no longer was adequate protection for them.

A national state system for the registration of many of the possible interests in land was established by the Land Charges Act 1925 (now consolidated with later amendments by the Land Charges Act 1972) and the old rules about notice no longer apply to registrable interests. Thus, a registrable right is void against a purchaser of the legal estate unless it is registered, even if the purchaser had notice of the interest.

NOTE: Where title to land is registered under the Land Registration Act 1925 (as amended) (*see* **6** below), such interests (called *minor interests*) must be protected by an entry on the Charges Register. The old rules on notice similarly do not apply.

The system of registering interests in land applies mainly to equitable interest, e.g. estate contracts, restrictive covenants and equitable charges, for these are the more vulnerable of the two types. However, some important legal interests are also registrable, e.g. a legal mortgage of unregistered land which is not supported by a deposit of the title deeds with the mortgagee (a *puisne mortgage*)—this is a common security taken by a banker to secure an overdraft.

Equitable interests incapable of registration are *overreached* on a sale of the land, e.g. the interest of a life tenant. This means that a purchaser of the legal estate, even one with notice, takes free from the equitable interest. This now attaches to the proceeds of the sale and no longer to the land itself.

5. The Land Charges Register. Registration of charges under the Land Charges Act 1925 (consolidated with amendments in the Land Charges Act 1972) superceded the doctrine of notice. An unregistered charge is void against a purchaser for value. A *mortgagee* is a "purchaser".

There are five registers of different registrable interests, the first being the most important.

(*a*) *Register of land charges.* This is divided into six classes, C and D being the most important.

(*i*) *Classes A and B*. These contain charges arising under certain Acts of Parliament, mainly in connection with agricultural land improvements.

(*ii*) *Class C*.

(1) A puisne mortgage, i.e. a legal mortgage unprotected by a deposit of title deeds.

(2) A limited owner's charge, i.e. an equitable charge in favour of a life tenant who has discharged some liability in con-

nection with the estate from his own pocket when it should have been paid from the estate. The life tenant is entitled to a charge on the land in the same way as if he had lent money to the estate on mortgage.

(3) A general equitable charge, e.g. an equitable mortgage of a legal estate (*see* 7:**6**).

(4) An estate contract (*see* **4** above).

(*iii*) *Class D.*

(1) A charge for death duties.

(2) A restrictive covenant entered into after 1925 and not one between a lessor and a lessee.

(3) An equitable easement created after 1925.

(*iv*) *Class E.* Annuities created but not registered before 1926. (Few such annuities exist.)

(*v*) *Class F.* A spouse's right to occupy a house owned by the other spouse: Matrimonial Homes Act 1983, and a spouse's "matrimonial rights" over trust property: Matrimonial Homes and Property Act 1981.

(*b*) *Register of pending actions.* Bankruptcy petitions are registrable pending actions.

(*c*) *Register of Writs and Orders affecting Land.* Writs and orders registrable here are those which enforce judgments and orders of the court, e.g. a bankruptcy order.

(*d*) *Register of Deeds of Arrangement.* (*See* 5:**18–20**).

(*e*) *Register of Annuities.* Very few registered annuities now exist.

6. The Local Land Charges Register. This is kept at the registering local authority and records charges acquired by the local authority under statutory authority, e.g. charges for making up roads or laying drains, and intended compulsory purchase orders.

Title and its transfer

7. Registration of title to land.

(*a*) *Introduction.* The registration system is governed by the Land Registration Act 1925, as amended. It deals with the *whole* title to the land and not just individual transactions. It replaces the separate investigation of title necessary on every conveyance of *unregistered land* with a state investigated and guaranteed title. Many incumbrances or charges affecting the land are also shown on the register.

If title to land is *registered*, the system of registering land charges in the Land Charges Register (*see* 5 above) does not apply.

NOTE: Whether title to land is registered or unregistered, charges acquired by any local authority by statute must still be registered in the Local Land Charges Registers. Such charges are public as opposed to private rights, e.g. restrictions on the use of land and compulsory purchase proceedings. Similarly, most charges over land created by a company also require registration in the Companies Register: Companies Act 1985, s.395 (*see* 4:**29**).

(*b*) *Registered interests.* Only the two legal estates (*see* 3 above) can be registered, but restrictions exist on the registration of a lease: *see* below.

(*c*) *Overriding interests.* Overriding interests are those which could be discovered from enquiries of the occupier or by an inspection of the land itself, and not (if title to the land were unregistered) from the title deeds and documents relating to the land. Examples include (*i*) legal easements and profits à prendre; (*ii*) rights of a person in actual occupation, including a beneficiary under a trust; (*iii*) local land charges; and (*iv*) leases for terms of twenty-one years or less.

They bind the purchaser of registered land even though he has no notice of them and they are not mentioned in the register.

NOTE: The Registrar is only under an obligation to enter a notice of the existence of an overriding interest created by an instrument which appears on the title at the time of *first* registration.

Enquiries into possible rights of occupation are essential to a would-be purchaser or mortgagee.

EXAMPLE: In *Hodgson* v. *Marks* (1971), the plaintiff transferred her house to E. E subsequently sold it to the defendant who mortgaged it to a building society. The plaintiff remained in the house throughout the period, the original transfer to E, her lodger, being intended to prevent her nephew turning him out. HELD: despite E's apparent occupation of the house, the Court of Appeal held the plaintiff to be in *actual occupation* within the meaning of the Land Registration Act 1925, s.70. Hence, the house could only be transferred subject to her overriding interest.

NOTE: In *Williams & Glyn's Bank Ltd.* v. *Boland and another* (1980), a wife made substantial contributions to the matrimonial home on land of which the husband was registered as the sole proprietor. He mortgaged it to the bank without his wife's knowledge and no caution, restriction or notice to protect her interest was registered as a consequence. HELD: (H.L.) the wife had an overriding interest as she was in *actual occupation*. The bank's charge was therefore subject to her interest and its action for possession failed. The principle would also protect a husband, or anybody, who could establish a financial stake in the property and who was in actual occupation. The decision would seem to apply to all land, registered and unregistered, and not just matrimonial homes or other dwelling houses. It is clearly of the greatest importance to bankers.

(*d*) *Minor interests*. These consist of all interests in registered land other than registrable interests and charges, and overriding interests. They require protection by an entry on the register. However, even when registered, not all minor interests bind a purchaser, e.g. the equitable interest of a beneficiary under a trust.

Minor interests can be divided into four types. (*i*) Those protected by entry of a *notice* on the charges register (*see* below) of the title effected. These automatically bind the transferee of the land. Examples include restrictive covenants and a spouse's rights in the matrimonial home. (*ii*) Those protected by entry of a *caution* on the proprietorship register. This ensures that the cautioner receives notice of any proposed dealings with the land and gives him a specified period, usually fourteen days, in which to object. Examples include equitable mortgages, whether or not protected by a deposit of the land certificate and interests under a trust for sale. (*iii*) Those protected by entry of a *restriction* on the proprietorship register. The entry is made by or with the consent of the registered proprietor and restricts his power to dispose of the property without first fulfilling some specified requirement. (Such minor interests would rarely affect a bank.) (*iv*) Those protected by entry of an *inhibition* on the proprietorship register. The entry can only be made by court order or by the Registrar and prevents any dealings with the land during a specified period. An example is a bankruptcy inhibition entered when a bankruptcy order is made against the registered proprietor.

NOTE: These four methods protect interests roughly correspond-ing to charges registrable under the Land Charges Act 1972.

(e) *The Register.* This is divided into three parts.

(i) *The Property Register.* This describes the land and the estate for which it is held, refers to a map or plan showing the land and notes any interest held for the benefit of the land, e.g. easements or restrictive covenants.

(ii) *The Proprietorship Register.* This gives the nature of the title (*see* below) and the name, address and occupation of the registered proprietor. It sets out any cautions, inhibitions or restrictions affecting his right to deal with the land (*see* above).

(iii) *The Charges Register.* This contains entries relating to rights against the land, e.g. mortgages and restrictive covenants, and notices protecting rights over the land, e.g. a spouse's rights in the matrimonial home (*see* above).

Each registered proprietor is given a *land certificate* containing a copy of these entries. This is his document of title which he will keep until he sells or charges the land. Proof of title is, however, the Register itself because the land certificate may become out of date through subsequent entries on the Register.

The Land Register, unlike the Registers of Land Charges, is not open to public inspection. In general only the proprietor of the land or of a charge over it may make a search, or a person with his written authority to do so.

(f) *Registration.* This is still not compulsory in all areas of the country. Even in a compulsory registration area, registration is only necessary on a conveyance on sale of a freehold or the creation or assignment on sale of certain leases.

Registration of a lease is only compulsory where:

(i) the lease is granted for a term of forty years or more, or a lease with forty or more years to run is assigned on sale in a compulsory registration area; or

(ii) a lease is granted for more than twenty-one years from an estate which has itself been registered, whether or not the land is in a compulsory registration area.

A lease *cannot* be registered if:

(i) it is granted for a term of twenty-one years or less; or

(ii) it forbids assignment; or

(*iii*) it is a mortgage term still subject to a right of redemption (*see* 7:**19**).

NOTE: A transaction does not convey the legal estate in a compulsory registration area unless an application for registration is made within two months, or such longer period allowed by the court or the Registrar. A non-registered transaction only creates a *minor interest*: *see* above.

A caution may be lodged with the Registrar by anyone who thinks that he may be prejudiced by an application to register title to a particular piece of land. If any such application is made, the cautioner will be informed of this by the Registrar and he can then object to the registration.

(*g*) *Registered titles*. Four types of registered title exist.

(*i*) *Absolute*. This title is state-guaranteed and subject only to entries on the charges register and overriding interests.

Absolute title applies to a leasehold where the freehold out of which the term is created is itself registered with absolute title. It also guarantees that the lease was validly granted.

(*ii*) *Qualified*. This title is granted following an application for registration of an absolute title where the title can only be established for a limited period or subject to certain reservations. A qualified title is very rare.

(*iii*) *Possessory*. This arises where the proprietor has produced only *prima facie* evidence of his title. The title is not guaranteed prior to its first registration and must, therefore, be investigated by a prospective purchaser as though the title was unregistered.

Provided that the proprietor satisfies the Registrar that he is in possession of the land, the Registrar must convert a possessory title to absolute title in the case of a freehold after fifteen years, and to good leasehold title in the case of a leasehold after ten years.

(*iv*) *Good leasehold*. This applies only to leaseholds. It is evidence that the leaseholder's title is good, but it does not guarantee title to the freehold from which the lease was granted.

An absolute title *may*, however, be granted by the Registrar after ten years' possession.

NOTE: The registrar *may* convert qualified, possessory or good leasehold to absolute or good leasehold (as the case may be) if the land is transferred for value.

8. The transfer of title to land. The method by which title to land is transferred depends upon whether the title is unregistered or registered.

(*a*) *Unregistered land.*

(*i*) *Freehold.* The freehold title to unregistered land is evidenced by a collection of deeds and documents. Together these show a chain of title concluding with that of the present owner. They are known as the *title deeds*.

Transfer is effected in two stages:

(1) the *contract*—this binds vendor and purchaser to complete the transfer;

(2) the *conveyance*—this transfers the legal estate to the purchaser. (By the Law of Property Act 1925, s.52(1), the conveyance must be by *deed*.)

A contract for the sale of land is subject to the usual rules of contract law, although it must be in writing or evidenced by a signed memorandum in writing to be enforceable: Law of Property Act 1925, s.40. In practice, the method adopted is usually an "exchange of contracts".

The contract may be *formal* or *open*. The basic difference between them is that a formal contract contains all the requisite terms in detail, while an open contract leaves all but the most essential terms—the parties, the property and the consideration (the price)— to be implied by law.

Under an open contract, the vendor must produce for the purchaser's inspection, an abstract of title showing evidence of title going back at least fifteen years to a good root of title. This may be:

(1) a *conveyance*—a deed transferring the legal estate to freehold land from the existing freeholder to a purchaser or donee;

(2) a *mortgage*;

(3) an *assent*—a signed document transferring the legal estate in land from the personal representatives of a deceased holder to the person who inherits the land under the will or intestacy.

A shorter or longer period than the statutory fifteen years may be agreed by the parties in a formal contract. Stipulation of a shorter period is dangerous to a purchaser because he will be bound by existing legal interests, and he is deemed to have constructive notice of any equitable interests which an investigation of the fifteen-year period would have disclosed.

From the time that the contracts are exchanged, the purchaser becomes the equitable owner, since an order for specific performance of the conveyance will normally be granted if the vendor refuses to execute it voluntarily.

Following the exchange of contracts, the purchaser (usually his solicitor) will examine the deeds, making such enquiries as he considers to be necessary.

Arrangements are then made for completion, at which the conveyance executed by both parties is handed over with the title deeds (of which the conveyance now forms part) in exchange for the purchase price—usually in the form of a bank draft.

NOTE: The system of unregistered conveyancing has the disadvantage that the process of investigating the title has to be repeated each time it is transferred.

(ii) *Leasehold.* A leaseholder can dispose of his legal estate by assigning to another person the whole of his remaining term unless he is prohibited from doing so by the terms of his lease. (An *assignment* is a deed transferring the legal estate in leasehold land. It is similar to the *conveyance* used to transfer title to unregistered freehold land.)

Subject to the same proviso, a leaseholder may grant a *sub-lease* for a term shorter than that which he himself holds. Leases frequently contain restrictions on the lessee's right to assign or to sub-let. It is quite usual for the lessor's prior permission to be necessary.

A leasehold title to unregistered land is also evidenced by title deeds, but the lease itself may be the only document.

Under an open contract for the grant or sale of a lease, the prospective lessee cannot demand proof of the freehold title.

NOTE: An open contract for a lease must contain the commencement date and duration of the lease.

A prospective assignee of an existing lease is entitled to the production of the actual lease, no matter how old, and to inspect the title under which it has been held for the last fifteen years. He cannot demand, however, proof of the freehold reversion.

Under a formal contract, the parties may agree to increase these requirements.

Completion is similar to completion on a sale of freehold land. The lease will be delivered against a draft for the consideration moneys or payment of the rent. A copy of the lease will be placed with the title deeds. An assignment of an existing lease will similarly be delivered with other relevant documents against payment.

(*b*) *Registered land*. Transfer of a registered title is effected by a short, simple form of registered transfer. This replaces the conveyance or assignment necessary to transfer title to unregistered land.

At completion, the vendor hands to the purchaser the land certificate and a registered transfer signed by him against payment.

The land certificate and transfer are sent to the Land Registry where the new proprietor is entered on the register and on the land certificate. The land certificate is then returned to the new proprietor as his evidence of title.

Progress test 6

1. Distinguish between real and personal property. (**1**)

2. Explain the relationship between estates and tenures. (**2**)

3. State and explain the full legal terminology for freehold and leasehold estates. (**3**)

4. What is the difference between an estate and an interest in land? (**4**)

5. Explain the difference between legal and equitable interests in land. (**4**)

6. List the five types of legal interest in land. (**4**)

7. What is a restrictive covenant? (**4**)

8. Explain the importance of the Land Charges Act 1972. (**5**)

9. In what circumstances can a lease for less than three years create a legal estate even though the term was not granted by deed? (**7**)

10. What is an overriding interest under the Land Registration Act 1925? (**7**)

11. Explain the importance of a caution lodged at the Land Registry. (**7**)

12. What is a land certificate? (**7**)

13. What are the four possible titles with which land can be registered? Distinguish between them. (**7**)

14. Distinguish between the contract and the conveyance in the transfer of title to land. (**8**)

15. What are the requirements of the Law of Property Act 1925, s.40? (**8**)

7
Land as security

Securities generally

1. Meaning of "security". A security is some right or interest in property given to a creditor. In the event of the debtor failing to pay his debt as and when due, the creditor may reimburse himself for the debt out of the property charged. Both real and personal property (*see* 6:**1**) may be charged with repayment of a debt in this way.

2. The nature of a mortgage. A mortgage is a conveyance of a legal or equitable interest in property with a provision for redemption, i.e. upon repayment of a loan, or the performance of some other obligation, the conveyance shall become void or the interest shall be reconveyed.

Possession of the property mortgaged remains with the *mortgagor* (the borrower), while the *mortgagee* (the lender) obtains some or all of the rights of ownership, or the right to obtain ownership, if the borrower defaults in repayment.

Land is the form of property most usually mortgaged, but *choses in action* (rights to property as opposed to actual physical property itself), e.g. a life assurance policy, can be mortgaged by assignment, and *goods* by a conditional bill of sale, both subject to a condition that on repayment the property shall be reassigned to the mortgagor. A mortgage of goods is rare.

3. Other forms of security.

(*a*) *Pledges.* A pledge is a *deposit of goods*, or documents of title to them, or negotiable instruments with a lender as security for a debt.

It differs from a mortgage in that the lender obtains possession of the property, while the borrower retains ownership.

(b) *Liens*. A lien is a right to retain property belonging to another until a debt is paid (a possessory lien) or a right to seek a court order for sale of the property (an equitable lien). They differ from mortgages and pledges in that they arise by operation of law from certain situations. Mortgages and pledges are the result of express agreements between borrowers and lenders.

(c) *Charges*. A charge is usually regarded as a type of mortgage. However, a mortgage conveys an interest in the property mortgaged subject to a right of redemption, whereas a charge merely gives certain rights over the property charged as security for a loan, it conveys no interest in the property.

Mortgages of land

4. Introduction: legal and equitable interests. In English property law, a distinction is drawn between *legal* and *equitable* interests in property. The former are enforceable in any court and against any person, the latter are personal rights against a particular individual or individuals. (Legal and equitable interests in land were discussed in **6:4**.)

Legal interests can only be created in the correct form for the particular type of property involved, e.g. a deed in the case of land. An equitable interest is either (a) the result of an informal creation, e.g. a conveyance of an interest in and otherwise than by deed, or (b) the result of a transfer of an existing equitable interest.

Both legal and equitable interests in land (or other types of property) can be used as security for loans, but the limited enforceability of equitable interests makes them less acceptable securities.

Mortgages of land may similarly be either legal or equitable. A legal mortgagee acquires rights against the property itself in addition to the personal action available against the mortgagor for the principal and interest due. An equitable mortgage gives no rights against the property, only personal rights against the borrower, principally a right to share in the proceeds of sale of the property when sold, and a right to seek the court's aid in enforcing this right. The wider and more effective range of remedies enjoyed by a legal mortgagee is today the most important practical distinction between legal and equitable mortgages (*see* **14–18** below).

5. Legal mortgages. A legal mortgage can be effected in two ways, both *by deed*.

(*a*) *By a lease to the mortgagee for a term of years*, subject to a proviso that the lease will terminate upon repayment of the debt (cessor on redemption).

If it is a leasehold to be mortgaged, there must be a sub-lease for a term less by one or more days than the head lease. It is usual to make the term ten days shorter in order to allow for second and subsequent mortgages.

The term granted is long, normally 3,000 years, but on repayment the term automatically ceases.

(*b*) *A charge by deed expressed to be by way of legal mortgage.* This is commonly known as a *legal charge*. It is a creation of the Law of Property Act 1925.

A legal charge gives the mortgagee no term of years, but he obtains the same protection, powers and remedies as a legal mortgagee by grant of a term of years. A legal charge has the following advantages.

(*i*) Freeholds and leaseholds can be conveniently mortgaged together. Duplication of forms is avoided, the security can be taken by merely listing the properties in the schedule to the charge.

(*ii*) A charge of leasehold property creates no sub-lease and therefore does not infringe any covenant against sub-letting in the lease.

(*iii*) The form of a legal charge is short and simple.

(*c*) *Keeping the mortgage deed.* In the case of *unregistered* land, the mortgage will normally be retained by a bank with the other title deeds which will have been previously obtained from the prospective borrower. In the case of *registered* land, the mortgage (charge form) must be sent with a duplicate and the land certificate to the Land Registry. The Registrar will enter the charge on the Charges Register, retain the land certificate and issue a charge certificate which includes one sewn-in copy of the mortgage.

6. Equitable mortgages. An equitable mortgage does not convey a legal interest in the property to the mortgagee. Consequently, he cannot enforce it without the consent of the court. For this reason, a banker will normally take a *written memorandum of deposit* in which the mortgagor undertakes to execute a legal mortgage as and when called upon to do so by the banker.

An equitable mortgage can be created by the following.

(*a*) *An agreement to create a legal mortgage.* (If the mortgagor defaults in his repayments, the mortgagee can seek specific performance of the borrower's undertaking to execute a legal mortgage.)

(*b*) *A deposit of title deeds or land certificate.* Provided the deposit is intended to be used as security, this will be sufficient to create an equitable mortgage even though a memorandum of deposit is not taken.

(*c*) *An equitable charge.* This can be created by any written memorandum, no matter how informal, in which the borrower states that his property shall be security for the money advanced.

The charge creates no interest in the property, but the chargee (e.g. a banker) can seek the court's sanction for the sale of the property if repayment is not made.

7. Bank forms of mortgage.

(*a*) *Introduction.* Bank mortgages are not intended to be investments and, therefore, they must possess as far as possible the same degree of liquidity found in other forms of security taken by bankers. Hence, they will be made repayable on demand and enable a banker to realise the security with a minimum of formality on the mortgagor's default in repayment.

(*b*) *Legal mortgages.* It is usual for the mortgage form to contain the following clauses.

(*i*) *An all-moneys clause.* The mortgage thereby covers all liabilities which may be owed to the bank at any time and on any account. This includes interest and commission payments, and any expenses incurred by the bank in taking and enforcing the security.

(*ii*) *A clause making the advance repayable on demand.* Without this provision, time would begin to run under the Limitation Act 1980 from the date on which the mortgage was created. With the provision, time runs from the demand for repayment.

(*iii*) *A continuing security clause.* This ensures that the mortgage secures the outstanding balance at any given time. This provision is required to prevent a possible operation of the Rule in *Clayton's Case* (1816) to a banker's detriment, i.e. the initial secured borrowing would be reduced by payments-in while subsequent debits would be unsecured.

(*iv*) *The mortgagor's undertaking to keep the property in good repair and insured against fire.*

NOTE: In *Halifax Building Society* v. *Keighley* (1931), it was held that the mortgagee was not entitled to sums paid to the mortgagor for fire damage under an insurance of the mortgaged property effected quite separately from his statutory and mortgage obligations to insure. Thus, the clause will expressly provide that the mortgagor's obligation to use moneys received under an insurance policy on the property to make good the relevant loss or damage, or in discharge of the mortgage debt, applies whether or not the mortgagor is bound to maintain the insurance policy under the terms of the mortgage deed.

(*v*) *A covenant to observe all the provisions of the lease* in the case of a mortgage of a leasehold.

(*vi*) *A provision excluding s.103 of the Law of Property Act 1925.* This allows the banker to exercise his power to sell the mortgaged property or to appoint a receiver (*see* **15** below) immediately, or after a minimum period of notice (usually one month), should a demand for repayment be unsatisfied. Under s.103, a period of three months must elapse between the demand for repayment and the exercise of the power.

(*vii*) *An exclusion of s.93 of the Law of Property Act 1925.* If not excluded, s.93 would prevent the bank from consolidating two or more mortgages on different properties taken from the same mortgagor. Consolidation prevents the mortgagor from redeeming a valuable mortgage while unsatisfactory ones are left outstanding. The bank can therefore prevent the mortgagor redeeming one mortgage in advance of others.

(*viii*) *An exclusion of ss.99 and 100 of the Law of Property Act 1925.* This deprives the mortgagor of his right to grant or surrender leases without the bank's consent. The grant of a lease on the mortgaged property would clearly prejudice a sale of the security and a surrender of an existing lease could lessen its value. A lease granted in contravention of the clause does not bind the bank. The clause does not, however, apply to a morgage of agricultural land, provided the lease is granted in good faith: Agricultural Holdings Act 1948.

NOTE: If a banker (or any other mortgagee) is relying on the vacant possession value of the security, e.g. when making a temporary advance to enable his customer to complete the purchase of a house with a building society mortgage, it is important to ensure that the premises are not let on or before the date on which the mortgage is executed. In *Universal Permanent Building Society* v. *Cooke* (1952), for example, C exchanged contracts for certain premises but had no right to possession before the completion date. She nevertheless let the premises, the tenant taking possession before completion. The day after completion, C mortgaged the premises to the plaintiff, the mortgage excluding her power to grant leases. C defaulted on repayments and the plaintiff sought possession of the premises. HELD: the tenancy was protected because the tenant's title was completed by estoppel in the one day in which C had a right to grant a lease free from the restriction of the mortgage.

(*c*) *Equitable mortgages*. A banker will wish to take an equitable mortgage by a deposit of the title deeds or land certificate accompanied by a written memorandum of deposit.

NOTE: An equitable charge can be created by deposit of the title deeds or land certificate alone, or by a written document under hand or under seal (by deed) charging the relevant property without a deposit of the title deeds or the land certificate.

A memorandum of deposit will avoid any possible dispute over the nature of the deposit, i.e. that the deposit was purely for safe custody purposes, and include the same or similar provisions to those contained in the usual legal mortgage form (*see* above).

In addition, the customer usually undertakes to execute a legal mortgage of the property to the bank when requested to do so, thereby extending the remedies available to his banker.

A memorandum of deposit under seal is sometimes taken. This will incorporate either (*i*) an irrevocable power of attorney, or (*ii*) a declaration of trust in the bank's favour. The former enables a banker to sell, or execute a legal mortgage of the property in the mortgagor's place if he proves to be uncooperative. Incorporated in a uitably worded deed, the latter empowers a banker to replace the mortgagor as trustee with his own nominee, thereby enabling him to deal with the property should the mortgagor be similarly un-cooperative.

If the memorandum of deposit is not under seal, and does not contain such provisions, the mortgagee must seek the court's aid in any action against the property (*see* **16** below).

3. Second mortgages.

(*a*) *Introduction.* It is possible for any number of mortgages, legal or equitable, to exist at the same time over one piece of land. A banker may be prepared to accept a second mortgage as security for an advance if the value of the property is sufficient to repay both the first mortgage and the proposed second mortgage, i.e. there is sufficient *equity* in the property.

The main disadvantage of a second mortgage is that the first mortgagee may exercise his legal remedies, e.g. his power of sale, without reference to, and therefore to the detriment of, the second mortgagee.

A sale of the mortgaged property by the first mortgagee extinguishes the second mortgage and, whilst the second mortgagee is entitled to the surplus proceeds of the sale, it might not realise sufficient moneys to repay both debts in full.

NOTE: A second mortgagee can obtain complete control of the security by paying off the first mortgage.

(*b*) *Creation of second mortgages.* A second *legal* mortgage is created by:

(*i*) a charge by way of legal mortgage; or

(*ii*) a lease for a term longer by one day than the term granted to the first mortgagee in the case of a freehold; or a sub-lease for a term longer by one day than that granted to the first mortgagee in the case of a leasehold.

A second *equitable* mortgage is created by:

(*i*) a general equitable charge; or

(*ii*) an agreement to create a legal mortgage.

(*See* generally **5–6** above.)

4. Sub-mortgages.

(*a*) *The nature of a sub-mortgage.* A sub-mortgage is a mortgage of a mortgage debt and of the security for that debt.

A sub-mortgage is quite distinct from a second mortgage. In the latter type of agreement, an *additional* mortgage is created on the same property in favour of either a different mortgagee or the existing mortgagee.

A sub-mortgage can be a very good security because of its three fold nature. To the personal obligation of the sub-mortgagor (the banker's customer) is added the personal obligation of the original mortgagor which is supported by a mortgage of the land itself.

(*b*) *The form of a sub-mortgage.* A sub-mortgage of an existing legal mortgage may be legal or equitable, but if the original mortgage is equitable, the sub-mortgage can only be equitable.

(*i*) A *legal* sub-mortgage is drafted according to the nature of the head (first or original) mortgage. If this was created by a grant of a term of years, the sub-mortgage can be by either a legal charge or the grant of a sub-lease for a term less by one day than the term held by the head mortgagee. In both cases, the mortgage must contain an assignment of the debt due under the head mortgage.

If the head mortgage was created by legal charge, a sub-mortgage should be taken by a transfer of the benefit of the head mortgage to the bank (the sub-mortgagee).

(*ii*) An *equitable* sub-mortgage can be taken by (1) a deposit of the head mortgage, normally with a memorandum of deposit, or (2) a general equitable charge.

(*See* generally **5–6** above.)

10. Procedure on taking a bank mortgage. (*N.B.* This section is intended as an introduction only; no attempt is made to detail the practice of different bankers.)

(*a*) *Investigation of title.* It is essential to ensure that the prospective mortgagor has a good title to the property that he offers as security. If there is any doubt, or if the process of investigation could prove to be complicated, the investigation should be entrusted to a solicitor. This is more likely to be the case where the title to the property offered is not registered.

A search must be made of (*i*) the Land Charges Register (unregistered land), or the Land Registry Registers (registered land), (*ii*) the Local Land Charges Register, and (*iii*) the Registrar of Companies Register of Charges (where applicable), to ensure that the proposed security and the customer's title to it are not subject to unacceptable adverse claims, e.g. a spouse's right of occupation (*see* **6:5–7**, and **4:29**).

(*b*) *Valuation.* The value of the property to be mortgaged must be sufficient to cover the advance. If a banker is considering taking a second mortgage on the property, it is essential to ensure that there is sufficient *equity* in the property after the first mortgage has been repaid in full.

The valuation is often undertaken by the manager or a senior member of staff, but a professional surveyor may be employed, particularly when business or unusual property is offered as security.

A mortgage of leasehold property requires particular care. The inevitable drop in value as the lease nears expiry must be taken into account. There should be no onerous covenants on the land, and rents and receipts for it must be checked.

(*c*) *Insurance.* A banker's mortgage form imposes an obligation on the mortgagor to maintain adequate fire insurance on the property with a company approved by the bank and to produce receipts for payment when requested to do so.

The mortgage will further provide that, if the mortgagor fails to maintain adequate insurance, the banker can do so at the mortgagor's expense.

Notice of the bank's interest must be given to the company concerned and the policy kept with the documents of title.

(*d*) *Execution of mortgage.* On a mortgage of *unregistered* land, the mortgagor must sign the bank's appropriate mortgage forms and acknowledge receipt of the advance in writing. The title deeds to the land, if available, must be deposited with the bank. If the deeds are not available, e.g. where a second mortgage is taken, the bank must register the mortgage in Class C of the Land Charges Register (*see* **6:5**).

On a mortgage of *registered* land, the mortgagor must execute the appropriate charge and stamp it. The charge must be registered at the Land Registry (*see* **6:7**).

(Registration and protection of mortgages is considered generally in **12–13** below.)

NOTE: If the property to be mortgaged is vested in the names of joint tenants, e.g. husband and wife, and one signs a legal charge, forging the other's signature, the genuine signature creates an equitable interest over the signatory's interest in the property. The other co-owner is not liable on the mortgage: *First National Securities Ltd*. v. *Hegarty* (1982).

(*e*) *Second mortgages*. Title, value and fire insurance arrangements must be investigated and approved. This is normally done by sending a list of relevant questions, together with the customer's written permission to answer them, to the first mortgagee.

The answers will usually be accepted without further investigation if the first mortgagee is another bank, a building society, an insurance company, a local authority, or other similarly reputable organisation.

A banker must give formal notice of his mortgage to the first mortgagee, asking him to state the amount of his loan and to confirm that his mortgage does not impose on him an obligation to make further advances.

This last enquiry is made because the Law of Property Act 1925, s.94(1), entitles a mortgagee under such an obligation to *tack* (add) these advances on to the original advance in priority to the second mortgage, irrespective of notice of it.

Such an obligation must be a term of the mortgage. It does not arise merely because the first mortgage is expressed to be a continuing security as is the case in bank mortgages.

NOTE: In a bank mortgage the obligation may be encountered where the mortgage secures an advance to finance the construction of a building, its payment being made in stages. Without such a right, notice of a second mortgage when the building is still incomplete would prevent the bank gaining priority on subsequent advances while holding an almost certainly unsaleable security.

Notice to the first mortgagee is important for two reasons.

(*i*) *Further advances*. It prevents a first mortgagee, other than one under an obligation to make further advances, from making further advances which will rank in priority to the second mortgage. In particular, a first mortgagee whose security expressly covers further advances is not under an obligation to make a search before increasing his mortgage advance: Law of Property Act 1925, s.94(2). This would be the case in a bank mortgage securing an overdrawn current account or a fluctuating loan account.

NOTE: (1) This concession to bankers applies only to mortgages, e.g. registration of a bankruptcy petition or a bankruptcy order would constitute actual notice. (2) If a search is made and discloses a second mortgage in these circumstances, the first mortgagee is considered to have had actual notice of the second mortgage. (3) Where title to the property is registered, the Registrar will have sent prior notice of the second mortgage to a first mortgagee whose security expressly covers further advances: Land Registration Act 1925, s.30(1).

(*ii*) *Documents of title*. When his mortgage is discharged, notice of the second mortgage imposes a duty on the first mortgagee to hand over the title deeds or land certificate to the second mortgagee. Direct notice is necessary to ensure that this is done because a mortgagee is under no obligation to make a search for subsequent mortages on the discharge of his own mortgage.

(*f*) *Notice of a second mortgage*. (This important matter is considered here a little out of context to achieve greater coherence in the consideration of second mortgages.)

Since a bank mortgage never imposes an obligation to make further advances, it is not possible for a bank to tack further advances onto existing borrowing once notice of a second mortgage has been received. The bank's mortgage is terminated as a continuing security and action must be taken to protect its interests. The mortgagor's account must be broken and a fresh account opened through which all subsequent transactions must be passed.

This action will preserve the priority of the debt existing when the notice was received over the subsequent mortgage by preventing the Rule in *Clayton's Case* (1816) working to the bank's detriment. Under the Rule further advances on the original account could not be charged against the security in priority to the second mortgage and subsequent credits to the account would reduce and perhaps ultimately extinguish the amount secured by the mortgage.

EXAMPLE: in *Deeley* v. *Lloyds Bank Ltd*. (1912), the bank had advanced money against a second mortgage and was held to have had notice of a third mortgage to X, its customer's sister. The bank did not break the account as its own procedure required, however, and subsequent credits totalled more than its customer's debt to the bank. Its customer was subsequently adjudicated bankrupt and the bank sold the property for a sum just sufficient to repay the first and second mortgages. HELD: (1) Payments to the credit of the account after notice of the mortgage to X wiped out the advance outstanding at the time of the notice; (2) X's mortgage had priority over fresh advances; (3) X was consequently entitled to the proceeds of the sale after repayment of the first mortgage.

A spouse's right of occupation, registered according to the Matrimonial Homes Act 1983, has the same effect for the purposes of s.94 of the Law of Property Act 1925 as a second or subsequent mortgage. Hence, a banker must protect his position as first mortgagee in the same way.

(g) *Sub-mortgages*. In addition to the general considerations covered above, the original mortgagor must be given notice of the sub-mortgage, requesting his acknowledgment of it and seeking his confirmation of the amount outstanding. This notice is necessary to ensure that all instalments of the mortgage debt are paid to the bank (the sub-mortgagee) and not to the mortgagee (the customer).

11. Advantages and disadvantages as security.

(a) *Advantages*.

(i) A mortgage of land possesses one overriding advantage: land never completely loses its value. Indeed, a first legal mortgage of freehold land is the surest security that a banker can take.

(ii) Land has historically always appreciated in value.

(b) *Disadvantages*.

(i) Land is sometimes difficult to value for security purposes.

(ii) Greater difficulty and formality attach to a mortgage of land than to other forms of security.

(iii) Land is not an easily realisable security. In addition, realisation of the security can possibly bring bad publicity to the bank.

(iv) A second mortgage is subject to the rights of the first mortgagee (*see* **8** above).

(v) An equitable mortgagee must seek the court's sanction in any action for realisation of the security.

Registration and protection of mortgages

12. Unregistered land.

(a) *Accompanied by a deposit of the title deeds*. A mortgage of unregistered land, whether legal or equitable, accompanied by a deposit of the title deeds *cannot* be registered.

An exception exists where the mortgage is given by a company. In this case it must be registered in accordance with s.395 of the Companies Act 1985 (*see* 4:31).

(b) *Not accompanied by a deposit of the title deeds*. Any mortgage which is unaccompanied by a deposit of the title deeds requires registration at the Land Charges Registry. If legal it is registered as a *puisne mortgage*, if equitable as a *general equitable* charge (*see* 6:5). Most such mortgages are second mortgages.

NOTE: If the mortgage is a *floating charge* created by a company, it can only be registered with the Registrar of Companies.

A puisne mortgage or a general equitable charge is *void* against a purchaser of the land charged unless it is registered before completion of the purchase: Land Charges Act 1972, s.4.

NOTE: Although seldom used by bankers, a prospective mortgagee can lodge a *priority notice* of his intention to register a charge with the Registrar. Provided the actual registration takes place within thirty days of lodging the priority notice and refers to it, the charge will be deemed to have been registered at the time the charge was executed.

13. Registered land.

(a) *Legal mortgage*. This must be protected by sending to the Land Registry the land certificate, the original charge certificate and a duplicate, an application form and the Land Registry fee.

The Registrar will register the charge, retain the duplicate and the cover of the land certificate, and return the charge certificate to the bank. This consists of the remainder of the original land certificate sewn in with the original charge form. (A charge certificate is easily distinguishable from a land certificate by its cover, the former being plain while the latter is ornate.)

A second or subsequent mortgage is similarly protected by a charge at the Land Registry, a search certificate being sent in place of the land certificate. Details of earlier charges will appear on the charge certificate.

A sub-mortgage is protected by registering a sub-charge. This is submitted in duplicate with the original charge certificate and the appropriate fee. A certificate of sub-charge is issued. Alternatively, a caution may be lodged, but the sub-mortgage will then only take effect in equity until actually registered (*see* below).

(*b*) *Equitable mortgage.* This is usually created by a deposit of the land certificate with the bank together with a memorandum of deposit. The bank acquires a lien on the land certificate which takes effect subject to overriding interests, registered interests and any existing entries on the register: Land Registration Act 1925, s.66.

The mortgage must be protected by sending a notice of deposit of a land certificate to the Land Registry signed by the mortgagor or his solicitor. The land certificate should also be sent so it can be endorsed with the notice of deposit. After endorsement, it will be returned to the bank. An equitable sub-mortgage, by deposit of the head mortgage, is protected by notice of deposit of a charge certificate.

Having lodged a notice of deposit, the Registrar must give the mortgagee fourteen days' notice of any proposed dealings with the land. In this period, a banker can take further steps to protect his interests, e.g. by taking and registering a legal mortgage, the mortgagor having undertaken to execute a legal mortgage on the bank's request in the memorandum of deposit.

However, entry of the notice is itself complete protection of the bank's equitable interest because subsequent chargees cannot claim to be without notice of it.

NOTE: A banker is often prepared to have a legal charge form executed but hold it unregistered to save his customer the Land Registry fees. Such an arrangement creates only an equitable mortgage, however, and must be protected by a notice of deposit of a land certificate. The legal charge can, nevertheless, be registered at any time. This would be done within fourteen days of the Registrar giving notice to the bank of any proposed dealings with the land. (This procedure is also applicable to sub-mortgages.)

Protection of an equitable mortgage where the land certificate is temporarily unavailable is effected by lodging a notice of intended deposit at the Land Registry. This situation would arise, for example, where transfer of title to the mortgagor has not been completed.

When available, the land certificate will be sent direct to the bank. The original notice of intended deposit still stands and a banker need take no further action unless he considers it advisable to take a legal charge on the property.

Where the land certificate is not going to be available at all, an equitable mortgage must be protected by a notice or caution on the Proprietorship Register. This would be the case where a banker takes a second equitable mortgage. Until protected in this way, it is capable of being overridden as a minor interest (*see* 6:**7**).

An equitable mortgage by a company must also be registered with the Registrar of Companies.

The remedies of a mortgagee

14. Introduction. Bank mortgages ensure that all possible remedies are available to a banker should his security have to be realised. In particular, provisions are included to exclude certain sections of the Law of Property Act 1925 which would otherwise delay the realisation (*see* generally **4** above).

A legal mortgagee's rights are superior to those of an equitable mortgagee. A legal mortgage confers a right *in rem*, i.e. a right to the property itself, in addition to the right *in personam*, i.e. a personal right, against the mortgagor, while an equitable mortgage gives only a right *in personam*. Thus, an equitable mortgagee cannot take action against the property itself without the court's sanction and help.

15. Legal mortgagee. A legal mortgagee has five remedies available to him. These remedies are *cumulative* and *concurrent*. In other words, they may be used in combination at the same time to ensure that the full debt (but not more) is recovered.

(*a*) *An action for the debt.* This is a personal action against the mortgagor to recover the capital sum and any interest owed. It avoids the delay and effort involved in realising the security but is only suitable where non-payment is the result of unwillingness rather than inability. This remedy is, of course a general remedy and it is available to an unsecured creditor.

After judgment is obtained a banker may serve a *statutory demand* on the mortgagor (*see* 5:1–3 above). The threat of bankruptcy proceedings can be an effective method of ensuring payment.

(b) *Sale of the property.* Every mortgage made by deed (legal or equitable) confers on the mortgagee the power to sell the mortgaged property: Law of Property Act 1925, s.101.

By s.103, however, the power may not be exercised until (i) a demand for repayment has been made and the borrower has been in default for three months; (ii) some interest under the mortgage is two or more months in arrears: or (iii) the mortgagor has broken some other term of the mortgage.

Although rarely done, this power may be curtailed or excluded in the mortgage itself. This would *never* be the case in bank mortgages. Indeed, they exclude s.103 and provide for repayment on demand or after a minimum period of default. A banker thereby strengthens his position as mortgagee against his customer.

NOTE: If the power of sale arises solely on account of the customer's bankruptcy, the sale requires the leave of the court: Law of Property Act 1925, s.110(1). This section does not, however, affect the mortgagee's power of sale (or appointment of a receiver) when the requirements of s.103 are satisfied.

The conveyance on sale can be completed by the bank, and a purchaser obtains a valid title free from any second or subsequent mortgage that may be outstanding: Law of Property Act 1925, s.104(1). Second or subsequent mortgages are extinguished.

NOTE: A mortgagee cannot prevent the sale by repaying the loan once the bank has entered into a binding contract with the purchaser: *Waring* v. *London & Manchester Assurance Co.* (1935).

A mortgagee has considerable discretion with regard to the arrangements for the sale, but he must act in *good faith*, e.g. he cannot buy the property himself. Where there is a conflict of interests, however, he is entitled to give preference to his own. He is not trustee of the power of sale for the mortgagor: *Cuckmere Brick Co. Ltd.* v. *Mutual Finance Ltd.* (1971) (*see* below).

NOTE: If there is a second mortgage on the property, it is usual practice for a banker to invite the second mortgagee to take over the first mortgage before exercising his power of sale.

A mortgagee is under a duty to take reasonable care to obtain the true value of the property.

EXAMPLE: In *Cuckmere Brick Co. Ltd.* v. *Mutual Finance Ltd.* (1971), a piece of land with planning permission for houses and subsequently for flats was mortgaged to the defendants. In exercising their power of sale, the defendants did not state in advertisements for the property that planning permission for flats existed. This permission made the land more valuable. HELD (C.A.): the defendants had been negligent, and their counter-claim for the balance of the advance was unsuccessful.

There is, however, no obligation on the bank to wait for an improvement in the market or keep a business running pending sale: *Bank of Cyprus (London)* v. *Gill* (1979).

A banker is *trustee* of the proceeds of the sale. He must apply them:

    (*i*) to the costs of the sale:

    (*ii*) in repayment of the mortgage debt and interest;

    (*iii*) if surplus proceeds remain, in payment to subsequent mortgagees, or, if there are none, to the customer himself.

It is necessary, therefore, to search the Register of Land Charges for second mortgages where title to the property is unregistered, because registration of a charge is equivalent to actual notice of it.

If title to the property is registered, a search is unnecessary provided the bank's mortgage was drawn to cover further advances. This is because the Registrar is required to give a mortgagee notice of a subsequent charge in such circumstances: Land Registration Act 1925, s.30(1) (*see* **10** above).

(*c*) *Appointment of a receiver.* A receiver is appointed to collect the income from the mortgaged property. He must be appointed in writing.

A banker would appoint a receiver (*i*) where a sale is imprac-ticable, e.g. where the property is let, or (*ii*) where the property market is depressed and a sale would be unlikely to realise sufficient to repay the advance.

This power to appoint a receiver arises when the mortgagee

becomes entitled to exercise his power of sale: Law of Property Act 1925, s.101 (*see* above).

The receiver is the agent of the mortgagor, not of the mortgagee. Therefore, the mortgagor is responsible for his actions and stands the cost of the receivership. For this reason the appointment of a receiver is a more attractive remedy to pursue than entry into possession (*see* below).

The income collected by the receiver is applied:

(*i*) in payment of outgoings such as rates and taxes;

(*ii*) in payment of interest on prior charges (if any);

(*iii*) in payment of insurances required by law or by the mortgage, and of his own commission;

(*iv*) in payment of interest due to the bank;

(*v*) if directed in writing by the mortgagee, towards repayment of the principal debt due. (Such a direction is always included when a banker appoints a receiver.)

NOTE: If a receiver is appointed under a mortgage granted by a company, his appointment must be filed at Companies House within seven days.

(*d*) *Foreclosure*. Foreclosure deprives the mortgagor of his equitable right to redeem the mortgaged property (*see* **19** below), and the property becomes the mortgagee's absolutely. It makes no difference if the value of the property greatly exceeds the debt outstanding.

Under a bank mortgage, the right to foreclose arises after a demand for repayment has been made and a reasonable time has elapsed without repayment having been made.

In other mortgages it arises after the contractual (legal) redemption date stated in the mortgage has passed. (Bank mortgages are usually expressed to be repayable on demand.)

Foreclosure requires the consent of the court, and proceedings must be started for an order *nisi*. This order will not be made *absolute* until six months have passed without repayment having been made.

In practice, the court will usually prefer to make an order for the sale of the property because foreclosure is very harsh on the mortgagor, particularly where the debt is small, and may give an excessive profit to the mortgagee. Thus, foreclosure orders are very rare.

NOTE: A foreclosure order absolute extinguishes the rights of subsequent mortgages. Therefore, any person interested in the mortgagor's *equity of redemption* (*see* **19** below) must be made a party to the action and given the opportunity of paying off the debt.

(*e*) *Taking possession of the property.* A mortgagee has the power to take possession of the property because a mortgage by demise gives him a term of years, and a mortgage by legal charge gives the same protection, powers and remedies as a mortgage by demise: Law of Property Act 1925, s.87(1).

Theoretically, a mortgagee can exercise this right even if there has not been a breach of the mortgage. It is usual, however, for the mortgagee to provide that the right shall not be exercised unless the mortgagor defaults in repayment.

Whether a mortgagee takes possession directly or constructively, i.e. by receiving income where the property is let, he does so at his own expense. He is also accountable to the mortgagor for any income which would have been received but for his actions.

EXAMPLE: In *White* v. *City of London Brewery Co.* (1889), the defendants took possession of the plaintiff's public house and let it as a *tied house*. A higher rent would have been obtained had it been let as a *free house*, i.e. one which could order supplies of beer from any source and not just from the defendants. HELD: the defendants were accountable to the plaintiffs for the higher rent which could have been obtained.

A banker will seldom take possession of mortgaged property because appointing a receiver (see above) achieves the same results without the expense and accountability involved in taking possession.

NOTE: Of the five remedies available, three are mainly used to recover the principal sum due and to put an end to the security. These are (1) an action for the debt, (2) sale, and (3) foreclosure. The other two: (4) appointing a receiver, and (5) taking possession, are designed primarily to recover the interest due.

16. Equitable mortgagee.

(*a*) *Mortgage under hand (in writing).* An equitable mortgagee who holds a mortgage executed under hand has only a right *in personam* (a personal right) against the mortgagor. Thus, a banker holding an equitable mortgage under hand cannot take direct action against the property mortgaged by his customer; he must obtain the court's sanction and aid to realise the security.

A banker's memorandum of deposit or charge form details the remedies available. These will include:

(*i*) an action for the money due;

(*ii*) an action for specific performance of the mortgagee's undertaking to execute a legal mortgage when requested to do so by the bank;

(*iii*) an action for the sale of the property;

(*iv*) the right to apply to the court for the appointment of a receiver;

(*v*) an action for foreclosure; (An equitable mortgage created by an equitable charge, however, gives no right of foreclosure because the charge conveys no interest in the security: *see* 3 above.)

(*vi*) a possible right to take possession: this right only exists if expressly given in the mortgage because an equitable mortgage conveys no legal estate in the property to the mortgagee. (An equitable chargee can never take possession.)

(*b*) *Mortgage under seal (by deed)*. For practical purposes, an equitable mortgage under seal puts the mortgagee in the same position as a legal mortgage because s. 101 of the Law of Property Act 1925 provides that any mortgage by deed gives the mortgagee the power of sale and the power to appoint a receiver. These are the two most useful remedies to a banker.

Furthermore, a banker's equitable mortgage under the seal will always include a power of attorney or a declaration of trust with the power to replace the mortgagor as trustee (*see* 7 above). This enables a banker to convey the legal estate to the purchaser without recourse to the court. Without such provisions, a banker could not convey the legal estate because he himself has only an equitable interest in the property.

NOTE: Any equitable mortgage is subject to prior equities. These cannot be overriden in the way that is possible when a legal mortgage is taken. A possible example which would affect a banker would be where one spouse gives an equitable mortgage over the matrimonial home held in his or her sole name when the other spouse has an equitable interest in it by virtue of having contributed to its purchase. (See also *William & Glyn's Bank Ltd.* v. *Boland and another* (1980): **6:7**.)

17. Second mortgagee. A second mortgagee's remedies are very similar to those of the first mortgagee.

He may sell the property without recourse to the first mortgagee. This will probably prove to be difficult, however, because the land would still be subject to the first mortgage. Therefore, a second mortgagee will usually seek to join the first mortgagee in the sale, the proceeds being applied in discharge of both mortgages.

NOTE: Under s.50 of the Law of Property Act 1925, a second mortgagee can apply to the court to free the property from the first mortgagee after paying a sum of money sufficient to repay the first mortgage into court.

Should a receiver be appointed, interest on the first mortgage must be paid before that on the second mortgage. The same applies to income received by taking possession of the property.

A foreclosure order absolute vests the property in the mortgagee subject to the first mortgage.

18. Sub-mortgagee. A sub-mortgagee has the following remedies.

(*a*) He may bring an action for the money due;

(*b*) He may sell the debt (if anyone can be found to buy it). This power is exercisable after a default on the sub-mortgage and a purchaser takes subject to the head mortgagor's right of redemption (*see* **19** below).

(*c*) He may exercise the powers conferred by the head mortgage. However, he may do this only where there has been default under both the head mortgage and sub-mortgage.

If the property is sold—the most usual remedy—the purchaser takes free from any claim by either mortgagor.

A sale by an equitable sub-mortgagee requires the consent of the court.

Redemption and discharge of mortgages

19. Redemption.

(*a*) *Introduction.* A mortgage is redeemed by the mortgagor repaying the advance. Once the mortgagee acknowledges receipt of the money the mortgage automatically terminates: Law of Property Act 1925, s.115.

(*b*) *The equity of redemption.* A mortgagor has a legal (contractual) right to redeem his property on the date stipulated in the mortgage. After this he loses his contractual right to take back his property.

Equity (the principles developed and applied in the old Court of Chancery), however, began to recognise a mortgagor's right to redeem his property by (*i*) giving reasonable notice and (*ii*) paying off the principal, interest and costs, even though the legal redemption date had passed. This became known as the *equity of redemption.*

Equity took the view that the mortgage was given only as a *security* and it was never intended to transfer the land to the mortgagee unless the mortgagor had no reasonable chance of repaying the loan.

In modern mortgages, the contractual date for redemption is usually six months after the execution of the mortgage. Hence, in the vast majority of cases, the mortgagor relies on his equitable right of redemption.

The equity of redemption is an *equitable interest in land.* It can be sold, left by will or otherwise assigned.

(*i*) *"Clogs" on the equity.* The equity cannot be *clogged,* i.e. the mortgagor cannot be prevented from eventually redeeming his property, or be made to take back his property still subject to claims by the mortgagee. Any agreement purporting to clog the equity in such ways is *void.*

NOTE: A limited company is not protected by this rule. A *debenture* may be wholly or partly irredeemable and an ordinary mortgage by a company is a debenture: *Knightsbridge Estates Trust Ltd.* v. *Byrne* (1940) (*see* 4:**32–35**).

It is, however, possible in a commercial transaction to *postpone* repayment for a reasonable period; what is reasonable being a question of fact. An exception is a regulated agreement under the Consumer Credit Act 1974. This provides that the borrower may complete payments ahead of the time stipulated in the case of security for a regulated agreement and that there can no be contracting out of this right.

(*ii*) *Loss of the equity.* It can be lost in the four following circumstances:

(1) when released by the mortgagor;

(2) by foreclosure;

(3) by lapse of time, when the mortgagee has taken and remained in possession of the land for twelve years: Limitation Act 1980;

(4) when the land is sold by the mortgagee acting under his statutory power of sale.

20. Discharge of legal mortgages.

(*a*) *Unregistered land.* A legal mortgage of unregistered land can be discharged by a *simple receipt* for the principal and interest: Law of Property Act 1925, s. 115. This may be endorsed upon or attached to the mortgage deed. (Bank mortgages usually include a printed form of receipt ready for completion when required.) A bank will complete the receipt under seal, although it is not actually necessary to do so.

Should a third party repay the advance, the receipt will acknowledge this. It will then operate as a transfer of the mortgage to him, e.g. where a guarantor pays off the whole debt and thereby becomes entitled to have all securities deposited by the principal debtor transferred to him.

Alternatively, the mortgagor can ask for a *formal reconveyance* of the property to him. This form of discharge is most likely to be used (*i*) where several properties were mortgaged together and only one is being released, or (*ii*) where only a part of the amount outstanding is being repaid.

If the mortgage to be discharged was unsupported by a deposit of the title deeds, it will have been registered as a puisne mortgage on the Land Charges Register. This registration must be removed by filing the appropriate form.

A banker who holds the title deeds may return them to his customer unless he has had express notice of a subsequent charge. He is not required to make a search for subsequent charges.

A second mortgagee (certainly a banker) should give express notice of his charge to the first mortgagee. A banker *receiving* such notice must then deliver the title deeds to the second mortgagee when his own first mortgage is discharged.

NOTE: This must be distinguished from a mortgagee's duty to

make a search for subsequent charges when he has exercised his power of sale (*see* **15** above).

A legal mortgage, even though discharged, remains part of the chain of title to registered land and it must be retained with the other deeds by the owner of the property.

(*b*) *Registered land*. A mortgage of registered land is almost always discharged by completing the Land Registry's Form 53, and sending this with the charge certificate to the Registry Office. The entry on the register is then discharged. The charge certificate is cancelled and the land certificate, written up to date, is re-issued in its place.

Suitably amended, Form 53 can also be used where only part of the security is to be released.

Alternatively but rarely, the discharge may be effected by a receipt for the money due in the form of a reconveyance.

Should the mortgagor sell the property (either voluntarily or after the pressure from his bank), Form 55 is used. This is a combined form of transfer and discharge. The mortgagor executes the form as proprietor of the land charged and the mortgagee as proprietor of the charge. Hence, the property is transferred to the purchaser free from the charge.

Bank mortgages expressly cover further advances, and the Registrar is therefore required to give a banker notice of any subsequent charge: Land Registration Act 1925, s.30(1). Thus, it is unnecessary for a banker to search the charges register before returning the land certificate or the surplus proceeds, if he has exercised his power of sale, to his customer.

21. Discharge of equitable mortgages.

(*a*) *Method*. Equitable mortgages, whether under seal or under hand, are usually discharged by cancelling the memorandum of deposit. This is not a link in the chain of title and it can be retained by the mortgagee.

An alternative, but uncommon, method of discharge is by simple receipt.

The title deeds or land certificate are then returned to the customer.

(*b*) *Removal of entries on relevant registers*.

(*i*) *Unregistered land*. An equitable mortgage unsupported by a deposit of title deeds, e.g. a second equitable mortgage, must be registered at the Land Charges Registry as a general equitable charge (*see* 12 above). This entry must be removed.

(*ii*) *Registered land.* An equitable mortgage of registered land will have been protected by a notice of deposit of a land certificate (*see* 13 above). This notice is removed by the Registrar on receipt of the mortgagee's written request to do so accompanied by the land certificate. A banker makes this request by signing the reverse of his copy of the notice.

22. Discharge of mortgages given by companies. Company mortgages must be registered at Companies House. This entry must be removed in addition to any relevant entry considered in 12 and 13 above.

The company can file a memorandum of satisfaction with the Registrar and, although this is not obligatory, it is clearly advisable. The memorandum must be accompanied by a statutory declaration by the secretary and one director attesting the truth of the details it contains.

Progress test 7

1. Define a mortgage. What is its main characteristic? (**2**)
2. Distinguish a mortgage from the following types of security: (*a*) a pledge, (*b*) a lien, (*c*) a charge. (**3**)
3. State and explain the most important and practical distinction between legal and equitable mortgages. (**4 and 14**)
4. What are the ways in which a legal mortgage of land can be effected? (**5**)
5. In what ways can an equitable mortgage be created? (**6**)
6. Why does a banker's memorandum of deposit contain an undertaking by the borrower to execute a legal mortgage when asked to do so? (**6**)
7. List the clauses which are usually found in bank mortgages. Briefly explain the purpose and effect of each. (**7**)
8. Why is a memorandum of deposit under seal sometimes taken by a banker? (**7**)
9. What is the main disadvantage of a second mortgage? (**8**)

10. Define a sub-mortgage. Distinguish it from a second mortgage. (**9**)

11. What is tacking? (**10**)

12. When a banker takes a second mortgage as security, why is it important for him to give direct notice of his interest to the first mortgagee? (**10**)

13. Why must the mortgagor's account be broken when notice of a second mortgage is received? (**10**)

14. State the main advantages and disadvantages of a mortgage of land as a security. (**11**)

15. Can a mortgage of unregistered land by deposit of title deeds be registered? (**12**)

16. How is a mortgage of registered land protected? (**13**)

17. In what circumstances would a banker lodge a notice of intended deposit of a land certificate? (**13**)

18. List the five remedies available to a legal mortgagee. Which of these remedies is not a right *in rem* and which are primarily designed to recover the interest due. (**15**)

19. Which remedies are usually most favoured by bankers? (**15**)

20. Why is the appointment of a receiver to be preferred as a remedy to taking possession of the mortgaged property? (**15**)

21. What is meant by the equity of redemption? (**19**)

22. In what circumstances is the equity lost? (**19**)

23. Outline the usual method of discharging a legal mortgage of unregistered land. (**20**)

24. In what circumstances are Land Registry Forms 53 and 55 used to discharge mortgages? (**20**)

25. What is the usual method of discharging equitable mortgages? (**21**)

8

Life insurance policies

Life policies: the general law

1. Definition. A life insurance policy is a contract in which the insurer, in return for the payment of premiums, agrees to pay to the proposer a given sum of money on the death of the person whose life is insured, or on a specified date before this.

NOTE: To be strictly correct, a life policy is one of *assurance* not insurance because the latter term refers to contracts of indemnity, e.g. motor or fire insurance, under which a claim may never arise. Payment at some time is *assured* under a life policy. However, the terms are used interchangeably today, and the term *life insurance* is the more common.

2. Types of life policies. There are two main types.

(*a*) *Whole life policies*. The sum assured is only payable on the death of the person whose life is insured.

Premiums are lower than for an endowment policy (*see* below) because a claim will not usually arise for many years.

Whole life policies have declined in popularity because a proposer insuring his own life can never enjoy the benefit of the policy.

(*b*) *Endowment policies*. The sum assured is payable on a certain date or on the death of the life insured, whichever occurs first.

(*c*) *"With profits"* or *"without profits"*. Both whole life and endowment policies can either be "with profits" or "without profits" policies. The former type share in the profits of the issuing company, the latter type do not.

The premium for a with profits policy will be the higher of the two, for considerably more will be payable on maturity.

Although it is impossible to do so accurately, insurance companies will usually give an estimate of the maturity value of with profits policies based on the continued payment of bonuses at the current rate.

(*d*) *Policies covered by the Married Women's Property Act 1882, s.11.* Policies covered by s.11 are usually effected by a husband on his own life for the benefit of his wife, his children, or both, although s.11 also covers corresponding policies effected by a wife.

NOTE: These policies must be considered separately because of the problems which can arise if one is offered as security (*see* **7** below).

Policies under s.11 create *trusts* in favour of the persons named in them. The proceeds of such a policy do not, therefore, form part of the policyholder's estate.

Any mortgage of a policy to which s.11 applies requires the consent of the beneficiaries and their signatures on the mortgage.

3. Insurable interest.

(*a*) *Introduction.* The person intending to take out the policy (the proposer) must have an *insurable interest* in the life insured: Life Assurance Act 1774, s.1. A policy is void if no such interest can be shown.

A person always has an insurable interest in his own life and in that of his or her spouse, but in other situations the insurable interest required must be a *pecuniary interest*, i.e. the financial loss which would be suffered by the proposer on the death of the person whose life he or she insures: *Halford* v. *Kymer* (1830).

The sum assured in such cases is limited to the amount of the pecuniary interest: s.3 of the 1774 Act; but where a person insures his or her own life or that of his or her spouse, i.e. where the insurable interest is not a pecuniary interest, the policy may be for any amount.

NOTE: The insurable interest distinguishes a life policy from a *wager*, for they are similar in so far as they both provide for the payment of a sum of money on the happening of a future uncertain event. However, a wager creates the risk of loss, while a life insurance contract guards against the consequences of a loss.

A life policy may be *assigned* (*see* **6** below) to someone who has no insurable interest in the life insured: *Ashley* v. *Ashley* (1892). (This rule is important because sale of the policy may be a more profitable alternative to surrender if the policy holder wishes, or is compelled to realise the value of the policy before its maturity.)

(*b*) *Examples of insurable interests.*

(*i*) The interest of a creditor in the life of his debtor (to the amount of the debt).

(*ii*) The interest of a guarantor in the life of the principal debtor (to the amount of his guarantee).

(*iii*) The interest of an employer in the life of his employee, and vice versa.

NOTE: A parent has no insurable interest in the life of a child, nor vice versa, purely on the grounds of parentage: a pecuniary interest must be shown. A father would, for example, have an insurable interest in the life of a daughter who acted as his housekeeper. A parent may, however, effect a policy for a child in the child's name.

(*c*) *Termination of the insurable interest.* Since the Life Assurance Act 1774, s. 1, only requires an insurable interest to exist at the time the policy is taken out, the policy is not invalidated if the insurable interest subsequently ceases, e.g. when an employee leaves his employment or when a debtor repays an advance guaranteed by the proposer: *Dalby* v. *India and London Life Assurnce Co.* (1854).

4. "Uberrima fides".

(*a*) *Meaning.* All insurance contracts are contracts *uberrimae fidei* (of the utmost good faith). Both the proposer and the insurer are under a duty to disclose all *material facts* (*see* below) and failure by one party to do so makes the contract voidable at the option of the other. This rule applies however innocent the failure to disclose.

In practice, it is the proposer who is most affected by the rule, since he alone is in a position to know all the facts which might influence his insurer.

(*b*) *Material facts.* A material fact is, therefore, one which would influence the judgment of a prudent insurer in fixing the premium or in determining whether to accept the proposal: Marine Insurance Act 1906, s. 18. (This Act applies to all types of insurance contract:

Locker and Wolff v. *Western Australian Insurance Co.* (1936).)
Whether or not a particular fact is material is a question of fact.

EXAMPLE: In *Woolcott* v. *Sun Alliance and London Insurance Ltd.*
(1978), the defendants issued a block-policy of insurance to a
building society. The insured were the building society and their
mortgagors. The building society application form asked no
specific question about applicants' characters but asked: "Are
there any other matters which you wish to be taken into account?"
The plaintiff in applying for a mortgage advance answered that
there were not, failing to disclose that he had served a long prison
sentence for robbery. A claim arose on the policy. The defendants
satisfied the society's claim to the extent of their interest but
refused to pay the plaintiff's claim because he had not disclosed
his criminal record. HELD: they were entitled to do so. It made no
difference to the duty of disclosure that the policy was effected
through a block proposal and not through individual proposal
forms.

(*c*) *Modifications of the rule.* The common law rule on non-
disclosure may be modified by the proposal form. This may provide
that the inaccuracy of *any* statement made by the proposer will
constitute grounds on which to avoid the policy, whether or not the
statement is material to the assessment of the risk.

Conversely, it may be provided that only fraudulent non-disclosure
will constitute grounds for avoiding the contract.

It is usual, however, for the proposal form to specify that the
questions it contains are to be the basis of the contract. Where this is
so, the duty of disclosure is limited to these questions.

NOTE: The *uberrima fides* rule is important to the use of a life policy
as a security. Should a policy held as security be invalidated for
non-disclosure of a material fact, the mortgagee's interest is
similarly invalidated. Hence, a life policy can never be an
absolutely safe security.

5. Suicide. It is a general principle of insurance law that a policyholder cannot claim for deliberately self-inflicted loss. The principle
would probably defeat a claim on a policy by the representatives of a
policyholder who commits *suicide while sane* unless the policy

expressly provides otherwise. *Insane suicide* is not considered to be a deliberate act.

Most life policies do in fact expressly provide that suicide will not affect a claim providing it takes place a given number of years after the policy is taken out.

Whether or not a particular policy contains a suicide clause is a relevant factor for a banker to consider should it be offered as a security. It is, however, quite common for a policy not containing a suicide clause to expressly permit an assignee for value to claim on it to the extent of his interest should the policyholder commit suicide while sane.

A banker who accepts a life policy as security for an advance is, for example, an *assignee for value*.

6. Assignment of life policies.

(a) *Introduction.* The right to claim under the policy may be transferred by the policyholder to another person, i.e. it may be *assigned*. The assignee is not required to have an insurable interest in the life insured: Life Assurance Act 1774, s.1.

(b) *Policies of Assurance Act 1867.* An assignment of a life policy must comply with this Act. Section 5 requires that the assignment must be by either (i) an indorsement on the policy itself, or (ii) by a separate document of assignment in the form laid down in the Act.

An assignee of a policy may sue in his own name for the policy moneys (s.1.), but this right is subject to two conditions.

(i) *He takes subject to equities.* This means that any defence which would have been available against the policyholder (the assignor) is available against the assignee, e.g. invalidation of a policy by non-disclosure of material facts: s.2. (A banker must bear this in mind when he is offered a life policy as a security.)

(ii) *Notice in writing of the assignment* must be given to the company which issued the policy: s.3. This notice is necessary to vest legal title to the policy in the assignee.

If there are *second or subsequent assignments*, priority of interests between assignees is determined by the date on which notice of assignment was received by the issuing company.

EXCEPTIONS: A mortgagee who has *actual* or *constructive notice* of a prior assignment is postponed to it even though notice of the prior assignment was not given to the issuing company. In *Spencer* v. *Clarke* (1978), for example, the plaintiff took as security an assignment of a policy which the defendant said that he had left at home but would produce the following day. Notice of the assignment was duly given to the issuing company. The defendant had, in fact, already deposited the policy under a previous assignment, of which notice had not been given. HELD: the first mortgagee's claim had priority because the mortgagor's failure to produce the policy constituted *constructive notice* of the prior assignment. On the facts, possession of the policy was more important than notice to the issuing company. (A banker must, therefore, insist on the production of the policy before accepting a mortgage of a life policy as security.)

An assignee loses his claim against the issuing company if it pays the policy moneys in good faith to the assignor before notice of an assignment is received.

A life policy will state where notices of assignment are to be given, usually the company's principal place of business. The issuing company is bound by the Act to give written acknowledgement of the notice if requested in writing to do so by the assignee. A small fee is payable for this acknowledgement, although it is often waived.

Life policies as security

7. Inspection of the policy. Policies offered as security must be inspected in the following respects.

(*a*) *The life assurance company.* Most policies offered as security will have been issued by a reputable British company which will present few problems. Policies of little known or recently formed companies are not favoured as securities. Any policy issued by a foreign company must be made payable in sterling at its London office:

(*b*) *Special restrictions in the policy.* These may relate to
   (*i*) suicide (*see* 5 above);
   (*ii*) foreign travel;
   (*iii*) hazardous occupations;
   (*iv*) sporting activities;
   (*v*) residence.

Any restrictions on assignment in a life policy will prevent its use as a security.

NOTE: Restrictions on assignment are, however, only common in *industrial policies*, and these are not suitable securities since small weekly premiums are payable on them involving a banker in disproportionate effort to check that they have been properly paid.

(*c*) *Financial provisions*. A banker is primarily interested in the *surrender value* of a policy, for this represents his security. This will be checked along with the capital sum assured and the amount and frequency of the premiums.

Endowment policies are preferred to whole life policies because they mature on a specified date. A *paid-up policy* is an even better security because no further premiums are payable and it will steadily increase in value.

(*d*) *Admission of age*. A policy will normally state either "Age admitted" or "Age not admitted". This refers to the formal production of the insured's birth certificate to the issuing company as proof of his or her age; the mere mention in the policy of the age or date of birth of the insured does not mean that age has been admitted.

The insured's age *must be admitted* before the company will make any payment under the policy since premiums are related to age. The value of the policy is affected by an incorrect statement of the insured's age.

If a banker accepts as security a policy in which age is not admitted, he should obtain a copy of his customer's birth certificate and send it with the policy to the life office for admission of age to be indorsed on the policy.

(*e*) *Beneficiaries*. All the beneficiaries named in a policy to which the Married Women's Property Act 1882, s.11, applies (*see* 2 above) must join the policyholder in effecting the assignment to the bank.

If all the possible beneficiaries are not identified with reasonable certainty, or if any are under 18 years of age, no effective charge can be taken.

A plea of *undue influence* is always a possibility should a banker seek to realise such a policy. To avoid the risk of losing his security, a banker should ensure that a wife or "child" receives sound advice on the effect of a proposed mortgage before they join in the assignment. At the very least, a *free will clause* should be added to the charge.

(*f*) *Ancillary matters.* A banker must also check that (*i*) premiums have been paid up to date, and (*ii*) whether or not there are existing charges on the policy.

If a previous assignment (the document of charge duly reassigned) comes with the policy, it forms a link in the chain of title to the policy and it must be carefully kept with it.

8. Legal mortgage. A banker will take a legal mortgage of a life policy by an *assignment under seal* of the mortgagor's rights to the policy moneys.

A typical bank mortgage will contain the following clauses:

(*a*) An assignment of the policy to the bank, together with any accrued bonuses attaching to it.

(*b*) A clause providing for the re-assignment of the policy to the customer (the mortgagor) when he has repaid the advance.

(*c*) An all-moneys clause.

(*d*) A clause making the advance repayable on demand.

(*e*) A continuing security clause.

(*f*) An undertaking by the customer to abide by the terms of the policy, and to do nothing which would invalidate it. This includes the punctual payment of premiums and the production of receipts for them. If the premiums are not paid, the mortgage gives the bank the power to pay them and debit the customer's account accordingly.

(*g*) A clause giving the bank power to exercise its statutory rights under the Law of Property Act 1925, and under the policy itself (*see* **10** below) without his customer's consent.

(*h*) Exclusions of ss.93 and 103 of the Law of Property Act 1925.

(*i*) Where the mortgage secures the account of another person (a *third party charge*), clauses:

(*i*) giving details of the account secured;

(*ii*) granting the bank the right to vary arrangements with the debtor without prejudicing its security;

(*iii*) allowing the bank to put any money received under the mortgage into a suspense account.

(*iv*) enabling the bank to give a valid discharge for the proceeds of the policy.

Many of these clauses are identical or very similar in purpose to those contained in a banker's form of legal mortgage over land. They are discussed fully in 7:7.

NOTE: When a legal mortgage of a *duplicate policy* is offered as security, the possibility of fraud always arises, even though the issuing company will have made its own inquiries before issuing the duplicate. For example, a legal assignment of the original policy may exist of which notice as required by the Policies of Assurance Act 1867 was not given, the assignment thereby creating an equitable interest only (*see* **9** below). Thus, a banker must receive a very good explanation for the policy's destruction to avoid being fixed with *constructive notice* of the prior charge: *see* **6** above, *Spencer* v. *Clarke* (1878).

9. Equitable mortgage. A banker will take an equitable mortgage of a life policy by deposit of the policy, usually supported by a memorandum of deposit. The memorandum is important because it will set out the purpose of the deposit, the terms of the mortgage (*see* **8** above) and the rights of the bank as mortgagee (*see* **10** below).

In particular, the mortgage will be made a continuing security, and it will contain the customer's undertakings to execute a legal assignment on the banks' request, and to pay the premiums as they fall due, the bank being empowered to pay them on his behalf if he does not.

NOTE: An equitable mortgage by deposit of the policy without a memorandum of deposit is good against the mortgagor's trustee in bankruptcy. This is because the policy vests in the trustee subject to all equities existing at the date of the commencement of the bankruptcy: *Re Wallis* (1902).

There is no enactment requiring notice of an equitable mortgage of a life policy to be given to the issuing company, nor for the company to recognise an equitable interest. However, most companies will acknowledge notice if it is sent. This will give the mortgagee priority over previous equitable mortgagees provided that he did not have actual or constructive notice of the prior interest at the time he made the advance. A banker will, therefore, always give notice of any equitable mortgage that he takes.

Where notice is not given, priority between equitable mortgages is determined by their date.

NOTE: An equitable mortgage of a life policy is comparatively rare because a legal mortgage is easily effected and provides a much better security: (*see* **13** below).

10. Remedies of a mortgagee.

(*a*) *Introduction.* Enforcing the security will never realise the potential value of the policy and it will inevitably involve the mortgagor in considerable loss. A banker will, therefore, allow a customer every latitude before exercising his rights as mortgagee.

(*b*) *Legal mortgagee.* If the policy moneys have become payable, i.e. the insured has died or the policy has matured, the mortgagee can claim the policy moneys from the company, proof of death being required.

If the policy moneys are not yet payable, the mortgagee may do one of the following.

(*i*) *Surrender the policy* to the company. This right is expressly given in a bank's mortgage form.

(*ii*) *Obtain a loan* from the insurance company against the policy. The mortgagor's co-operation is necessary to do this because *he* must make the application to the company and authorise payment of the loan direct to the bank in exchange for the policy and the mortgage duly discharged.

(*iii*) *Sell the policy.* Sale is an alternative to surrender of the policy and it may realise a considerably larger sum.

If a friend or relation cannot be found who is willing to buy the policy, it can be sold to one of a number of companies that specialise in the purchase of life policies as investments. The purchaser (assignee) need not have an insurable interest in the life insured (*see* **3** above).

Since s. 103 of the Law of Property Act 1925 is excluded in bank mortgages, the power of sale can be exercised as soon as the customer defaults in repayment.

(*iv*) *Convert the policy into a paid-up policy* for a smaller capital sum. This remedy is useful when the customer is unable to pay the premiums. The surrender value of the policy is seldom affected.

(*c*) *Equitable mortgagee.* If the policy moneys are payable, the insured or, if he has died, his personal representatives must join with the bank in a receipt for the policy moneys. This is because the *legal title* is still vested in the insured or became vested in his personal representatives on his death.

If the policy moneys are not yet payable, the mortgagee may do one of the following.

(*i*) *Ask the mortgagor to execute a legal assignment of the policy.* The customer's undertaking to do this is included in a bank's memorandum of deposit. (This would enable a banker to exercise the more extensive rights of a legal mortgagee.)

(*ii*) *Seek the mortgagor's agreement to the sale or surrender of the policy.*

(*iii*) *Apply to the court for an order of sale or a foreclosure order* (*see* 7:15) if the customer proves to be uncooperative.

An order for sale is far more common than a foreclosure order, but should the latter be granted the policy becomes the mortgagee's absolutely (subject to prior equities), and he can then surrender it.

A sale must be effected in good faith, and reasonable care must be taken to obtain the best possible price for the policy.

(*iv*) *Seek the mortgagor's consent and aid in converting the security into a paid-up policy, or in obtaining a loan from the issuing company sufficient to pay off the advance.* This latter course of action keeps the policy alive.

11. Discharge of the mortgage.

(*a*) *Legal mortgage.* The policy must be *reassigned under seal*. Bank mortgages of life policies generally have a standard form of re-assignment printed on them ready for use.

Notice of the re-assignment must be given to the issuing company.

NOTE: The discharged mortgage forms a link in the chain of title to the policy. It must be retained carefully with the policy for production when a claim is made on it.

(*b*) *Equitable mortgage.* Cancellation of the memorandum is a sufficient discharge of the mortgage. No re-assignment is necessary because legal title to the property remains with the mortgagor throughout.

If notice of the mortgage was given to the issuing company, notice of the discharge must also be given.

12. Notice of a subsequent charge. The customer's account must

be broken to prevent the Rule in *Clayton's Case* (1816) working to the bank's detriment (*see* 3:**18**). A new account must be opened through which all transactions must pass. This account must be kept in credit or fresh security taken.

If a banker is forced to *realise* the security, he must pay surplus proceeds to the second assignee after repaying himself. If the advance is *repaid*, he must re-assign the policy and deliver it with the original assignment to the second assignee.

NOTE: Since a banker will retain the policy and the assignment of it when taking the security, his customer will find it difficult to find anybody willing to take a second assignment of the policy as security. It is, therefore, uncommon to receive notice of a second charge on a life policy.

13. Advantages and disadvantages.

(*a*) *Legal or equitable mortgage?* Life policies are both a very common and a very acceptable type of security. However, it is uncommon for a banker to take an equitable mortgage of a life policy because a legal mortgage can be effected easily and cheaply (compare land: *see* 7:**10**), and offers considerable advantages, particularly the following.

(*i*) The issuing company *must recognise* a legal assignment if requested to do so by the assignee; it need not recognise equitable interests.

(*ii*) A legal assignee has an *absolute right to surrender or sell the policy*; an equitable mortgagee needs the co-operation of his customer or the consent of the court.

(*iii*) A legal assignee can *give a valid discharge for the policy moneys in his own name*; an equitable mortgagee must join with the insured or his personal representatives in the discharge.

NOTE: These latter two advantages of a legal mortgage arise because title to the policy vests in a legal assignee.

(*b*) *Advantages.*

(*i*) The *value* of a life policy can be easily ascertained, does not fluctuate with market forces and steadily increases.

(*ii*) *Title* to the policy can be easily checked.

(*iii*) The security can be *easily taken*.

(*iv*) *Realisation* of the security by a legal mortgagee is quick and simple.

(*c*) *Disadvantages.*

(*i*) The mortgagor's *possible inability to pay the premiums*. A banker must continue to pay these in order to keep the policy alive if the advance has been allowed to exceed the current surrender value of the policy.

(*ii*) *Possible invalidation of the policy*, and hence the loss of the security, through (1) the customer's breach of the *uberrima fides* obligation, or of the conditions in the policy, or (2) through the customer's lack of an insurable interest when he effected the policy, although this is very unlikely to arise in practice.

(*iii*) Some life policies are linked to unit trust investments and these can and do *fluctuate in value* in line with the general value of stock market investment. Thus, their surrender values can be reduced if stock market values are particularly depressed.

Progress test 8

1. Define a life policy. (**1**)
2. Distinguish between whole life and endowment policies. (**2**)
3. To what policies does the Married Women's Property Act 1882, s.11, apply? How does this section affect the use of such policies for security purposes? (**2**)
4. Explain what is meant by an insurable interest. Give examples. (**3**)
5. Explain the principle of *uberrima fides* as applied to life policies. How can it affect a banker holding a life policy as security? (**4**)
6. What is a material fact in the context of the *uberrima fides* principle? (**4**)
7. Does an assignee for value lose his claim on the policy if the insured commits suicide while sane? (**5**)
8. What is meant by assigning a life policy? (**6**)
9. State the provisions of the Policies of Assurance Act 1867 in regard to assignments of life policies. (**6**)
10. In what respects must a life policy be investigated before it is accepted as a security? List them. (**7**)
11. What form does a banker's legal mortgage of a life policy take? (**8**)

12. List the usual clauses to be found in a legal mortgage of a life policy. Explain the purpose of each. (**8**)

13. How does a banker effect an equitable mortgage of a life policy? (**9**)

14. Why should a banker send notice of an equitable mortgage to the issuing company? (**9**)

15. List a legal mortgagee's rights if the policy moneys have not become payable. (**10**)

16. List the remedies of an equitable mortgagee. How do they differ from those of a legal mortgagee? (**10**)

17. How is (*a*) a legal mortgage, and (*b*) an equitable mortgage of a life policy discharged? (**11**)

18. Outline the procedure which a banker should follow after receiving notice of a second mortgage of a life policy. Explain why the procedure is necessary. (**12**)

19. Why does a banker prefer a legal mortgage of a life policy to an equitable mortgage? (**13**)

20. List the main advantages and disadvantages of life policies as security. (**13**)

9

Stocks and shares

Types of stocks and shares

1. Introduction. The term "stocks and shares" is used in this chapter to embrace a variety of securities taken by bankers in addition to those issued by companies. Included are unit trust holdings, shares in building societies, national savings securities and government and local authority stock.

2. Company securities.

(*a*) *Stocks and shares.* The number of shares or the amount of stock which a person holds in a company is the measure of his interest in that company.

A company must initially raise its financial capital by the issue of shares but, once issued, fully paid-up shares may be converted into stock. Each shareholder then receives an amount of stock equivalent to the nominal value of his shares.

(The different types of shares have been considered in 4:**19** and the distinction between shares and stock in 4:**20**. You should now refer back to these sections.)

(*b*) *Debentures and debenture stock.* This is *loan* capital, not invested capital. Hence, debenture holders are creditors of the company and not members of it.

(Debentures have been discussed fully in 4:**32–40** and debenture stock in 4:**20**. You should once again refer back to these sections at this point.)

3. Unit trust holdings. A unit trust is established by a trust deed. It is a *trust* in the true legal sense of the word.

The trust's investments are handled by *managers*, often a limited company formed for the purpose, and the investments are held on behalf of the unit holders by a *trustee*, usually a banker or an insurance company.

The units are not bought on a stock exchange but direct from the managers to whom they may be resold. Daily *bid* and *offered* prices are quoted by them. These are the prices at which the managers will buy and sell the units.

The managers invest the funds of the trust in a portfolio of securities in accordance with the provisions of the trust deed. Some trusts are set up to hold a general portfolio, others concentrate on either high income or capital growth, and others are mainly devoted to one particular sphere of investment, e.g. banking or mining.

Unit trusts enable an investor to have an indirect holding in a wide portfolio of investments. He also gains the advantage of having his investment managed by persons with a specialist knowledge of the stock market.

4. Building societies. A person can either *subscribe for shares* in, or *lend money on deposit* to a building society.

Depositors are entitled to priority in repayment of their investment should the society be wound up. They therefore receive a marginally lower rate of interest on their accounts.

Building societies have become a very popular investment with the "man in the street", because they offer easy realisation of the investment, a good rate of interest and excellent security.

5. Government and local authority loan stock. These may be *dated*, i.e. repayable on or by a specific date, or *undated*, but they always bear interest at a fixed rate on the nominal value of the stock.

Such stocks are always repaid at their nominal value. Thus, a person who buys at less than the nominal value and holds the stock to maturity will receive a capital profit in addition to regular interest.

British Government stocks are known as *gilt edged* stock, and they are guaranteed by the state. Their value does fluctuate, however, in particular undated stock which carries a low rate of interest such as 3½ per cent War Stock.

The stock issued by local authorities and major Commonwealth governments is regarded as being almost as safe as *gilts*. Confidence in stock issued by other foreign governments is determined by the market's assessment of the *risk* involved.

6. National savings securities. The most important securities in this category are:

(a) National Savings Certificates;
(b) Premium Savings Bonds;
(c) British Savings Bonds.

These securities are guaranteed by the state.

Title and its transfer

7. Introduction. The types of stocks and shares were classified above according to the type of organisation which issued them. Alternatively, they can be classified by the method by which title to them is established and transferred.

A banker must view these classifications as being complimentary, rather than mutually exclusive, because both are important when "stocks and shares" are offered as security for an advance.

8. Registered securities. These are the most common type.

(a) *Title*. The company or other organisation issuing the securities maintains a register in which the holder's name and address and the amount of his holding is recorded. The registered holder receives a certificate in his name. This is *prima facie* evidence of title.

Every company maintains its own register of shareholders and stockholders. The holders of British Government Stock and National Savings Securities are registered on either the National Savings Stock Register, and receive a certificate issued by the Director of Savings, or in books kept at the Bank of England and receive a certificate issued by the Bank.

Although the certificate issued is not a document of title, it must be surrendered when the shares are sold. A duplicate can only be issued when the original is lost or destroyed and proper inquiries must first be made. In most cases an indemnity from the holder is required before a duplicate will be issued.

(b) *Transfer of title*. Legal title to transferable registered securities is effected by lodging the transfer form (*see* below) signed by the transferor (and sometimes the transferee) and the relevant certificate with the issuing organisation for appropriate entries to be made on the register. A new certificate is then issued in favour of the transferee.

NOTE: National Savings Securities and the shares in some building societies are not transferable.

The form of transfer used is nearly always the simplified *stock transfer form* introduced by the Stock Transfer Act 1963. This form contains a statement of the consideration given (the price paid) for the shares, the names of the issuing company or other corporation, the number and value of the securities involved, and details of the registered holder and his signature. It is not signed by the transferee.

NOTE: The introduction on the Stock Exchange of a computerised accountancy system led to the introduction of the *Talisman* transfer form, a variant of the stock transfer form. This is used on a transfer by sale of shares in public companies. The transferee is always SEPON Limited when the form is used.

In a few cases, the 1963 Act prohibits the use of this stock transfer form, e.g. on the transfer of partly-paid shares, and a transfer must be *by deed* or by a *common form of transfer* signed by both parties. These alternative methods are almost identical to one another except that the latter is not sealed.

The *stamp duty* on the transfer of registered stocks and shares is at the rate of £1 per cent.

Units in *unit trusts* can be transferred by any method approved by the trustees. It is usual, however, for the holder to realise his investment by selling the units back to the managers of the trust by completing the form of renunciation on the back of his certificate.

9. Bearer securities.

(*a*) *Introduction.* Governments may issue *bearer bonds* and, if authorised by their articles of association, companies may issue *share warrants* to bearer in respect of fully paid-up shares or stock. They can also issue *bearer debentures*. No records are kept of the holders of bearer securities.

Bearer securities attract initial *stamp duty* of £3 per cent and their issue requires the Treasury's consent.

(*b*) *Transfer of title.* Bearer securities are *negotiable instruments* (*see* 11:1). As such title to them passes by mere delivery and a person who takes a transfer in good faith and for value acquires a good title, even though the transferor had either a defective title or no title at all.

(*i*) *Scrip certificates and letters of allotment.* Subscribers for Government stock receive a scrip certificate until all instalments have been paid. The certificate is then exchanged for the actual stock.

Companies now use letters of allotment instead of scrip certificates for the same purpose when issuing shares or debentures.

Scrip certificates are fully negotiable, but the form of renunciation contained in the letter of allotment must be completed and signed in order to pass title to the shares or debentures which the letter of allotment represents. The transferee is then able to complete the form of application and send it with the renounced allotment to the company.

(*ii*) *American and Canadian share certificates.* These are a cross between registered securities and bearer securities.

On the one hand, title to them is registered with the issuing organisation, usually in the name of a London stockbroker or trust company known as *good marking names*. On the other hand, by including a form of transfer and power of attorney signed by the registered owner, they are effectively *indorsed in blank* (*see* 11:**43**). They thereby become *quasi-negotiable* in that title to them is transferred by delivery.

However, they are not fully negotiable because a holder cannot enforce the rights represented by them in his own name (*see* 11:1).

10. Inscribed securities.

(*a*) *Introduction.* These are now rare and consequently seldom encountered by bankers but a few are still issued by Commonwealth governments. (In 1943 all inscribed British Government Stock was converted into registered stock and in 1949 local authority inscribed stock was similarly converted.)

(*b*) *Title.* Title to inscribed securities is evidenced only by entries in the books of the issuing organisations. A stock receipt may be issued to the registered owner, but this is not a document of title and has no value.

(*c*) *Transfer of title*. To effect a transfer of title, the owner or his attorney must normally attend at the office where the register is maintained but inscribed stocks registered at the Bank of England, e.g. those issued by Commonwealth governments, may be transferred by the use of a common form of transfer.

Stocks and shares as security

11. Registered stocks and shares.

(*a*) *Introduction*. These are the usual types of stocks and shares taken as security, stock exchange securities in particular.

Either a legal or an equitable mortgage can be taken. In both cases a memorandum of deposit setting out the terms of the mortgage will accompany the deposit of the certificate because it serves to clarify the purpose of the deposit.

The memorandum taken for a legal mortgage may list the securities held, or it may be phrased in general terms. This would be done where the mortgagor frequently changes his shareholding and the bank is willing to substitute new shares for those originally taken.

NOTE: It is not strictly correct to call the document a "memorandum of deposit" when it accompanies a legal mortgage. This is because *legal title* is transferred to the bank (usually its nominee company) by a legal mortgage and therefore a banker does not rely on the deposit as his security. In addition, he can realise the securities without the need for any express written statement of his power to do so.

(*b*) *The contents of the memorandum*. A memorandum will usually contain the following clauses.

(*i*) An all moneys clause.

(*ii*) A clause making the advance repayable on demand.

(*iii*) A continuing security clause.

(*iv*) An exclusion of s. 103 of the Law of Property Act 1925.

(These clauses have been discussed fully in 7:**7**. You should now refer back to that section.)

(*v*) The mortgagor's undertaking to complete on demand any formalities necessary to perfect the bank's title to the securities. (This clause is only found where an equitable mortgage is taken.)

(*vi*) A specified margin of cover clause. By this clause, the customer undertakes to maintain the value of the shares deposited at a given level above that of the advance secured.

(*vii*) In the memorandum for an equitable mortgage, the mortgager's undertaking to deliver to the bank all bonus and rights issues received (*see* **17** below). (These would automatically be received by the bank when a legal mortgage has been taken.)

(*viii*) The mortgagor's agreement not to insist on redelivery of the actual shares mortgaged on repayment of the advance. (A banker can therefore redeliver shares of the same type and value. This avoids potential inconvenience.)

(*ix*) Where the account secured is that of a third party, the memorandum will:

(1) give details of the account secured;

(2) allow the bank to vary arrangements with the debtor without prejudicing its security; and

(3) allow the bank to put any money received under the mortgage into a suspense account.

(*x*) A re-pledge clause, enabling the bank to use the securities deposited to secure its own borrowing. (This clause is associated with the memoranda of *merchant banks*.)

NOTE: A memorandum signed by the joint holders of securities only covers the joint holding. Should securities held separately also be deposited, additional memoranda must be signed in order for the separate holdings to secure the joint liability. Similarly, a jointly signed memorandum does not cover separate liabilities.

If a limited company charges its shares as security, the memorandum must be authorised by resolution of the company, and a certified copy of this should be retained with the memorandum.

NOTE: A specific charge on stocks and shares by a limited company does not require registration with the Registrar of Companies: Companies Act 1985, s.396.

(*c*) *Legal mortgage*. A legal mortgage is effected by transferring legal title to the shares to the bank or, more usually, its nominee company (*see* **8** above).

The transfer of company shares will state a nominal consideration—usually 50 pence—and will thereby attract a fixed stamp duty of 50 pence instead of the normal duty of £1 per cent. The same applies to the retransfer of the securities when the mortgage is discharged. A transfer of government and local authority stocks is exempt from stamp duty.

Letters of allotment are occasionally taken as security provided they are in favour of the customer and fully paid.

When the form of renunciation is signed the allotment letter effectively becomes a bearer security and can be mortgaged by deposit with the usual memorandum of deposit. A banker is then able to complete the acceptance form and obtain a legal mortgage of the shares by having them registered in the name of its nominee company.

Alternatively, if repayment is not made, he is able to sell the shares by delivering the letter of allotment with renunciation in blank to the purchaser, who is then able to complete the form of acceptance himself and thereby acquire legal title to the shares.

NOTE: Most banks will prefer to take an equitable mortgage and a blank transfer (*see* below) rather than a legal mortgage. This avoids the administrative cost which would follow from being registered as the holder of the shares and therefore receiving all communications from the company to its shareholders.

(*d*) *Equitable mortgage.* An equitable mortgage is created by a mere deposit of the share certificates. It is, however, standard practice to take a memorandum of deposit.

In addition, a banker will often take a *blank transfer*, i.e. a transfer incomplete in a material particular, in order to strengthen his position should the advance not be repaid. The blank transfer will usually bear only the mortgagor's signature as transferor and details of the securities concerned: the transferee will not be stated. It is also known as an *undated unstamped transfer*.

A blank transfer enables a bank to transfer legal ownership of the securities to its nominee company by inserting its name as transferee (thereby completing the document) and registering the transfer whenever it considers it necessary to do so. Alternatively, the transfer may be completed in favour of a purchaser if the bank exercises its power of sale under the mortgage.

A banker holding an equitable mortgage *without* a blank transfer would have to obtain a court order for the sale of the securities if his customer was uncooperative.

NOTE: Until completed and registered, a blank transfer is subject to prior equitable interests. Once notice of any such interest is received, priority cannot be obtained by completing and registering the transfer, i.e. by acquiring legal title to the securities.

In the very few cases where transfer of title must be by deed (*see* **8** above), a blank transfer cannot be used. This is because a deed must be completed at the *time of its delivery*.

A deed completed subsequently will only transfer an equitable interest, and the transferee will take subject to prior equities, e.g. where the securities turn out to be trust property, those of the beneficiaries of that trust.

NOTE: Should such circumstances occur, the bank's interest would be good against the mortgagor's trustee in bankruptcy, who would probably be willing to repay the advance in order to obtain the securities and thereby augment the estate available for distribution.

An equitable mortgage is taken of letters of allotment by deposit accompanied by a memorandum. The form of renunciation need not be completed by the mortgagor because the shares can only be exchanged for the letter and a banker can therefore easily obtain possession of them.

A blank transfer may also be taken to strengthen the bank's position when the actual shares are obtained.

(*e*) *Protecting an equitable mortgage.* In practice, a banker will never accept an equitable mortgage of stocks and shares where he has any doubt at all about his customer's ability to repay the advance. He would insist on a legal mortgage in such circumstances. Thus, when an equitable mortgage is taken, it is unlikely to be protected.

Two methods of protection for an equitable mortgage of *company securities* do exist, however, although neither is completely effective.

(*i*) *Notice of lien.* This is given by letter informing the company of the interest and requesting acknowledgment of it. In the letter, a banker will enquire whether (1) prior equitable interests exist over the securities, and (2) whether the company's articles of association give it a first and paramount lien over them for any debts owed to it by the shareholders.

NOTE: A company whose fully paid-up shares are quoted on a

stock exchange cannot have such a lien. Thus it is restricted to those securities which are the least likely to be accepted as security by a banker, i.e. *unquoted* or *partly-paid* shares.

The company can ignore or acknowledge the notice, or state that by the Companies Act 1985, s.360 it cannot record a notice of a trust on its register.

Nevertheless, three advantages are gained by sending notice of a lien.

(1) On receipt, the company is prevented from exercising its own lien in priority to the bank's interest: *Bradford Banking Co. Ltd. v. Henry Braggs, Son & Co. Ltd.* (1866).

(2) Prior equitable interests will be discovered if the company keeps a record of them.

(3) If the company records equitable mortgages of its shares, protection is gained against the possibility of the mortgagor fraudulently obtaining duplicate certificates, and then selling them to the detriment of the bank's interest.

(*ii*) *Notice in lieu of distringas*. A legal process by which a banker applies to the High Court for a notice to be served on the company requiring it to give him eight clear days' notice of any proposed transfer of the shares. This period enables him to take steps through the court to protect his position.

The cost and technicality of the process mean that it is seldom used.

(*f*) *Realising the security*.

(*i*) *Legal mortgage*. The memorandum (or letter) of deposit gives the bank the right to sell the securities on default in repayment. The advance is usually repayable on demand.

(*ii*) *Equitable mortgage*. If a blank transfer was not taken with the security, either the mortgagor's consent and co-operation or a court order is required for the sale of the security.

The memorandum will, however, contain the mortgagor's undertaking to effect a legal mortgage when requested to do so by the bank.

If a blank transfer was taken, realisation is much easier. Merely depositing share certificates with a blank transfer confers an *implied* power of sale on the lender, the power being exercisable after reasonable notice to the borrower. If a memorandum of deposit was also taken, this will confer an *express* power of sale on the banker.

(g) *Discharging the mortgage.*

(*i*) *Legal mortgage.* Title to the shares must be re-transferred from the bank or its nominee company to its customer. Nominal stamp duty and the company's own registration fee are payable.

(*ii*) *Equitable mortgage.* The certificates are returned and the memorandum of deposit is cancelled. If a blank transfer was taken, this must be destroyed. Notice of lien, or notice in lieu of distringas, if lodged, must be discharged.

12. Inscribed securities. A legal mortgage of inscribed stock is effected by transferring the stock into the name of the bank or its nominee company. It is usual to take a memorandum of deposit to clarify the nature of the transfer.

An equitable mortgage is not possible because the stock receipt issued is not documentary evidence of title, and its deposit creates no equitable interest.

In the rare event of inscribed stock being offered as security and the banker not wishing to take a legal mortgage, he must:

(*a*) insist that the stock be first *registered* at the Bank of England, after which an equitable mortgage by deposit of the certificate issued and a memorandum of deposit is possible; or

(*b*) rely on the customer's integrity and take an *equitable charge* containing the customer's undertaking not to deal with the stock without the bank's consent.

In this latter situation, a power of attorney may also be taken. This enables the bank to sell the stock without reference to its customer.

NOTE: Relying on the customer's integrity and the equitable charge is a very poor security because there is nothing to prevent the customer subsequently transferring legal title to a third party; not even the stock certificate has to be produced.

13. Bearer securities.

(*a*) *Taking the security.* Bearer securities are charged by *pledge* (*see* 7:**3**) and not by mortgage.

Bearer securities are negotiable instruments and their deposit alone is sufficient to transfer legal title to them. However, a banker will usually take a memorandum of deposit because this sets out the bank's rights in the transaction.

Provided that the securities are taken in good faith and for value (this includes securing an *existing* debt: Bills of Exchange Act 1882, s.27: *see* 11:**21**), and without notice of any defect in the customer's title, a perfect legal title is obtained.

The doctrine of constructive notice does not apply to negotiable instruments. This means that a banker is under no duty to enquire into the pledgor's title unless he is aware of suspicious circumstances which merit investigation.

EXAMPLE: In *London Joint Stock Bank* v. *Simmons* (1892), a stockbroker pledged bearer securities belonging to Simmons, a client, to secure his own overdraft. Simmons sued the bank for their return. He argued that, knowing the business of its customer, the bank should have enquired into their ownership before accepting the pledge. HELD: the bank had a perfect title to them. On the facts there were no suspicious circumstances involved in the transaction and the bank was therefore under no duty to make inquiries.

(*b*) *American and Canadian style certificates*. Since these are only *quasi-negotiable* (*see* **9** above), a deposit as security is an equitable mortgage and not a pledge.

A legal mortgage is effected by transferring the certificates into the name of the bank's nominee company—normally it would be a *good marking name*.

(*c*) *Discharging the security*. This is achieved by cancelling the memorandum of deposit.

14. National savings securities. These are *not transferrable*, and therefore only an equitable mortgage of them is possible.

Thus, a banker is largely dependent on the honesty of his customer because it is possible to obtain duplicates of the securities deposited and obtain repayment.

Equitable mortgages are obtained over:

(*a*) *British Savings Bonds* by the deposit of the bond book accompanied by a memorandum of deposit (an *encashment note* should also be signed by the customer);

(*b*) *Premium Savings Bonds* by their deposit with a memorandum of deposit and a *repayment form* signed by the holder;

(*c*) *National Savings Certificates* by the deposit of the certificates with a memorandum of deposit and a *repayment form* signed in blank by the holder.

15. Unit trusts. Only an *equitable mortgage* of unit trust certificates is possible because the holder has only an equitable interest himself.

The mortgage can be created in two ways:

(*a*) *by transferring the units* into the name of the bank's nominee company and taking a memorandum of deposit; or

(*b*) *by depositing the certificates* with a memorandum of deposit.

The form of renunciation on the back of the certificate should be signed by the mortgagor because this will enable the bank to send the certificates to the managers of the trust and obtain repayment.

Notice of the charge should be sent to the managers who will acknowledge and record it.

16. Building society shares.

(*a*) *Legal mortgage.* Providing the rules of the building society allow the transfer of its shares, a legal mortgage is obtained by transferring the shares to the bank or to its nominee company on the society's special form. A memorandum of deposit will also be taken.

(*b*) *Equitable mortgage.* This is effected by depositing the pass-book or share certificate and taking a memorandum of deposit. A repayment form, completed in the banks's favour save for the date, may also be taken.

Notice of the deposit should be sent to the society, enquiring (*i*) if it claims a *lien* on the account for money owed to it by the share-holder, (*ii*) whether it has received *notice of withdrawal*, and (*iii*) whether it has received *notice of any prior claim* on the account.

17. Advantages and disadvantages as security.

(*a*) *Legal or equitable mortgage?* A *legal mortgage* has the following important advantages.

(*i*) It ranks before prior equitable interests, provided it was taken in good faith.

(*ii*) All dividends will be paid directly to the bank.

(*iii*) All rights and bonus issues will be made directly to the bank (the importance of this is explained below).

NOTE: A *rights issue* is the sale of shares to existing shareholders at less than their market price. A *bonus issue* is the issue of shares fully paid-up to existing shareholders, i.e. no payment is made for them.

(*iv*) Should the customer not make repayment, the bank has the right to sell the shares and transfer legal title to them to the purchaser.

A legal mortgage has the following disadvantages. These are not nearly so significant, however, and should be avoidable by good banking practice.

(*i*) The customer may be unwilling to pay the registration fees involved.

(*ii*) The customer may be reluctant to let the company know he is mortgaging his shares. This would most likely arise on the mortgage of shares in a private company.

(*iii*) Where the shares qualify the customer for a directorship, re-registration in the name of the bank's nominee company would disqualify him.

(*iv*) Extra administration in so far as the bank's nominee company as registered owner of the shares receives all communications from the company. These must be passed to the customer.

(*v*) The payment of calls on mortgaged partly-paid-up shares. The customer may not be able to reimburse the bank.

(*vi*) Possible forgery of the share certificate or the transfer form. (This latter problem can be avoided by insisting that the transfer be signed at the bank.)

A bank is liable to a company for any loss resulting from the registration of a forged transfer presented by the bank: *Sheffield Corporation* v. *Barclay* (1905).

The main advantage of an *equitable mortgage* is the ease and cheapness with which it can be taken; the mere deposit of a share certificate gives an equitable interest.

In the case of partly paid-up shares, an equitable mortgage would usually be preferred to a legal mortgage since the customer remains liable to pay calls and not the bank.

A private company's articles of association may restrict the transfer of its shares, and thereby enable only an equitable mortgage of them to be made.

Equitable mortgages have significant disadvantages.

(*i*) The mortgage will be postponed to any prior equitable interest in the securities, whether or not the bank had notice of it when taking the mortgage. There is no method of protection against this risk.

For example, the shares may have been held by the mortgagor as trustee, in which case the equitable interest of the beneficiaries would rank before that of the bank. (Shares held in joint names indicate a possible trust.)

NOTE: Completing and registering a previously taken blank transfer does not give a banker priority over equitable interests once he has knowledge of them (*see* generally **11** above).

(*ii*) The bank's interest would be similarly postponed if the company has a *lien* on the shares for money owed to it by its shareholder. (This is very unlikely to be encountered in practice.)

(*iii*) There is a possible loss of title, either (1) through forfeiture following non-payment of calls on partly paid-up shares, or (2) through the mortgagor fraudulently obtaining a duplicate certificate and selling it. A *bona fide* purchaser obtains a good legal title on registration.

NOTE: Such fraud is easiest in relation to National Savings Securities for the National Savings Stock Register will not record or acknowledge any notice of deposit or lien from a bank or other mortgagee.

(*iv*) There is no completely satisfactory method of protecting an equitable mortgage of stocks and shares.

(*v*) Notices from a company will be sent, dividends will be paid and rights and bonus issues will be made *to the mortgagor* (possibly without the bank's knowledge) and not to the bank.

NOTE: (1) A *bonus issue* made to the mortgagor may seriously devalue the securities held. A "one-for-one" bonus issue, for example, will usually halve the value of the shares held because each shareholder has his holding doubled. It follows that the security held by the bank will also be halved in value, while the mortgagor could sell the shares he received instead of depositing them to maintain the value of the security. (2) A *rights issue* will also reduce the value of each individual share and hence its value as security. A shareholder could similarly sell the rights issue.

Alternatively he could lose his rights, and thereby prejudice the bank, by failing to take up the issue in the prescribed time. In addition, a rights issue is often made payable by instalments. After payment of the first instalment, the shares become partly paid securities and can be forfeited by failure to pay the outstanding balance.

(*vi*) There may be difficulty in realising the security if the mortgagor refuses to co-operate and a blank transfer form is not held.

(*b*) *Advantages.*

(*i*) The customer's title to the securities can easily be established.

(*ii*) The current value of quoted stocks and shares can be ascertained easily and fairly precisely.

(*iii*) The security can be taken with little difficulty, formality or expense. (Compare charges over land.)

(*iv*) A legal mortgage can easily and effectively be protected by registering the mortgagee as holder of the shares in the books of the company or other organisation.

(*v*) Long-term stability in value, despite periodical setbacks. A mixed portfolio of shares as security enhances this advantage.

(*vi*) The security can be easily realised by selling on a stock exchange if a legal mortgage is held, or a blank transfer with an equitable mortgage.

(*vii*) Release of the security is simple.

(*viii*) *Bearer securities* have additional advantages:

(1) as negotiable instruments, title to them passes by mere delivery and a pledgee acquires a perfect title despite any defect in or even the non-existence of the pledgor's title;

(2) neither a pledge nor a transfer by sale incurs stamp duty;

(3) the pledge requires no formalities;

(4) the pledgee can always sell the shares without reference to the pledgor or to the court.

(*c*) *Disadvantages.* Certain disadvantages attach to certain types of stocks and shares and there is one general disadvantage.

(*i*) *Fluctuation in market value.* At best a forced sale in a depressed market would disadvantage the bank's customer, and at worst it could realise insufficient to repay the advance.

NOTE: National Savings and building society securities do not fluctuate in value, and the problem can be largely avoided with commercial securities by insisting on a suitable margin of cover and periodically revaluing the securities held.

(*ii*) *Partly paid-up shares*. These may be forfeited for non-payment of calls. If held as security, the bank may have to pay the call for its customer in order to retain its security. A legal mortgage renders the bank directly liable to pay. Such shares are, in addition, less marketable than fully paid-up shares.

NOTE: Partly paid-up shares are uncommon and very unlikely to be encountered as a security.

(*iii*) *Unquoted shares*. These are normally associated with private companies, but unquoted shares in public companies may sometimes be offered as security. They are difficult both to value and to realise. The shares may first have to be offered to existing company members who can to some extent, therefore, fix the selling price. Thus, the true value of the shares may not be realised and a mortgage of such shares is often considered as little more than evidence of a customer's means.

(*iv*) *Shares in private companies*. In addition to being difficult to value—they are unquoted—the company's articles of association will often affect their value as security. The articles may prevent their use as security altogether, prevent another registered company (i.e. the bank's nominee company) holding the shares—only an equitable mortgage is possible in such a case—and/or restrict their transfer, thereby affecting their realisability.

Progress test 9

1. Distinguish between registered, bearer, and inscribed securities. (**8–10**)

2. How is title to registered securities transferred? (**8**)

3. Give an example of a transfer of registered securities in which the simplified stock transfer form introduced by the Stock Transfer Act 1963 cannot be used. (**8**)

4. What initial rate of stamp duty do bearer securities attract? (**9**)

5. How is title to bearer securities transferred? Why? (**9**)

6. What are scrip certificates and letters of allotment? (**9**)

7. How do American and Canadian share certificates differ from other bearer securities?   (**9**)

8. How is title to inscribed securities transferred?   (**10**)

9. List the clauses usually found in a banker's memorandum of deposit for registered securities.   (**11**)

10. How is (*a*) a legal mortgage, and (*b*) an equitable mortgage of registered securities effected?   (**11**)

11. What is a blank transfer? Why is one often taken with an equitable mortgage of registered securities?   (**11**)

12. Why cannot a blank transfer be used when title to the securities must be transferred by deed?   (**11**)

13. What advantages are gained by an equitable mortgagee of company securities who gives notice of lien to the company?   (**11**)

14. How is a mortgage of registered securities discharged?   (**11**)

15. Explain why it is impossible to take an equitable mortgage of inscribed securities.   (**12**)

16. Explain the doctrine of constructive notice as it applies to a pledge of bearer securities.   (**13**)

17. Explain what kind of mortgage is possible of (*a*) National Savings Securities, (*b*) unit trusts, and (*c*) building society shares. (**14–16**)

18. State (*a*) the advantages of a legal mortgage, and (*b*) the disadvantages of an equitable mortgage of stocks and shares.   (**17**)

19. Explain fully why a rights or bonus issue on shares deposited with a banker under an equitable mortgage can seriously prejudice his position.   (**17**)

20. State (*a*) the advantages, and (*b*) the disadvantages of a mortgage of stocks and shares as security.   (**17**)

10
Guarantees

The general law

1. Definition. A guarantee is a promise to answer "for the debt, default or miscarriage of another" if that person fails to meet his obligation: Statute of Frauds 1677, s.4.

2. Main features of a guarantee. There are five main features of a guarantee.

(*a*) *Three parties* are involved: the creditor, the principal debtor and the guarantor (or surety) and *two separate contracts*.

(*b*) *A valid debt must exist* between the creditor and the principal debtor.

(*c*) Primary liability for the debt is incurred by the principal debtor, the *guarantor incurs only secondary liability*, i.e. he becomes liable only if the principal debtor fails to pay.

(*d*) the guarantor has *no direct interest* in the contract entered into by the creditor and the principal debtor.

(*e*) A guarantee must be *evidenced by a written note or memorandum* signed by the guarantor or his agent: Statute of Frauds 1677, s.4. Without such written evidence, a guarantee is unenforceable.

3. Consideration. In common with all other simple contracts, a contract of guarantee must be supported by consideration. The written note or memorandum, however, need not record the consideration given.

Bank guarantee forms always include a statement of the consideration.

NOTE: An existing overdraft is no consideration for a guarantee (i.e. past consideration is no consideration). However, a further advance, an extension of the repayment period, or a forbearance to enforce repayment already demanded would all be sufficient consideration.

4. Guarantees and indemnities. Under a guarantee, the guarantor incurs only secondary liability. Under an *indemnity* the indemnifier incurs *primary liability*.

EXAMPLE: If, when Mr Smith asks his banker for a loan, Mr Brown says, "Lend him the money he wants. If he doesn't pay you back, I will", Mr Brown is offering to guarantee the loan and would incur only *secondary* liability. If, however, Mr Brown says, "Lend him the money; I will see that you are repaid", he has offered to indemnify the bank and would incur *primary* liability.

The distinction is of practical importance in so far as an indemnity does not need to be evidenced in writing.

5. Legal capacity.

(*a*) *Principal debtor*. The principal debtor must be legally capable of incurring the debt or other obligation guaranteed. A legal nullity cannot be guaranteed.

Hence, unless the guarantee contains a specific and adequate provision to the contrary, i.e. an *ultra vires* clause: *see* **9** below, no action can be taken against either the principal debtor or the guarantor if the debt is void.

EXAMPLE: In *Coutts & Co.* v. *Browne-Lecky* (1947), the bank lent money to a minor on the security of a guarantee. The contract included a clause covering *ultra vires* borrowing by companies and other organisations. HELD: the guarantee was void because the loan to the minor was void under the Infants Relief Act 1874, and the *ultra vires* clause on which the bank relied did not cover loans to minors.

(*b*) *Guarantor*. The guarantor must have the legal capacity to enter into the guarantee, e.g. neither a minor nor a mentally disordered person can give a valid guarantee.

Special rules cover the following cases.

(*i*) *Co-guarantors*. A bank guarantee form will impose *joint and several liability* on two or more co-guarantors.

Joint liability enables the bank to claim against any one, or any combination of the co-guarantors, usually the one(s) in the best financial position, since each is liable for the full amount. It is then up to the guarantor(s) from whom the bank obtained payment to seek the appropriate contribution from the other(s). Should the bank not be repaid in full, it can still claim against the other(s) for the balance: Civil Liability (Contribution) Act 1978.

Several liability ensures that on the death or bankruptcy of a co-guarantor his estate remains liable on the guarantee. If liability was only joint, only the other co-guarantors would be liable for existing and future debts.

A joint guarantee must be signed by *all* the co-guarantors.

EXAMPLE: In *National Provincial Bank* v. *Brackenbury* (1906), three out of four guarantors signed the guarantee and the bank advanced money in anticipation of the remaining signature. The fourth guarantor died without signing. In an action to enforce the guarantee, the failure to obtain the fourth guarantor's signature was held to be sufficient to discharge the other three guarantors.

NOTE: A joint guarantor is not liable on a guarantee if the signature of another joint guarantor is forged: *James Graham & Co. (Timber) Ltd.* v. *Southgate-Sands* (1985).

Should one co-guarantor repay the whole debt, he has a right to compensation from his co-guarantors in proportion to their respective liabilities under the guarantee.

(*ii*) *Partners*. A partner has no implied authority to give a guarantee in the firm name unless giving guarantees is part of the firm's usual course of business (*see* 3:6). A banker should therefore ensure that any guarantee given by a partnership is signed by all the partners in the firm.

(*iii*) *Companies*. A registered company can only give a guarantee if power to do so is given in its memorandum of association. This is, in fact, usually the case.

A guarantee by a company must be accompanied by a certified copy of the board's resolution authorising it. Banks provide draft resolutions for this purpose.

NOTE: Where one or more directors has a personal interest in the giving of the guarantee, e.g. an inter-company guarantee, the resolution must be passed by a quorum of independent directors or by a general meeting of the company if this is not possible, unless the company's articles of association allow the interested directors to vote: *Victors Ltd.* v. *Lingard* (1927) (*see* 4:**13**).

Various statutory restrictions are imposed on a company's powers to give a guarantee. For example, the Companies Act 1985, s.151, prohibits, with exceptions, a company from giving a guarantee which enables a person to purchase or subscribe for its own shares or those of its holding company; and the Companies Act 1985, s.330, prohibits, with exceptions, a company guaranteeing a loan by a third person to one of its directors or a director of its holding company. Under Article 79 of Table A of the Companies Act 1948, the amount of any guarantee given by a company is included in calculating the limit of a director's borrowing powers (*see* 4:**26**).

6. Reality of consent.

(*a*) *Misrepresentation.* A misrepresentation of fact by the creditor which misleads the guarantor will entitle the guarantor to avoid his liability under the guarantee.

(*b*) *Undue influence.* If one of the parties to a contract was unable to exercise a free and independent judgment when he entered into the agreement, he may subsequently be able to avoid the contract on the grounds of undue influence.

In certain *confidential* or *fiduciary relationships* undue influence is presumed to exist, e.g. solicitor and client, trustee and beneficiary, parent and child; in all other relationships it must be proved by the party alleging its existence.

A banker should insist that a prospective guarantor receives independent legal advice before signing the guarantee form whenever the principal debtor may be in a position to influence his judgment. Proof of undue influence would render the guarantee voidable.

A *free will* clause is, therefore, often included in the guarantee form to the effect that the guarantor understands the nature of the document and the liability incurred under it. Such a clause should be witnessed by the guarantor's own solicitor who should sign the accompanying *attestation clause*. This states that he has explained to the guarantor the nature of the guarantee and the obligations incurred under it.

NOTE: In *O'Hara* v. *Allied Irish Banks and Another* (1984), it was held that a banker owes no duty to explain the terms and legal effects of a guarantee to a prospective guarantor who is *not a customer*.

No presumption of undue influence arises between husband and wife, although experience has shown that most problems concerning undue influence and guarantees occur when wives guarantee the accounts of their husbands.

NOTE: Since the passing of the Sex Discrimination Act 1975, any special treatment of a woman guarantor, e.g. including a free will clause in her guarantee, must be based upon inability to understand or appreciate the arrangement, and not upon the grounds of sex.

The bank itself may sometimes be in a position to exert considerable influence on a prospective guarantor who is also its customer: *Lloyds Bank* v. *Bundy* (1975) (*see* 1:5).

NOTE: In a decision welcome to bankers, the House of Lords held in *National Westminster Bank plc* v. *Morgan* (1985), that the principle of undue influence is based on the prevention of victimisation of one party by another. A presumption of undue influence will not arise *merely* because a confidential relationship exists between the parties; the transaction involved must be wrongful in that advantage was taken of the person subjected to the influence through the other party exercising undue influence to secure his agreement. Thus, while a banker must always be aware of his potential influence over a customer, the need for special care, e.g. insisting that the customer receives independent advice, only arises where a confidential relationship has probably arisen and where the transaction proposed is clearly to the bank's advantage and to the customer's disadvantage. The House stressed, however, that the jurisdiction to grant relief for undue influence is not precisely defined. Thus, it is better to err on the side of caution in such situations.

(*c*) *Mistake as to the nature of the document signed.* As a consequence of the decision in *Saunders* v. *Anglia Building Society* (1970), it is highly unlikely that a guarantor will ever be able to avoid his liability by a plea of *non est factum*, i.e. that he signed the guarantee in the mistaken belief that it was an entirely different type of document.

Such a plea will never succeed where he was negligent, e.g. where he signed the guarantee without reading it.

In practice this possible complication can easily be avoided by ensuring that the guarantee is signed and witnessed at the bank or attested by a solicitor. In addition, this simple precaution would subsequently prevent the guarantor from successfully pleading that his signature had been forged.

7. Disclosure of information. A guarantee is not a contract *uberrimae fidei* (of the utmost good faith). A bank is, therefore, under no duty to disclose to the guarantor all the facts known to him which may be relevant. A guarantor must obtain or ask for all the information he requires.

EXAMPLE: In *Cooper* v. *National Provincial Bank* (1945), the bank was held to be under no obligation to disclose to the guarantor of a wife's account that (1) her husband was an undischarged bankrupt, (2) that he had authority to draw on her account, and (3) that the account had previously been operated in an improper and irregular fashion.

The common law does, however, favour a guarantor. In *Royal Bank of Scotland* v. *Greenshields* (1914), it was held that in order to prevent a guarantor from being misled, and therefore from being able to avoid the contract:

(*a*) any information volunteered by the creditor to him must be complete and true;

(*b*) an entire misapprehension of the facts of the case on his part must be corrected by the creditor.

NOTE: To avoid breaching its duty of secrecy in this context, a bank should either obtain its customer's authority to disclose information or arrange a meeting with its customer and the prospective guarantor.

A guarantor is not entitled to inspect the debtor's account but he is entitled to know the extent of his liability. A guarantor of a regulated agreement (up to £15,000) under the Consumer Credit Act 1974 is always entitled to know the actual amount outstanding, even if it exceeds the guarantee. In other cases the debit balance should only be disclosed where it does not. Where it does, the guarantor should just be told that the guarantee is being fully relied upon.

A banker is not under a legal duty to advise a guarantor of any material change in the circumstances of the principal debtor.

EXAMPLE: In *National Provincial Bank* v. *Glanusk* (1913), a guarantor was unsuccessful in seeking to avoid liability on the grounds that the bank had not informed him when it knew that the overdraft guaranteed was being used for a purpose which he had not approved.

Should such a situation arise, a meeting with the customer and guarantor can again be arranged. If need be, pressure can be exerted on the customer by a threat to demand repayment if his co-operation is not forthcoming.

Bank guarantees

8. Introduction. Bank guarantees do four main things:

(*a*) precisely state the liability of the guarantor;

(*b*) prevent the operation of the Rule in *Clayton's Case* (1816) to the bank's detriment;

(*c*) specify the circumstances under which the guarantee can be determined;

(*d*) exclude all the guarantor's important common law rights and remedies against both the principal debtor and the bank. These extensive exclusions are necessary because the common law favours the guarantor.

The last of these four characteristics is the most important, the guarantor being left with only the following rights.

(*a*) To make repayment at any time after the principal debt is due and then to sue the principal debtor in the banker's name. (This is a rarely exercised right.)

(*b*) To require the banker to call upon the principal debtor to pay the debt at any time after it has become due.

(*c*) To know the extent to which his guarantee is being relied upon.

(*d*) To raise against the banker any defence, right of set-off or counterclaim available to the principal debtor.

(*e*) To sue the principal debtor in the place of the banker as soon as he (the guarantor) has paid off the debt. Technically, the guarantor is *subrogated* to all the banker's rights, including, for example, possible status as a preferential creditor.

(*f*) To any security held by the banker from the principal debtor, after he (the guarantor) has paid off the debt.

(*g*) To avoid the contract for misrepresentation.

9. Usual clauses in a bank guarantee form.

(*a*) The *whole* of the customer's indebtedness is guaranteed, but with a limit on the guarantor's liability.

EXAMPLE: If an advance of £20,000 is to be guaranteed, the guarantor will guarantee all liabilities of the customer with a *limit* of £20,000 on his actual liability. The guarantee will not be drawn specifically to cover the £20,000 advanced.

There are two reasons for drafting the guarantee in this way.

(*i*) Where the guarantee covers only part of the customer's debt, payment of that part entitles the guarantor to a proportionate share of any securities held by the creditor. A guarantor of the customer's total indebtedness cannot claim a part of any security held by the bank unless he meets all of the customer's indebtedness.

(*ii*) If the customer is made bankrupt, a guarantee covering his whole indebtedness prevents the guarantor proving against the customer's estate in competition with the bank: *Re Sass* (1896).

NOTE: Most bank guarantees expressly exclude the guarantor from entering a proof in competition with the bank.

The bank is able to put a guarantor's payment in discharge of his liability into a suspense account and enter a proof against its customer's estate for the entire amount owing. This means that the bank is able to recover more, perhaps all, of the debt, although the guarantor loses his right of proof.

EXAMPLE: Continuing the previous example, if the customer is made bankrupt owing £40,000 to the bank and a dividend of 50p in the £ is paid, a bank proving for the whole debt of £40,000 would receive £20,000. Adding this to the £20,000 held in a suspense account paid under the guarantee would mean that the bank would be repaid in full while the guarantor would lose the

£20,000 paid by him. Conversely, if the guarantor had guaranteed £20,000 and not the whole debt, his payment of £20,000 would have to be credited to the customer's account and both the bank and the guarantor would prove against the customer's estate for £20,000. Again assuming a dividend of 50p in the £, each would lose £10,000 on the transaction.

It is usual for the guarantor to bind his personal representatives for the whole debt. The guarantee then automatically remains in force should the guarantor die and it removes the necessity to break the customer's account to prevent the Rule in *Clayton's Case* (1816) acting to the bank's detriment.

(*b*) The guarantee is expressed to be a *continuing security* covering any amount owing on the debtor's account at any time, subject to the specified limit on the guarantor's actual liability.

This provision again excludes the Rule in *Clayton's Case* (1816). If not excluded, every payment into the customer's account would reduce the guarantor's liability and every payment out would be a fresh advance which would not be covered by the guarantee.

(*c*) The guarantor's liability arises on a *written demand for repayment* being made. By virtue of this provision, the six year limitation period under the Limitation Act 1980 does not commence running until a proper demand has been made.

(*d*) The guarantee is expressed to be *additional* to any other guarantee of the customer's indebtedness given by the guarantor to the bank. This prevents a contention that a subsequent additional guarantee was given in substitution for the original guarantee.

(*e*) The *consideration* is always expressed in such terms as "opening or continuing an account with (the principal) or giving accommodation or granting time to (the principal)". It is never stated to be the advance of a specific sum because this precise sum would have to be advanced in order for the guarantee to be valid.

(*f*) *Co-guarantors* undertake joint and several liability (*see* 5(*b*) above).

It is also provided that the bank can release any one of the co-guarantors without affecting its rights against the other(s).

(*g*) The guarantee will remain in force despite any change in the constitution of the parties, e.g. a change in the membership of a partnership, a reconstruction of a company or even the lending bank's merger with or take-over by another bank.

(*h*) The bank is given complete freedom to vary arrangements with the principal debtor. For example, (*i*) securities deposited by him may be released, (*ii*) he may be granted time to pay, and (*iii*) a voluntary composition outside the bankruptcy rules may be made with him.

At common law without such express provisions the guarantor would be released from his obligations by any material variation of the arrangement.

(*i*) The guarantor is required to give a specified period of notice, usually three months, before he can determine his guarantee. This allows the bank to make arrangements with its customer and the guarantor for repayment or the provision of alternative security.

(*j*) The guarantor agrees to accept the bank's statement of its customer's account as conclusive evidence of the amount owing by him to the bank. This clause is necessary to avoid possible problems in producing the necessary evidence to obtain judgment against the guarantor.

(*k*) It is usual to provide that the Rule in *Clayton's Case* (1816) will not apply in the event of the guarantee being determined. Such a provision makes it unnecessary to break the customer's account, and the guarantor remains liable for the balance at the time the guarantee was determined despite any subsequent payments into or out of the account.

NOTE: It is, however, usual to break the customer's account on the determination of the guarantee.

(*l*) On determination of the guarantee the bank is given the right to open a new account with its customer. Any credit balance or transaction on this account does not reduce the liability of the guarantor.

(*m*) The guarantor undertakes not to sue the debtor until the bank has been paid in full, nor to take security from him. Should such security be taken, the guarantor is deemed to hold this as trustee for the bank.

(*n*) The bank is given the right to keep the guarantee form uncancelled for a period of at least six months after all the moneys that it secures have been repaid. Such a clause is included in case the customer's repayment is held to be a fraudulent preference (*see* 5:**14**) and the bank has to refund the money to its customer's trustee in bankruptcy.

(o) The guarantor undertakes not to withdraw any cash deposit he made in support of his guarantee while he is still liable on it. On determination of the guarantee, immediate recourse can be made against the deposit without reference to the guarantor.

(p) The bank is able to place in a suspense account any sums paid by the guarantor in support of his guarantee or in reduction of his liability.

(q) An *ultra vires* clause will be included whenever there is doubt about the enforceability of the guarantee, e.g. when the customer is a minor. Under such a clause, the guarantor undertakes to accept primary liability as principal debtor for any sums which cannot be recovered from the customer by reason of any legal limitation, disability or incapacity. The contract thereby becomes one of indemnity as well as a guarantee.

(r) A free will clause will be included where there is a possibility that the guarantor may seek to avoid his liability on the grounds of undue influence (*see* **6** above).

An attestation clause, witnessing the guarantor's signature, may also be added.

NOTE: A guarantee taken to secure a regulated agreement under the Consumer Credit Act 1974 must conform to the statutory requirements in content and form.

10. Determination of a bank guarantee.

(a) *Introduction.* Bank guarantees are usually determined by agreement in accordance with the terms of the guarantee, the customer or the guarantor repaying the money owed to the bank.

(b) *Notice by the guarantor.* This must be given in accordance with the terms of the guarantee. After it has been given, he may discharge his liability by paying the amount due under the guarantee.

NOTE: A bank is probably entitled to make further advances to its customer during this period of notice. However, in order not to unfairly prejudice either the guarantor, by allowing its customer to take advantage of the situation, or its customer, who may have entered into obligations relying on the guarantee, a meeting with the guarantor and its customer to discuss the situation is often arranged. If its customer proves uncooperative, the bank can fix the guarantor's liability by demanding immediate repayment from its customer.

It is usual to break the customer's account when the guarantor gives notice of determination, although the Rule in *Clayton's Case* (1816) is usually excluded by the guarantee form.

Where one (or some) of a number of co-guarantors gives notice of determination or withdrawal, the remaining co-guarantors should sign a fresh guarantee, even though a bank guarantee allows the bank to release a co-guarantor without affecting the liability of the other(s).

Any payment made by the guarantor under the guarantee should be placed in a suspense account. This is possible under the usual terms of a bank guarantee. The same procedure should be adopted with part payment by co-guarantors.

(*c*) *Notice by the bank*. A bank's guarantee form gives it the right to make an immediate demand for repayment from the guarantor. This determines the guarantee.

While the terms of the guarantee usually make this unnecessary, the normal practice is to break the customer's account.

It is up to the guarantor and not to the bank to ensure that the principal debtor makes repayment. Hence, a banker need not first seek repayment from its customer before seeking repayment from the guarantor.

NOTE: In *Standard Chartered Bank* v. *Walker and Another* (1982), it was held (C.A.) that the duty owed by a mortgagee to the mortgagor to realise the best market price for a security, established in *Cuckmere Brick Co. Ltd.* v. *Mutual Finance Ltd.* (1971) (*see* 8:**14**), extends to a guarantor of the mortgagor's indebtedness.

(*d*) *Death*. The death of the principal debtor determines the guarantee and fixes the extent of the guarantor's liability.

Notice of the guarantor's death determines the guarantee unless he has bound his personal representatives to continue it. Such a provision is included in a bank guarantee form.

If no such provision is included, the customer's account must be broken to avoid the operation of the Rule in *Clayton's Case* (1816) to the bank's detriment. A new account must then be opened. This must be kept in credit, or suitable alternative security for any debit balance provided.

The personal representatives can themselves determine the guarantee in accordance with its terms.

NOTE: (1) The death of one co-surety does not end the continuing liability of the other(s) if they undertook joint and several liability. (This also applies to the mental disorder or bankruptcy of one co-surety.) (2) The commencement of the winding up of a company which is either the principal debtor or the guarantor will determine the guarantee.

(*e*) *Mental disorder.* Reliable notice of the mental disorder of the principal debtor or guarantor determines the guarantee. The customer's account should be broken.

(*f*) *Bankruptcy.* Notice of a bankruptcy petition or the making of a bankruptcy order against the guarantor determines the guarantee.

The customer's account must be stopped and a demand for repayment from him made. If he fails to repay the bank must pursue its claim against the guarantor in any voluntary arrangement or bankruptcy process which follows. Any part payment already made must be deducted from the bank's claim.

The guarantor's undertaking to guarantee the customer's whole indebtedness enables a bank to place into a suspense account any payments by him less than the total amount owed and prove for the whole debt in its customer's bankruptcy (*see* 10:**9**).

NOTE: (1) At common law a guarantee would also be determined in a number of other situations, e.g. a variation of the arrangements with the principal debtor, a change in the parties to the agreement, or a release of securities held from the principal debtor. Bank guarantee forms exclude the common law in these respects; only misrepresentation entitles the guarantor to set aside the contract at common law. (2) When a guarantor has paid off the whole debt, he is entitled to receive any securities deposited in support of the guarantee by the principal debtor or any third party.

11. Advantages and disadvantages as security.

(*a*) *Advantages.*

(*i*) A guarantee is a very simple security to take. No registration is involved and no complications concerning proof of title arise. (Compare mortgages.)

(*ii*) A guarantee can easily and immediately be enforced by court action.

(*iii*) As with any other security given by a third party (*collateral* security), it can be ignored when claiming against the principal debtor.

(*iv*) Since several parties can guarantee a loan, it is useful security where the principal debtor is unable to provide security but offers a viable business loan proposition.

(*b*) *Disadvantages.*

(*i*) Unless supported by a cash deposit or other security, a guarantee is always of an uncertain value as a security; a guarantor's financial position can change very quickly. A banker should only accept an unsupported guarantee after careful investigation into the proposed guarantor's financial circumstances.

(*ii*) Court action may be necessary to realise the security, and a technicality may possibly defeat the bank's claim. (Compare the position of a legal mortgagee of land: *see* 7:**15**.) For example, special rules apply to guarantees taken from partnerships and companies, although a defeat of the bank's claim would almost certainly be the result of carelessness when taking the security.

(*iii*) Enforcing a guarantee may cause bad feeling, particularly if the guarantor is a valued customer. However, should this happen, it would probably be the result of poor banking practice and failure to explain to the guarantor the obligations involved.

(*iv*) Litigation may be necessary to enforce payment where the guarantee was not supported by other (realisable) security.

Progress test 10

1. Define a guarantee. (**1**)
2. List the main features of a guarantee. (**2**)
3. Distinguish between a guarantee and an indemnity. (**4**)
4. State the reasons why co-guarantors should always undertake joint and several liability on the guarantee. (**5**)
5. Why must every co-guarantor sign the memorandum? (**5**)
6. Give reasons why care must be taken when a prospective guarantor is a registered company. (**5**)
7. What is the purpose of the free will clause in a bank guarantee form? (**6**)
8. To what extent must a banker disclose to the guarantor information about the circumstances surrounding the guarantee? (**7**)

9. List the four main things done by a bank's guarantee form. (**8**)

10. Explain why the whole of the customer's undebtedness is guaranteed by the surety. (**9**)

11. What is the purpose of the guarantor binding his personal representatives to the guarantee? (**9**)

12. Explain the effect of the Rule in *Clayton's Case* (1816) in the context of a bank guarantee. (**9**)

13. What is the purpose of providing that the guarantor's liability arises on a written demand for repayment being made? (**9**)

14. Explain the purpose of a bank guarantee form giving the bank the right to retain the guarantee form uncancelled for a minimum period of six months. (**9**)

15. What is the effect of an *ultra vires* clause in a bank guarantee form? (**9**)

16. To what extent may a bank make further advances to its customer after the guarantor has given notice to determination? (**10**)

17. Explain the effect of (*a*) death, (*b*) mental disorder, and (*c*) bankruptcy of the principal debtor or guarantor on a guarantee. (**10**)

18. State the advantages and disadvantages of a guarantee as a security for a banker's advance. (**11**)

11
Bills of exchange

The Bills of Exchange Act 1882 which governs this subject is reproduced in Appendix I. You should refer to it whenever a section is mentioned in the text without being quoted. Also reproduced is the Cheques Act 1957. It is good practice to annotate the Acts for future use. In this way, you will become familiar with the arrangement, wording and "feel" of the statutes.

Introduction

1. Negotiable instruments. These are documents used in commerce to secure the payment of money.

Negotiable instruments are *choses in action*, i.e. property which has no physical existence. Consequently, they cannot be physically possessed or protected and the right to them can only be enforced by legal action.

(*a*) *Main types.* The main types today are: bills of exchange; cheques (a specific type of bill of exchange); promissory notes, e.g. banknotes; dividend warrants; bearer debentures; and Treasury Bills.

(*b*) *Development.* The law relating to negotiable instruments developed from the practices of merchants, and the distinctive legal characteristics possessed by them can all be explained by their commercial origins. For example, a merchant would be unlikely to accept a negotiated bill of exchange instead of cash in settlement for a debt if he knew that his right to obtain payment of it could always be prejudiced by some defect in title of a prior party to the bill of which he was ignorant.

As such, negotiable instruments and the concept of negotiability are an extension of the concept of assignment. *Assignment* is the transfer of a right or interest to another. By the Law of Property Act 1925, s. 136, a legal assignment must be: (*i*) in writing and signed by the assignor; (*ii*) absolute; and (*iii*) notice in writing must be given to the debtor.

In comparison with negotiability there are two serious drawbacks to legal assignments from a merchant's point of view. First, its *formality*: the written transfer must be correct in form and detail and there must be evidence that the debtor received notice of the transfer. Secondly, *uncertainty*: the assignee has no better rights than the assignor had. He takes "subject to equities"; the debtor can set up any set-off, counterclaim or defence against the assignee that was available to him against the assignor.

NOTE: One particular informal or equitable assignment of debts is common in business. This is where a trader *factors* his trade debts by selling the right to collect them to a specialist factoring company.

(*c*) *Legal characteristics.*

(*i*) Title is transferable by delivery or, in the case of instruments payable to order, by indorsement completed by delivery;

(*ii*) A person taking a transfer of the instrument in good faith and for value (i.e. a holder in due course: *see* **31** below) is unaffected by any defects in the title of the transferor—he takes the instrument "free from equities". Thus, the transferee *can acquire a better title* than that held by the transferor. For example, a person who acquired the instrument by fraud has only a voidable title to it, but a *bona fide* transferee for value from him acquires a perfect title. Such a transferee also takes free from any defence, counterclaim or set-off which could have been raised against the transferor by the person liable on the instrument.

(*iii*) The holder can sue in his own name.

(*iv*) The holder need not give notice to prior parties to establish his title.

2. The nature of a bill of exchange.

(*a*) *A legally binding promise.* A bill of exchange constitutes a legally binding written promise by the drawer that the person who took it in payment will be paid in cash when he presents the bill for payment at the proper time and place.

The promise takes the form of an order by one person addressed to another.

(*b*) *Three parties.* Initially there are three parties to the transaction:

    (*i*) the *drawer*—the person who makes the order;

    (*ii*) the *drawee*—the person to whom the order is addressed, and who becomes the *acceptor* when he incurs liability on the bill by signing (accepting) it;

    (*iii*) the *payee*—the person to whom the bill is made payable.

If the bill is transferred (*negotiated*), other persons become parties to the bill (*see* **42** below).

NOTE: The acceptor is the party primarily liable on the bill, the drawer and any other person who has signed (indorsed) it are sureties for his payment.

The drawer and payee are sometimes the *same* person. This is often the case in bills used in overseas trade.

EXAMPLE:

£5,000   Manchester
                                      30 March 1985

Pay to me or to my order on presentation the sum of £5,000 for value received

                                     B. Brown

To A. Smith

Fig. 1   *A bill of exchange in which the drawer and the payee are the same person.*

Continuing the example in Fig. 1, if B. Brown in turn owed £5,000 to J. Jones, a bill could be drawn involving all three persons and settling both debts.

EXAMPLE:

£5,000   Manchester
                                          30 March 1985

One month after date pay~~s~~ Jo~~n~~s the sum of £5.000 for
value received

Accepted A. Smith   B. Brown

To A. Smith

Fig. 2   *A bill of exchange to which there are three parties. Note that the drawee
has accepted the bill by signing it.*

NOTE: If in Fig. 2, the bill was drawn payable on demand and
addressed to B. Brown's bank, the document would be a *cheque*:
Bills of Exchange Act 1882, s.73.

3. Bills of exchange in commerce.

(*a*) *Introduction.* Apart from cheques, bills of exchange are
seldom used in commercial transactions in the UK outside the City
of London.

In *international trade* the importance and use of the "pure" bill of
exchange has been diminished by newer forms of international
payment, e.g. bankers' commercial credits and bank transfers.

(*b*) *Advantages.* When used, however, bills of exchange have two
important advantages.

(*i*) As a method of payment, they avoid the need to transfer
large sums of money, particularly from one country to another.

(*ii*) The conflicting demands of buyer and seller can be satisfied.

Drawing a bill payable at a future date gives the buyer a useful,
perhaps essential, period of credit in which he can sell the goods and
pay the bill out of the proceeds.

Should the seller require immediate cash, the same bill can be
discounted (sold) for a little less than its face value.

NOTE: The seller can, of course, retain the bill until it *matures* (becomes payable) or negotiate it to any one of his own creditors who is willing to take it in settlement.

(*c*) *Functions of a bill.* It can be seen from the above that the two main functions of a bill are:

(*i*) providing credit;

(*ii*) settling debts.

(*d*) *Confidence in a bill.* "Confidence" is all important to the commercial value and use of a bill of exchange—confidence in the right to enforce payment and confidence in the ability to pay of at least one of the parties liable on it.

The first aspect of this "confidence" is provided by the law, the second by ensuring that a person or organisation of unquestionable financial standing has accepted liability on it. In many cases this is done by making a merchant bank a party to the bill.

(*e*) *The Consumer Credit Act 1974.* This Act restricts the extent to which negotiable instruments can be used to make payment or to provide security in consumer credit or consumer hire agreements (regulated agreements under the Act): ss.123–5.

NOTE: *Credit* includes a cash loan and any kind of financial accommodation: s.9(1).

There are the following restrictions.

(*i*) No negotiable instrument, other than a bank note or a cheque, may be taken by a creditor or owner in discharge of moneys payable under a regulated agreement.

(*ii*) A cheque taken in payment must be negotiated to a banker.

(*iii*) No negotiable instrument of any kind may be taken as a security, i.e. payment is to be made by some other method and action on the instrument would only be taken if this was not forthcoming.

Should the restrictions be infringed:

(*i*) the agreement may only be enforced against the debtor by court order;

(*ii*) a person taking a negotiated instrument in contravention of the Act is not a holder in due course (*see* **31** below);

(*iii*) the negotiation of a cheque in contravention of the Act constitutes a defect in title under the Bills of Exchange Act 1882, s.29(2)

NOTE: A subsequent holder in due course of the instrument can enforce it against the debtor but the latter is entitled to be indemnified by the creditor or owner for his liability on the bill.

The statutory definition

4. The Bills of Exchange Act 1882, s.3(1). This defines a bill of exchange as ". . . an unconditional order in writing, addressed by one person to another, signed by the person giving it, requiring the person to whom it is addressed to pay on demand or at a fixed or determinable future time a sum certain in money to or to the order of a specified person, or to bearer."

5. ". . . an unconditional order . . ."

(a) *An order*. A bill must contain an *order* to pay, not a mere *request*.

(b) *Unconditional*. The order must be unconditional between drawer and drawee. A conditional order is *not enforceable*.

EXAMPLE: In *Bavins Junior & Sims* v. *London & S. W. Bank* (1900), an instrument contained an order to pay: ". . . provided the receipt form at the foot thereof is duly signed, stamped and dated." HELD: the instrument failed to meet the requirements of s.3(1).

An order to pay which is dependent upon the happening of a future uncertain event—a *contingency*—is conditional: Bills of Exchange Act 1882, s.11. The subsequent happening of the specified event does not make the bill valid.

The drawer can include instructions as to payment on the bill, however, provided that on their true construction the order to the drawee remains unconditional.

EXAMPLE: A *direction* to pay from a particular fund is conditional, but an *indication* as to which account should be debited is unconditional provided the order to pay is itself unqualified: Bills of Exchange Act 1882, s.3(3).

6. ". . . in writing . . ." A bill may be written in any language on any substance (except metal) capable of delivery. (Many bankers have their own stories of unusual cheques!)

7. ". . . addressed by one person to another . . ." If the drawer and drawee are the same person, the instrument is a *promissory note* and not a bill of exchange: Bills of Exchange Act 1882, s.83(1).

NOTE: The drawee must be named or otherwise identified in a bill with reasonable certainty. A bill may be addressed to two or more drawees jointly, but not in the alternative nor in succession: Bills of Exchange Act 1882, s.6.

8. ". . . signed by the person giving it . . ." The signature must be that of the drawer or his agent. It may be in a *trade name*.

A *corporation's seal* is equivalent to a signature: Bills of Exchange Act 1882, s.91(2).

A *facsimile signature*, e.g. by a rubber stamp, probably satisfies s.3(1), provided that there is oral evidence that it was applied by the drawer or his agent.

NOTE: A signature is required for liability to be incurred on a bill of exchange.

9. ". . . on demand, or at a fixed or determinable future time . . ." A bill is payable on demand when:

(*a*) it is expressed to be payable on demand, at sight or on presentation; or

(*b*) no time for payment is given: Bills of Exchange Act 1882, s.10(1); or

(*c*) it is overdue as against the acceptor and any indorsers: Bills of Exchange Act 1882, s.10(2).

(Figure 1 is of a bill payable on demand and Fig. 2 of a bill payable at a fixed future time.)

NOTE: A cheque is a bill payable on demand.

Many bills are expressed to be payable "X days *after sight*", i.e. sight by the drawee of the bill when it is presented for acceptance. In these cases it is unnecessary for the date to be determinable when they are drawn.

Other bills are payable on the happening of a *certain future event*. In these cases the date of payment is not determinable even when they are accepted.

It must be possible *at some stage*, however, to fix or determine the date of payment in order to (*a*) establish the liability of the parties;

(*b*) present the bill for payment; and (*c*) if necessary, give notice of dishonour; all in accordance with the 1882 Act.

Thus, s.11 of the Act is not satisfied if a document contains a provision for payment at a *fixed period after acceptance*. It must be payable at a fixed period after date or sight in so many words. (*Acceptance* and *sight* are not the same thing.) It must be possible to determine the bill's date of maturity in the event of non-acceptance as well as acceptance.

NOTE: A holder may date an undated bill with what he believes to be the correct date: Bills of Exchange Act 1882, s.12.

10. ". . . a sum certain in money . . ." A sum of money is still certain within the meaning of the Act although it is to be paid:

(*a*) with interest;

(*b*) by stated instalments;

(*c*) according to a specified rate of exchange or according to a rate of exchange to be ascertained as directed by the bill: Bills of Exchange Act 1882, s.9(1).

If there is a discrepancy between the amount of the bill as it appears in figures and as it is written in words, the words take priority: Bills of Exchange Act 1882, s.9(2).

11. ". . . to or to the order of a specified person, or to bearer . . ."

(*a*) *Payable to order*. A bill is payable to order if it is expressed to be payable to a particular person or to somebody indicated by him, i.e. "Pay X" or "Pay X or order".

The payee must be named or indicated with reasonable certainty by the bill. It may, however, be made payable to two or more payees jointly or in the alternative to one of two, or one or some of several payees: Bills of Exchange Act 1882, s.7(2).

(*b*) *Payable to bearer*. A bill is payable to bearer if it is:

(*i*) drawn payable to bearer;

(*ii*) indorsed in blank, i.e. the payee or a subsequent holder signs the bill without designating an indorsee: Bills of Exchange Act 1882, s.8(3);

(*iii*) drawn payable to a fictitious or non-existing payee: Bills of Exchange Act 1882, s.7(3) (*see* **23** below).

12. Documents failing to meet the requirements. Although invalid as bills of exchange, a document outside the 1882 Act, s.3(1), may not be invalid for all purposes. For example, a customer may often present his own "cheque" made out to "Cash" to his own bank. Since it is not addressed to another person, it is not a bill of exchange and therefore not a cheque. However, it is a valid order to his banker to pay him the sum specified.

Types of bills

13. Sight and time bills. A *sight* (or demand) bill orders the drawee to make payment to the payee as soon as the document is presented to him.

A *time* bill orders payment to be made after the lapse of a specified time, e.g. 30 days after sight.

14. Order and bearer bills. A *bearer bill* is negotiated merely by delivery, an *order bill* by the indorsement of the holder completed by delivery: Bills of Exchange Act 1882, s.31(2) and (3).

(*See also* **11** above.)

15. Inland and foreign bills. An *inland bill* is a bill which is or on the face of it purports to be:

(*a*) both drawn and payable within the British Islands; or

(*b*) drawn within the British Islands upon some person resident therein: Bills of Exchange Act 1882, s.4(1).

Any other bill is a *foreign bill*.

Where a foreign bill has been dishonoured by non-acceptance it must be *protested* (*see* **44** below) in order to preserve the right of recourse against the drawer or any indorser.

16. Accommodation bills. An accommodation bill is a bill which is accepted gratuitously, i.e. *no consideration* is given for the acceptance.

Such bills are used to enable the drawer to raise money or to obtain a period of credit. The drawer is frequently the payee.

NOTE: In practice, if not at law, the drawer is the principal debtor because the intention of the transaction is that he and not the acceptor will pay the bill at its maturity. The acceptor fulfils the role of surety, signing the bill to enhance its commercial acceptability.

A person signing a bill as drawer, acceptor or indorser without receiving value in return is an *accommodation party*. He is liable on the bill to a holder for value: Bills of Exchange Act 1882, s.28.

17. Bills in a set. In international trade, bills are still occasionally drawn in a set, i.e. several copies of the same bill are sent by different posts. Bills are drawn in this way because a single bill may be lost in the post.

NOTE: Bankers' commercial credits have now rendered bills drawn in a set virtually obsolete.

While the drawer signs each part, the acceptor and any subsequent indorser must sign one part only. Should they sign more than one part, they will be liable to a holder in due course (*see* **31** below) of each part signed.

Similarly, the acceptor must only pay on the delivery to him of the one part that he signed. Payment on delivery of the other parts does not discharge his liability to the holder in due course of the signed part: Bills of Exchange Act 1882, s.71.

18. Domiciled bills. A bill is domiciled with a bank when its customer is the drawee or acceptor of it and arranges for the bill to be paid by the bank.

NOTE: A banker has no statutory protection if he pays a domiciled bill on a forged indorsement. (Compare cheques: *see* 12:**13**.) An indemnity is therefore usually required from the customer against liability for wrongly paying the bill.

19. Cheques. A cheque is a bill of exchange drawn on a banker payable on demand: Bills of Exchange Act 1882, s.73.

Consideration

20. Introduction. A bill of exchange must be supported by consideration, i.e. value must be given in return for the promise to pay.

Any consideration sufficient to support a simple contract will support a bill of exchange: Bills of Exchange Act 1882, s.27(1).

21. Special features. There are three special features of consideration in relation to bills of exchange.

(*a*) Consideration is presumed to have been given for the bill unless the contrary is proved: Bills of Exchange Act 1882, s.30(1).

(*b*) An antecedent debt or liability, i.e. *past* consideration, will support a bill of exchange: Bills of Exchange Act 1882, s.27(1).

Thus, a bill of exchange drawn in settlement of an existing debt is enforceable.

NOTE: Many bills, particularly cheques, are issued in payment for goods or services already supplied.

(*c*) The holder can enforce the bill provided value for it was given at some time; he need not provide the value himself, i.e. consideration need not move from the promisee: Bills of Exchange Act 1882, s.27(2).

EXAMPLE: If A draws a cheque in favour of B for goods supplied to him, and B negotiates the bill to C as a gift, the right to payment is transferred to C and he can enforce it against A, even though he himself gave no value for the cheque. C cannot, however, enforce the cheque against B, because consideration is still required for a bill to be enforceable between immediate parties to it.

22. Banker's lien. A banker acquires a lien on a bill which is deposited as security and he is deemed to have given value for it to the extent of the sum for which he has a lien: Bills of Exchange Act 1882, s.27(3).

Possible defects and irregularities in a bill

23. Fictitious or non-existing payee.

(*a*) *Bills of Exchange Act 1882, s.7(3)*. This provides that: "Where the payee is a fictitious or non-existing person the bill may be treated as payable to bearer."

(*b*) *Meaning*. A fictitious or non-existing person is a payee to whom the drawer never intended to make payment, it does not mean a person who literally does not exist.

EXAMPLE: In *Bank of England* v. *Vagliano Brothers* (1891), a clerk employed by the defendant merchant bank forged a number of bills drawn on his employers using an existing client as drawer and the name of a real company as payee. In the House of Lords it was held that because the fraudulent clerk—the drawer of the bills—intended that he and not the named payee should receive payment, the payee was a "fictitious person" within the meaning of s.7(3). The bills were therefore payable to bearer.

(c) *Indorsement of such a bill.* The bill is payable to bearer and therefore it can be transferred without the need for indorsement. Furthermore, any indorsement appearing on it can be ignored.

If the law required the bill to be indorsed, the right to payment could never be transferred because the indorsement of the payee could be nothing other than a forgery and therefore completely inoperative: Bills of Exchange Act 1882, s.24. (*See* **24** below.)

EXAMPLE: In *Vagliano's Case*, the fraudulent clerk used the defendant bank's usual office routine to get the bills accepted by them and then forged indorsements on them. He subsequently obtained payment in cash from the defendant's account at the Bank of England. HELD (H.L.): (1) The defendants were prevented from denying that the signatures were genuine because they had notified the Bank that the bills would be presented; (2) the Bank had not been negligent in paying the bills; and, since the bills were payable to bearer, (3) the indorsement could be ignored and the Bank of England was entitled to debit the defendant's account with the amount of the bills.

NOTE: In *Vinden* v. *Hughes* (1905), an employer signed cheques fraudulently prepared by his clerk in favour of existing customers. The clerk then forged the payee's indorsement and negotiated them to the defendant who took them in good faith and for value. On the facts the employer (the drawer) thought that he owed the money to the payees. HELD: (1) The cheques were not payable to bearer under s.7(3) because the drawer intended the payees to receive payment thinking that he owed them the money; (2) the forged indorsements could, therefore, not be ignored; and hence (3) the defendant was liable to repay the proceeds of the cheques that he had received.

24. Forged or unauthorised signatures.

(*a*) *Bills of Exchange Act 1882, s.24*. By this section such signatures are: "Subject to the provisions of this Act . . . wholly inoperative . . ." Thus, no rights can be acquired under them.

The provisos to this rule are:

(*i*) the protection given to a banker who pays a cheque bearing a forged indorsement (*see* 12:**13**);

(*ii*) estoppel (*see* **27–8** below).

(*b*) *Effects of a forged signature on a bill*.

(*i*) *Drawer's signature*. The forged signature is a nullity and the drawer is not liable on the bill. If, however, the bill was properly accepted and indorsed, the acceptor and the indorsers (as sureties) will be liable to the holder. The liability is based on *estoppel* under the Bills of Exchange Act 1882, ss.54 and 55.

NOTE: It is possible for the drawer to be estopped from denying the genuineness of his signature.

(*ii*) *Drawee's signature*. The drawee incurs no liability on the bill if his signature is forged—he has not accepted the bill. The holder of the bill can, however, enforce payment against the drawer and any indorsers, liability being based on estoppel under the Bills of Exchange Act 1882, s.55.

(*iii*) *Indorsement*. A forged indorsement does not make the payee or indorser whose signature it appears to be, liable on the bill. On an *order bill*, it fails to transfer legal title.

The transferee acquires *no right to payment* against parties prior to the forgery, i.e. the acceptor, drawer and any prior indorser. The forgery *breaks* the chain of title.

The holder of the bill can, however, enforce payment against any person signing (indorsing) the bill *after the forgery*, his liability being based on estoppel under the Bills of Exchange Act 1882, s.55(2).

NOTE: As the possessor of an order bill bearing a forged indorsement has no title to it, he would be liable in an action for conversion brought by its true owner.

(As to forged indorsements on *bearer bills*, *see* **23** above. Irregular indorsements are considered in **31** below.)

(*iv*) *Discharge*. Payment by the acceptor or drawer to the possessor of an order bill bearing a forged indorsement does not discharge their liability on the bill: Bills of Exchange Act 1882, s.24. They still remain liable to pay its true owner.

(Discharge of a bill is considered generally in **46** below.)

(*c*) *Banking considerations.*

(*i*) If a banker pays a cheque on which his customer's signature is forged, he *cannot* debit his account with the amount unless the customer is estopped from denying the genuineness of his signature (*see* **27–8** below).

(*ii*) Under the Bills of Exchange Act 1882, s.60, a banker who pays a bill bearing a forged indorsement is in certain circumstances protected from liability in conversion to its true owner (*see* 12:**13**).

(*iii*) The Cheques Act 1957, s.4, provides similar protection to a collecting banker in the case of cheques.

25. Inchoate instruments.

(*a*) *Meaning.* An inchoate instrument is a bill which has been *incompletely drawn* but which can be completed subsequently to make it a valid bill. For example, the payee's name or the amount of payment may be omitted. Such bills are commonly known as *skeleton bills*. A *blank cheque* is the most common example of such a bill.

(*b*) *Effect of issue.* Until it is proved otherwise, the person to whom it is issued has authority to complete the bill in any way he thinks fit: Bills of Exchange Act 1882, s.20(1). However, by s.20(2), to enforce an inchoate bill against a person who became a party to it before its completion, it must have been completed within a reasonable time and strictly in accordance with the authority given. To this the subsection provides an important *exception*. If the bill is negotiated to a holder in due course after its completion, he may enforce it even though it was completed in breach of authority and/or after unreasonable delay.

EXAMPLE: A signs a blank cheque and gives it to B with authority to complete it for £50. B completes the bill in favour of C for £100. C then negotiates it to D who takes as a holder in due course. D can enforce the bill against A for £100 even though B exceeded the authority given to him by A.

26. Effects on negotiability. A person who takes a transfer of a bill which is defective or irregular as described in the sections above,

cannot become a holder in due course of the bill (*see* **31** below). The bill of exchange, although still valid, loses the most important quality of negotiability: it cannot be transferred free from equities.

The role of estoppel in bills of exchange

27. The meaning of estoppel. Estoppel is a rule of evidence which prevents a person denying the truth of a statement he has previously made to a person who has relied on it and altered his position as a consequence.

NOTE: It is partly through the application of the doctrine of estoppel to bills of exchange that the "confidence" vital to the commercial value of a bill is created (*see* **3** above).

28. Instances of estoppel. There are five circumstances in which a person may be prevented from denying the genuineness of some part of a bill of exchange.

(*a*) *By affirming its genuineness and regularity.* In *Bank of England* v. *Vagliano Brothers* (1891), (*see* **23** above) the defendant's office routine included informing the Bank of England that the bills would be presented for payment in due course. This was an affirmation that the signatures on the bills were genuine and thus they could not subsequently deny this.

(*b*) *By failure to fulfil a legal duty.* This form of estoppel—estoppel by omission—occurs as a result of the banker-customer relationship.

The relationship gives rise to a number of contractual duties (*see* I, **6**), one of which requires the customer to inform his banker if he becomes aware that his signature on cheques is being forged.

A customer can be estopped from denying the genuineness of the signature if he fails to do so.

EXAMPLE: In *Greenwood* v. *Martins Bank* (1933), the plaintiff's wife held the cheque book for his account at the defendant bank and over a period of time drew a number of cheques by forging his signature. The plaintiff subsequently discovered this but did not inform the bank. After her death some eight months later he sought repayment from the bank of the amount of the forged cheques. HELD: he was estopped from denying the genuineness of the signatures and the bank was entitled to debit his account with the value of the cheques. However, in *Wealden Woodlands (Kent) Ltd.* v. *National Westminster Bank Ltd.* (1983), the bank's plea of estoppel failed. Here a trusted director had drawn twenty three cheques over a nine-month period by forging a co-director's "signature" on them. The bank argued that the company, by failing to query the payments on its bank statements, had adopted the transactions. On the facts, however, the company had not been in any way to blame for its failure to notice and query the transactions and could not be said to have adopted them.

(*c*) *Inchoate instruments.* (*See* 11:**25**.)

(*d*) *Through negligence.* A customer owes a contractual duty to his banker to draw his cheques with reasonable care. If a customer's careless drawing of a cheque enables it to be fraudulently altered and the bank relies on the alteration to its detriment, he will be liable on the cheque as altered. He is estopped from denying the validity of the cheque in its altered form.

EXAMPLE: In *London Joint Stock Bank Ltd.* v. *Macmillan and Arthur* (1918), a partner in the defendant firm signed a cheque payable to the payee or to bearer made out by a clerk for the sum of £2. The amount payable was shown in figures only. The clerk fraudulently altered the figures to read £120, wrote this amount on the cheque and obtained payment from the plaintiff, the firm's banker. HELD: the bank was entitled to debit the firm's account with the value of the cheque as altered.

Estoppel would not appear to apply when the drawer of the cheque leaves a space between the payee's name and the words "or Order" which enables the payee's name to be fraudulently altered: *Slingsby* v. *District Bank Ltd.* (1932).

The acceptor of a bill of exchange is not under a duty to take precautions against the subsequent alteration of a bill that he accepts.

EXAMPLE: In *Scholefield* v. *Earl of Londesbrough* (1896), the defendant accepted a bill drawn upon him for £500. The drawer subsequently altered the amount of the bill to £3,500 by using spaces that he had deliberately left in it. He indorsed the bill to a third party who negotiated it to the plaintiff. The plaintiff sued for payment of the bill as altered, i.e. £3,500. HELD: the acceptor was only liable to pay £500 on the bill.

(*e*) *Under ss.54 and 55 of the Bills of Exchange Act 1882.* These important sections are discussed fully in **35, 37–8** below.

Holder, holder for value and holder in due course

29. Holder.

(*a*) *Definition.* A holder is defined by the Bills of Exchange Act 1882, s.2, as: "The payee or indorsee of a bill who is in possession of it, or the bearer of a bearer bill."

The following points should be noted about this definition:

(*i*) The term includes an *unlawful* holder, i.e. a person to whom the bill is expressed to be payable but whose possession of it is unlawful. Examples include a finder or thief of a bearer bill and a person who obtained the bill's transfer to himself by fraud.

(*ii*) It follows that anyone in possession of a bearer bill is a holder. This includes a finder or a thief, although such a holder obtains no rights against the parties to the bill. A claim on the bill brought by him will fail on proof of his defective title.

(*iii*) The term does not include a *mere wrongful possessor*, for example a person who has stolen an order bill or a person holding under a forged indorsement—a forged signature is entirely inoperative: Bills of Exchange Act 1882, s.24.

These points are important (*a*) when a question of liability on the bill arises, for instance the acceptor does not pay and an action is taken against the drawer or indorser—only a holder can bring such an action; and (*b*) when the bill is paid, the liability of the parties to the bill will only be discharged if payment is made to the holder of the bill.

(*b*) *Duties of the holder.*

(*i*) To present the bill for acceptance.

(*ii*) To present the bill for payment.

(*iii*) To give notice of dishonour.

(*iv*) To note and protest a dishonoured bill.

(These duties are considered in context in **40–6** below.)

30. Holder for value.

(*a*) *Definition.* A holder for value is a holder of a bill for which value (consideration) has at some time been given. The value need not have been given by the holder himself.

A holder for value can enforce the bill against all persons who became parties to the bill prior to the value being given.

EXAMPLE: A draws a cheque in favour of B. B indorses it for value in favour of C who gives it as a gift to D. D is a holder for value (although he gives no value himself) and he can enforce it against A and B, but not against C because he gave no consideration for C's promise to pay.

The law presumes that a holder is a holder for value but he obtains no better title to the bill than that possessed by his transferor; he does not take free from equities. Thus, he does not enjoy a fundamental benefit of negotiability.

31. Holder in due course.

(a) *Definition.* Section 29(1) of the Act, defines a holder in due course as: ". . . a holder who has taken a bill, complete and regular on the face of it, under the following circumstances, namely: (a) that he became the holder of it before it was overdue, and without notice that it had been previously dishonoured, if such was the fact; (b) that he took the bill in good faith and for value, and that at the time the bill was negotiated to him he had no notice of any defect in the title of the person who negotiated it."

(b) *Requirements for a holder in due course.*

(i) The bill must be *complete and regular* on the face of it, i.e. technically correct. The face of the bill includes both sides: *Arab Bank* v. *Ross* (1952).

An *incomplete* bill is either (1) *undated*; (2) does not state an *amount*; or (3) lacks a required *signature*, e.g. an indorsement. A bill which merely lacks an *acceptance* is not incomplete.

An indorsement will be *irregular* where there is a clear and serious difference between the name of the payee or indorsee and his indorsement. The discrepancy must raise doubts about the genuineness of the indorsement.

EXAMPLE: In *Arab Bank* v. *Ross* (1952), the bank held two promissory notes drawn in favour of a firm "Fathi and Faysal Nabulsy Company". One partner had discounted them to the bank, indorsing them "Fathi and Faysal Nabulsy". HELD: omitting the word "Company" from the indorsement made the bill irregular. Thus, the bank was not a holder in due course of the notes, only a holder for value. (N.B. On the facts, their title as holder for value was valid and they were able to enforce the notes.)

(*ii*) The holder must have taken the bill *before* it was overdue.

(*iii*) The holder must have had *no notice* of any previous dishonour.

NOTE: A banker marking a cheque with a reason for dishonour clearly prevents subsequent parties from becoming holders in due course.

(*iv*) The holder must have taken the bill *in good faith*. Mere *negligence* is not the lack of good faith (Bills of Exchange Act 1882, s.90); the transferee must know or suspect that all is not as it should be concerning the bill.

EXAMPLE: In *Raphael and another* v. *Bank of England* (1855), the numbers of some stolen notes were circulated to bankers and exchange dealers, including the plaintiffs, to whom they were likely to be presented. One such note was changed by the plaintiff without consulting the file of notices of lost and stolen notes; he merely asked to see the presenter's passport and obtained his signature and address on the note. HELD: although he had been negligent, the plaintiff had taken the note in good faith and was therefore entitled to its value.

Knowledge that a bill is negotiated to him in circumstances that amount to a *preference* under s.101(4) of the Insolvency Act 1985 (*see* 4:**47**) prevents a person taking a bill in good faith: *Banca Popolare di Novaro* v. *John Livanos & Sons* (1965), a case involving a *fraudulent preference* under the Bankruptcy Act 1914.

(*v*) The holder must *himself* have given value for the bill. It is not enough that value has at some time been given. (Compare a holder for value.)

(*vi*) At the time of the bill's negotiation to him, the holder must have *no notice* of any defect in title of the person who negotiated it.

NOTE: This means actual notice, or knowledge of suspicious circumstances coupled with a deliberate omission to investigate them. Mere negligence is not enough: *Raphael and another* v. *Bank of England* (1855).

By s.29(2) of the Act, the title of a person negotiating a bill is *defective* if he obtained the bill or the acceptance of it by fraud, coercion or unlawful means, or for an illegal consideration, or when he negotiates it in breach of faith, or under such circumstances as amount to a fraud.

(*c*) *Important points to note.*

(*i*) Every holder is presumed to be a holder in due course until fraud or illegality is admitted or proved in the acceptance, issue or negotiation of the bill. The holder must then prove that value in good faith has subsequently been given for the bill.

(*ii*) A person who takes a transfer of a bearer bill from a thief can be a holder in due course.

(*iii*) The payee of a bill cannot be a holder in due course. The bill is *issued* to him, it is not negotiated: *Re Jones Ltd.* v. *Waring & Gillow Ltd.* (1926).

(*iv*) A person who takes an order bill bearing a forged indorsement cannot be a holder, and therefore not a holder in due course, he is merely a *wrongful possessor*. A forged signature is entirely inoperative: Bills of Exchange Act 1882, s.24.

(*v*) In the Bills of Exchange Act 1882, s.55(2), the term "holder in due course" has a special meaning, i.e. a person who would have been a holder in due course but for the forgery. He has the *rights* but not the status of a holder in due course against *certain parties* to the bill. Specifically, when a question of liability arises in this situation, persons signing the bill *after* the forgery are precluded from denying the genuineness of what is actually a forgery.

NOTE: A similar position arises under s.54(2). Here the acceptor is precluded from denying the genuineness of the drawer's signature on the bill.

(*See* also **38** below.)

(*d*) *Rights of the holder in due course.* His rights are the very essence of negotiability.

(*i*) He can *sue* in his own name any prior party to the bill.

(*ii*) He *takes* the bill free from equities. He can defeat any defences arising from defects in title, or from the dealings between prior parties to the bill: Bills of Exchange Act 1882, s.38(2).

He can, therefore, acquire a better title to the bill than that held by his transferor.

NOTE: Crossing a cheque "Not negotiable" prevents a person from becoming a holder in due course if there was any prior defect in title. The title remains permanently defective.

(*iii*) He can *transfer* his title as holder in due course to any person for value or as a gift, provided that that person was not a party to any defect which affected the bill; mere notice of the defect is not enough: Bills of Exchange Act 1882, s.29(3).

(*e*) *Defences against a holder in due course.* His position is extremely strong in an action brought by him to enforce payment of the bill. Unless it can be proved that he fails to satisfy the Bills of Exchange Act 1882, s.29(1), and is therefore not a holder in due course, only his rights against a *particular party* can be defeated.

The following grounds can be relied upon.

(*i*) *Lack of capacity*: neither a minor nor a corporation contracting *ultra vires* incur liability on a bill of exchange.

(*ii*) Sovereign or diplomatic *immunity*.

(*iii*) *Forgery* of that party's signature, unless he is estopped from denying its genuineness.

(*iv*) A plea of *non est factum* (*see* 10:**6**). (Such a plea is most unlikely to succeed today.)

(*v*) An express *exclusion of liability*, e.g. by signing the bill *sans recours* ("without recourse to me").

Liability of parties

32. Parties to a bill. A party to a bill of exchange is a person who has signed it and thereby incurred liability on it, i.e. the drawer, acceptor and any indorser.

33. Conditions for liability. In order to incur liability on a bill, a person must satisfy the following conditions.

(*i*) He must sign it: Bills of Exchange Act 1882, s.23.

An agent signing on behalf of his principal must make it clear that he signs in a representative capacity by adding the words "per pro" or "for and on behalf of", followed by his principal's name. He will incur personal liability if he does not make the nature of his representative capacity absolutely clear.

In addition, he can be held personally liable on the bill, and the words used can be ignored, if there is a clear agreement entered into between the parties to the effect that the agent should be personally liable on the bill: *Rolfe Lubell & Co.* v. *Keith and another* (1979).

NOTE: A forged or unauthorised signature is wholly inoperative: Bills of Exchange Act 1882, s.24.

(*ii*) He must deliver it: Bills of Exchange Act 1882, s.21(1).

There must be an actual or constructive transfer of possession of the bill from one person to another: Bills of Exchange Act 1882, s.2. Transfer to an agent is a *constructive* transfer.

Where, however, an acceptance is written on a bill and the acceptor notifies his acceptance to, or according to the directions of the person entitled to the bill, the acceptance becomes complete and irrevocable without delivery of the bill.

NOTE: In favour of a holder in due course, delivery is irrefutably presumed: Bills of Exchange Act 1882, s.21(2).

(*iii*) He must possess contractual capacity.

Capacity to incur liability as a party to a bill is co-extensive with capacity to contract: Bills of Exchange Act 1882, s.22(1).

The incapacity of the drawer or of any indorser will not, however, protect any other party to the bill from liability: Bills of Exchange Act 1882, s.22(2).

(*iv*) He must receive consideration.

A party to a bill must receive consideration for incurring liability, or be deemed to have so received consideration.

34. Order of liability. *Before acceptance* the drawer is the principal debtor and primarily liable on the bill. If the bill is negotiated, the indorser(s) incurs secondary liability as surety for payment by the drawer.

After acceptance the acceptor (drawee) becomes the principal debtor. The drawer and any indorsers become sureties for his payment. Thus, the bill can be enforced against the acceptor, drawer and any indorser. Each is liable for its full value and they can be sued individually or in any combination: they are *jointly and severally liable* on the bill.

35. The drawer. By s.55(1) of the Act:

(*a*) he promises that:
    (*i*) the bill will be duly accepted and paid when presented;

(*ii*) he will compensate any holder or indorser who has to pay if the bill is dishonoured, provided that the proper procedure for dishonour is followed;

(*b*) he cannot deny to a holder in due course (*i*) the payee's existence or (*ii*) his capacity to indorse the bill.

36. A drawee who does not accept. A drawee who does not accept a bill is not liable on it: Bills of Exchange Act 1882, s.53(1). Thus a banker who wrongfully dishonours his customer's cheque will not be liable to the holder, although he will, of course, be liable for breach of contract to his customer.

37. The acceptor. By the Bills of Exchange Act 1882, s.54, the acceptor:

(*a*) promises that he will pay the bill in accordance with his acceptance;

(*b*) cannot deny to a holder in due course (*i*) the drawer's existence, (*ii*) the genuineness of his signature; and (*iii*) his power to draw the bill;

(*c*) cannot deny the drawer's capacity to indorse the bill if it is payable to his order;

(*d*) cannot deny (*i*) the existence, or (*ii*) the capacity to indorse of a third person to whom the bill is made payable.

NOTE: The acceptor does not warrant that an indorsement is either genuine or valid. He can set up a forged indorsement as a defence against a person seeking to enforce the bill against him.

38. An indorser. By the Bills of Exchange Act 1882, s.55(2), an indorser:

(*a*) promises that the bill will be duly accepted and paid when presented;

(*b*) promises to compensate any party who has had to pay as a result of its dishonour, provided that the proper procedure for dishonour is followed;

(*c*) cannot deny to a holder in due course the genuineness and regularity of the drawer's signature, or of any indorsement prior to his own;

(*d*) cannot deny to a subsequent indorsee (*i*) that it was a valid bill when he indorsed it, nor (*ii*) that his title to it was good.

NOTE: The drawer and any indorser can add words expressly excluding or limiting their liability on the bill, e.g. *sans recours*: Bills of Exchange Act 1882, s.16(1).

A person signing a bill other than as drawer or acceptor incurs the liabilities of an indorser to a holder in due course: Bills of Exchange Act 1882, s.56. An example would be a director of a company who personally indorses a bill to which his company is a party.

A forged indorsement on an order bill does not transfer title to the bill. The transferee has no claim against parties prior to the forgery: Bills of Exchange Act 1882, s.24. A forged indorsement on a bearer bill can be ignored.

Under s.55(2) of the Act, however, estoppel will make the bill valid and enforceable between the parties subsequent to the forgery. Thus, the ultimate possessor will usually be able to obtain payment from the person who transferred the bill to him and he in turn will be able to claim from the person who negotiated the bill to him and so on. The loss will eventually lie with the person who first took the bill when it bore a forged indorsement. He will bear the loss unless he can trace and recover from the forger.

39. A transfer by delivery. A person who negotiates a bearer bill without indorsing it is a transferor by delivery: Bills of Exchange Act 1882, s.58(1).

He is not liable on the bill, but he warrants to a holder for value to whom *he* transfers the bill, i.e. his immediate transferee, that: (i) the bill is what it purports to be, i.e. not a forgery; (*ii*) he has a right to transfer it; and, (*iii*) at the time of transfer he is unaware of any fact which makes it valueless: Bills of Exchange Act 1882, s.58(2) and (3).

He cannot be sued by remoter transferees.

NOTE: A transferee giving value for the bill acquires the right to have the bill indorsed by the transferor: Bills of Exchange Act 1882, s.31(4).

The progress of a bill of exchange

40. Introduction. The drawer may put the bill into circulation before or after it has been accepted by the drawee. The advantage of doing so after acceptance is that the bill will offer greater security to the payee or a subsequent holder who takes it from him in payment.

Some bills must be presented for acceptance before payment can be demanded, others do not need to be.

The bill may be treated as dishonoured if acceptance or payment is refused.

41. Acceptance.

(*a*) *Meaning.* By the Bills of Exchange Act 1882, s.17(1): "The acceptance of a bill is the signification by the drawee of his assent to the order of the drawer." The acceptance must be written on the bill and be signed by the drawee. His signature alone is a sufficient acceptance.

By accepting the bill, the drawee promises to pay the bill when payment becomes due: Bills of Exchange Act 1882, s.54(1). Provided consideration has been given for the bill by the payee or a subsequent holder, he incurs primary liability on the bill to its holder.

Acceptance may be made before the drawer has signed the bill, or when it is overdue or has been previously dishonoured. If the drawee subsequently accepts a sight bill after it was dishonoured by non-acceptance, the holder is entitled to have the acceptance backdated to the date when it was first presented for acceptance: Bills of Exchange Act 1882, s.18(3).

(*b*) *Presentment for acceptance.* This is only necessary where:

(*i*) the bill is payable after sight for here acceptance is necessary to fix the date on which the bill becomes payable: Bills of Exchange Act 1882, s.39(1);

(*ii*) presentment is expressly stipulated;

(*iii*) the bill is payable elsewhere than at the residence or place of business of the drawee, e.g. a bank: Bills of Exchange Act 1882, s.39(2).

Under the Bills of Exchange Act 1882, s.41(2), presentment for acceptance is *excused* and the bill is treated as dishonoured by non-acceptance where:

(*i*) the drawee is dead or bankrupt, or is a fictitious person, or lacks the contractual capacity to accept the bill;

(*ii*) presentment is impossible, e.g. where the drawee cannot be found after the exercise of reasonable diligence.

NOTE: For two reasons, presentment for acceptance is advisable in all cases: (1) the drawee becomes liable on the bill when he accepts: (2) if acceptance is refused, the holder gains an immediate right of recourse against prior parties.

A bill payable at a specified date must be presented for acceptance before it is overdue: Bills of Exchange Act 1882, s.41(1)(*a*).

A bill payable after sight must be presented for acceptance or negotiated within a reasonable time—this is a question of fact. Failure to do so discharges the drawer and any prior indorsers (Bills of Exchange Act 1882, s.40(2)) because the longer the bill is left unaccepted the greater is the risk incurred by them, i.e. the risk of the drawee becoming insolvent.

Presentment must be made by the holder or his agent to the drawee or his agent at a reasonable hour on a business day.

Provided it is authorised by agreement or usage, presentment by post is sufficient: Bills of Exchange Act 1882, s.41(1)(*e*).

(*c*) *General or qualified acceptance.* By the Bills of Exchange Act 1882, s.19, a general acceptance is an unqualified assent to the order as drawn, whereas a qualified acceptance in some way varies the effect of the bill as drawn.

There are five types of qualified acceptance.

(*i*) *Conditional*: Payment by the acceptor is made subject to a condition.

EXAMPLE: "Accepted if the bills of lading are handed over."

(*ii*) *Partial*: an acceptance to pay only part of the sum specified.

(*iii*) *Local*: an acceptance to pay *only* at a particular place.

EXAMPLE: "Accepted payable at Southtown Bank, High Street." is a general acceptance; whereas "Accepted payable at Southtown Bank, High Street only." is a qualified acceptance.

(*iv*) *Qualified as to time.*

EXAMPLE: "Accepted payable in 60 days." where the bill was drawn payable in 30 days.

(v) *Accepted by some* but not all of several joint drawees.

The holder may treat the bill as dishonoured if only a qualified acceptance is given: Bills of Exchange Act 1882, s.44(1).

If the holder takes a qualified acceptance, the drawer and any indorser who did not authorise or agree to the qualified acceptance is discharged: Bills of Exchange Act 1882, s.44(2).

If, however, the holder gives notice to prior parties of his intention to take a qualified acceptance, they are deemed to have agreed to it unless they notify their dissent to him within a reasonable time: Bills of Exchange Act 1882, s.44(3).

42. Negotiation of a bill. A bill is negotiated when it is transferred in such a way as to make the transferee the holder of it: Bills of Exchange Act 1882, s.31(1).

A *bearer bill* is negotiated by delivery.

An *order bill* is negotiated by the indorsement of the holder completed by delivery.

NOTE: A bill is *assigned*, not negotiated, where the holder of an order bill transfers it for value without indorsing it. The transferee only acquires such title to the bill as the transferor had and he cannot sue on the bill in his own name. He does, however, acquire the right to have the bill indorsed by the transferor: Bills of Exchange Act 1882, s.31(4).

A bill continues to be negotiable until it has been (a) restrictively indorsed (*see* **43** below) or (b) discharged by payment or otherwise (*see* **46** below): Bills of Exchange Act 1882, s.36(1).

Although an overdue bill can still be negotiated, a transferee takes it subject to any defects in title affecting it at its maturity: Bills of Exchange Act 1882, s.36(2). He cannot become a holder in due course.

43. Indorsements.

(a) *Meaning.* An indorsement is the signature of the indorser of the bill, i.e. the payee or a subsequent holder.

Unless the contrary is proved, indorsements on a bill are deemed to have been made in the order in which they appear.

NOTE: Through the nature of their use and the Cheques Act 1957, indorsements are rarely found on cheques.

(*b*) *Essentials*. An indorsement must satisfy the Bills of Exchange Act 1882, s.32.

(*i*) It must be *written* on the back of the bill.

(*ii*) It must be of the *entire bill* and not part.

(*iii*) If there are two or more payees *all must endorse*, unless one is authorised to indorse for the others, e.g. a partner.

(*iv*) It should *correspond exactly* with the drawing or previous indorsement, e.g. if the payee's name was misspelt, he should indorse it with the same spelling, adding his proper signature if he wishes.

NOTE: An indorsement which does not exactly correspond with the previous designation on the bill is not invalid: *Arab Bank* v. *Ross* (1952). However, an irregular indorsement—a question of fact—will prevent a transferee from becoming a holder in due course. In addition, banks will usually refuse to pay order bills on which the indorsement does not correspond exactly with the name of the payee or previous indorsee.

(*c*) *Types*.

(*i*) *Indorsement in blank*. This consists of a signature only. No indorsee is specified. The bill becomes payable to bearer.

(*ii*) *Special indorsement*. This consists of a direction to pay a particular person accompanied by the indorser's signature. The bill becomes payable to, or to the order of, the person specified.

The holder can convert a blank indorsement into a special indorsement by writing above the signature a direction to pay himself or some other person: Bills of Exchange Act 1882, s.34(4).

NOTE: Blank and special indorsements enable an order bill to be converted into a bearer bill and vice versa.

(*iii*) *Restrictive indorsement*. This prohibits or restricts further negotiation of the bill: Bills of Exchange Act 1882, s.35(1).

EXAMPLE: An indorsement "Pay X only" prohibits further negotiation; while an indorsement "Pay X for the account of Y" entitles X to receive the sum paid to hold as agent for Y; in other words, it does not transfer ownership of the bill but merely gives the indorsee authority to deal with it for the specified limited purpose.

The restrictive indorsement transfers the rights to receive payment and to enforce the bill against prior parties but the transferee cannot transfer his rights unless the indorsement expressly authorises him to do so: Bills of Exchange Act 1882, s.35(2). Since the bill is no longer negotiable (merely transferable), a subsequent transferee cannot become a holder in due course.

NOTE: (1) Should a holder purport to indorse a bill *conditionally*, the condition may be disregarded by the payer. Payment by him is valid whether or not the condition has been fulfilled: Bills of Exchange Act 1882, s.33. This provision is of practical importance to a banker. (2) On bills other than cheques, a marking "Not negotiable" prevents the bill's transfer. On cheques, it merely prevents the transferee obtaining a better title than that possessed by the transferor (*see* 12:**8**).

44. Payment.

(*a*) *Rules for presentation for payment.*

(*i*) *Sight or time bills.* Presentment must be made on the date fixed by the bill, e.g. three months after acceptance or after sight: Bills of Exchange 1882, s.45(1).

(*ii*) *Demand bills.* Presentment must be made within a reasonable time after its issue to render the drawer liable and within a reasonable time of indorsement to render the indorser liable: Bills of Exchange Act 1882, s.45(2).

(*iii*) *Method.* Presentment must be made by the holder or his agent to the payer or his agent at the proper place at a reasonable time on a business day: Bills of Exchange Act 1882, s.45(3).

(*iv*) *Post.* Presentment by post is sufficient where authorised by agreement or by usage: Bills of Exchange Act 1882, s.45(8).

NOTE: Banks may present cheques through the post, as may a person drawing a cheque payable to himself on his own account.

(*v*) *Delay in presentation.* Delay is excused where it is caused by circumstances beyond the holder's control and not by his default, misconduct or negligence: Bills of Exchange Act 1882, s.46(1). Presentation must be made with reasonable diligence when the cause of the delay ceases to operate.

(*vi*) *Presentation excused.* Under the Bills of Exchange Act 1882, s.46(2), presentation is dispensed with when:

(1) it cannot reasonably be made, e.g. the acceptor cannot be found;

(2) the drawee is a fictitious person;

(3) it has been waived.

Failure to present the bill in accordance with the Bills of Exchange Act 1882, s.45, will discharge the drawer and any indorser. Unless excused under s.46, a delay of one day in presenting is a sufficient failure: *Yeoman Credit* v. *Gregory* (1963); as is a presentment on the day before maturity of the bill.

(*b*) *Dishonour by non-payment.* A bill is dishonoured by non-payment when:

(*i*) it is duly presented for payment and payment is refused or cannot be obtained; or

(*ii*) when presentment is excused and the bill is overdue and unpaid: Bills of Exchange Act 1882, s.47(1).

The bill is not discharged.

NOTE: Banks frequently act as agents for collection of bills and a banker must ensure that he follows the proper procedure to secure acceptance and payment. He must similarly ensure that he takes the proper steps if the bill is dishonoured. (Dishonour is discussed generally in **45** below.)

(*c*) *Payment.*

(*i*) *Payment in due course.* This is payment at or after the bill's maturity to its holder in good faith and without notice that his title to the bill is defective: Bills of Exchange Act 1882, s.59(1). Such payment discharges the bill. All parties are released from liability on it.

(*ii*) *Payment before maturity.* This constitutes a purchase of the bill, and the acceptor could theoretically re-issue it.

The bill is not discharged and except to the acceptor, prior parties remain liable on the bill.

(*iii*) *Part payment.* An offer of part payment when the bill is presented for payment may be treated as dishonour.

If the holder takes part payment in full discharge from the acceptor, but expressly reserves his rights against the drawer and any indorser, they are not discharged because their own rights against the acceptor are thereby preserved.

(*d*) *Time of payment.* A sight bill must be paid on the *last day* of the time for payment as fixed by the bill. If that day is a non-business day, it must be paid on the next business day: Bills of Exchange Act 1882, s.14(1).

In calculating the date of payment, the day on which time begins to run is excluded from the calculation and the day of payment is included. Time begins to run on a sight bill from the date of acceptance or, if this is refused, from the date of noting and protest. The term month means a calendar month.

45. Dishonour.

(a) *Introduction*. A bill of exchange can be dishonoured (i) by non-acceptance: Bills of Exchange Act 1882, s.43; or (ii) by non-payment: Bills of Exchange Act 1882, s.47.

(b) *Notice of dishonour*.

(i) *Failure to give notice*. This discharges the drawer and any indorsers from liability on the bill: Bills of Exchange Act 1882, s.48.

NOTE: (1) The rights of a holder in due course taking the bill after an omission to give notice following dishonour by non-acceptance are not prejudiced by the omission. He must, of course, give appropriate notice himself when he is refused acceptance or payment. (2) Indorsers can rely on notice of dishonour given by the holder of the bill.

(ii) *Delay in giving notice*. This is excused when it is caused by circumstances beyond the control of the party giving notice and not by his default, misconduct or negligence: Bills of Exchange Act 1882, s.50(1).

Notice must be given with reasonable diligence once the cause of the delay ceases to operate.

(iii) *Notice unnecessary*. Notice of dishonour is dispensed with in the following circumstances.

(1) When after reasonable diligence it cannot be *given* e.g. the person to whom it is to be given cannot be found.

(2) When it is expressly or impliedly waived.

(3) As regards the *drawer*: (a) where the drawer and drawee are the same person; (b) where the drawee is a fictitious person or lacks contractual capacity; (c) where the drawer is the person to whom the bill was presented; (d) where the drawee or acceptor was under no obligation to the drawer to accept or pay the bill, e.g. where a cheque is drawn on an account with insufficient funds to meet it and no overdraft facility exists; (e) where the drawer has countermanded payment.

NOTE: The combination of the last two circumstances above means that there is seldom any need for the holder of a cheque to give notice of dishonour when it is dishonoured by non-payment.

(4) As regards the *indorser*: (*a*) where the drawee is a fictitious person or lacks contractual capacity and the indorser was aware of this when he indorsed; (*b*) where the indorser is the person to whom the bill was presented; (*c*) where the bill was only made and accepted for the indorser's accommodation.

(*c*) *Method of giving notice.* Provided it clearly identifies the bill, notice of dishonour of an inland bill can be in any form. A *foreign bill* must be noted and protested when it is dishonoured: *see* below.

Very strict time limits are applied to giving notice despite the words "may be given as soon as the bill is dishonoured, and must be given within a reasonable time thereafter" in the Bills of Exchange Act 1882, s.29(12).

(*i*) Where the parties live in the *same place* (this probably means the same postal district), it must be given or sent off *to reach* the other party on the day after the bill's dishonour.

(*ii*) If the parties live in *different places*, the notice must be *sent off* on the day after the bill's dishonour provided that there is a convenient post on that day and, if not, by the next convenient post thereafter.

Notice of dishonour is treated as given when it is *received* not when it is sent. Thus, notice is invalid if received before the bill is dishonoured although it is not invalidated merely because it was posted too soon.

EXAMPLE: In *Eaglehill Ltd.* v. *J. Needham Builders Ltd.* (1973), the plaintiff knew that a bill would be dishonoured when presented and prepared a postdated notice of dishonour accordingly. By mistake, the notice was posted too soon and arrived on the day the bill was dishonoured and at about the same time. HELD: the notice was valid because there was no evidence that it had been received before the bill was dishonoured.

NOTE: If a bill when dishonoured is in the hands of an agent, he may either give notice himself or he may give notice to his principal. The agent has the same time to give notice to his principal as if he were the holder. The principal on receipt of it has the same time in which to give notice as if he and his agent were independent parties to the bill: Bills of Exchange Act 1882, s.49(13). This section is of practical importance to bankers collecting cheques and bills for their customers. Under it they are able to return dishonoured instruments to them.

(*d*) *Noting and protest*. Noting is the formal representation of a dishonoured bill by a *notary public* for acceptance or for payment. The reply given is noted on the bill. The protest takes the form of a formal declaration signed by the notary attesting the dishonour and containing the relevant facts: Bills of Exchange Act 1882, s.51(7). This and a copy of the noted bill are then sent to the party from whom payment is sought.

Noting and protest provide formal evidence of dishonour which will be universally recognised and accepted.

Where the services of a notary cannot be obtained, a *householder* in the presence of two witnesses may give a certificate signed by them attesting the dishonour of the bill. This certificate operates as if it were a formal protest: Bills of Exchange Act 1882, s.94.

Any dishonoured bill may be noted and protested but it is only necessary where:

(*i*) a foreign bill is dishonoured: Bills of Exchange Act 1882, s.51(2);

(*ii*) acceptance or payment for honour are sought (*see* below): Bills of Exchange Act 1882, s.65(1) and s.67(1);

(*iii*) a bill is dishonoured by an acceptor for honour (*see* below): Bills of Exchange Act 1882, s.67(4).

A bill requiring noting must be noted on the day that it is dishonoured or on the next business day. The protest, being an extension of the noting, can be done later: Bills of Exchange Act 1882, s.51(4). Failure to protest discharges the drawer and indorsers.

NOTE: A protest is dispensed with and delay excused under exactly the same terms and conditions as apply to notice of dishonour: Bills of Exchange Act 1882, s.59(1). (*See* above.)

A bill may be protested for better security by a notary engaged by the holder where the acceptor becomes bankrupt or insolvent or suspends payment of his debts before the bill matures. The notary first demands better security and issues the protest if this is refused: Bills of Exchange Act 1882, s.51(5).

Such a protest confers no right of action, but enables the bill to be accepted for honour *supra* protest.

(*e*) *Acceptance and payment for honour.* A bill of exchange which has been (*i*) protested for dishonour by non-acceptance or (*ii*) protested for better security may be accepted for honour for part or all of the amount by any person who is not already a party to it.

The bill must be overdue and the holder must consent to the acceptance for honour: Bills of Exchange Act 1882, s.65(1) and (2). The acceptance must be written on the bill, must be signed by the acceptor for honour and must indicate that it is an acceptance for honour. The acceptance prevents the holder exercising his rights of recourse against other parties to the bill.

An acceptor for honour is liable to the holder of the bill and to all persons who became parties to it after the party for whose honour he accepts: Bills of Exchange Act 1882, s.66(2).

He undertakes to pay the bill provided it is protested following the drawee's failure to pay after a proper presentation for payment to him: Bills of Exchange Act 1882, s.66(1).

If the acceptor for honour does not make payment, the bill must be protested for non-payment by him.

A bill must also be protested for non-payment when payment is sought from a *referee in case of need*, i.e. a person designated on the bill by the drawer or indorser from whom the holder *may* apply for payment if the drawee dishonours the bill: Bills of Exchange Act 1882, s.68.

Under the Bills of Exchange Act 1882, s.68, payment for honour takes place when a person intervenes and pays the bill after the bill has been protested for non-payment.

The payer, who may already be a party to the bill, may pay for the honour of any party liable on the bill or the person for whose account it was drawn, e.g. where an agent draws a bill for his principal. Payment for honour can take place after the bill is overdue.

If the holder refuses the payment, he loses his right of recourse against all parties who would have been discharged by the payment.

A person who pays for honour is *subrogated* to the rights of the holder against the party for whose honour he pays, and all parties liable to that party: Bills of Exchange Act 1882, s.68(5).

(*f*) *Damages for dishonour.* Under the Bills of Exchange Act 1882, s.57, the measure of damages is:

(*i*) the amount of the bill;

(*ii*) interest on it from the time of presentment for payment if the bill is payable on demand, and from the maturity of the bill in any other case;

(*iii*) the expenses of noting and protest.

The holder can sue any party to the bill and the party sued can in turn sue any prior party until liability rests with the acceptor or, if the bill was not accepted, with the drawer.

46. Discharge.

(*a*) *By payment in due course.* This is defined by the Bills of Exchange Act 1882, s.59(1) as payment: (*i*) by or on behalf of the drawee or acceptor; (*ii*) at or after the bill's maturity; (*iii*) to its holder; (*iv*) in good faith; and (*v*) without notice that his title to the bill is defective.

NOTE: The meaning of the term "holder" is explained in **29** above.

Payment in due course by any other party will not discharge the bill unless it is an accommodation bill and payment is made by the party accommodated: Bills of Exchange Act 1882, s.59(3).

NOTE: Under s.60 of the Act, a bank's payment of a cheque bearing a forged or unauthorised indorsement (the presenter cannot, therefore, be its holder) is deemed to be payment in due course provided the payment was made in good faith and in the ordinary course of business. Such payment *discharges the cheque*. (This section is dealt with generally in 12:**13**.)

(*b*) *By merger.* This occurs when the acceptor is or becomes the holder of the bill in his own right at or after its maturity: Bills of Exchange Act 1882, s.61.

If the acceptor becomes the holder before maturity, it is possible for him to re-issue the bill, although he will not retain his rights against prior parties.

(*c*) *By renunciation.* At or after a bill's maturity the holder may absolutely and unconditionally renounce his rights against the acceptor in writing or by giving the bill to him: Bills of Exchange Act 1882, s.62(1).

The holder may similarly renounce his rights against specific prior parties before, at or after the bill's maturity. Such renunciation, however, does not affect the rights of a holder in due course without notice of it: Bills of Exchange Act 1882, s.62(2).

(*d*) *By cancellation.* The cancellation must: (*i*) be made by the holder or his agent; (*ii*) be made intentionally; and (*iii*) be apparent: Bills of Exchange Act 1882, s.63(1).

An unintentional, mistaken or unauthorised cancellation is inoperative but the person who maintains that the cancellation is inoperative must prove it.

The holder may cancel the bill as a whole or the signature of one prior party. The latter cancellation discharges that person's liability together with all indorsers who would have had a right of recourse against him.

(*e*) *By material alteration.* An alteration is material if it has the effect of changing the operation or business effect of the instrument or the liabilities of the parties.

Such alterations include those of: (*i*) the date; (*ii*) the sum payable; (*iii*) the time of payment; (*iv*) the place of payment; and (*v*) the addition of a place of payment without the acceptor's consent where the bill has been accepted generally: Bills of Exchange Act 1882, s.64(2).

NOTE: (1) Section 78 of the Act provides that altering the crossing on a cheque is a material alteration. (2) A customer owes a duty to his bank to draw his cheques with reasonable care in order to avoid fraudulent alterations of them: *London Joint Stock Bank* v. *Macmillan and Arthur* (1918) (*see* **28** above).

A material alteration will render a bill void against all parties except the one who made, authorised or consented to the alteration, and any party who indorsed the bill after its alteration: Bills of Exchange Act 1882, s.64(1).

If the alteration is *not* apparent, a holder in due course may enforce the bill for the original amount as if it had not been altered.

Progress test 11

1. List the main types of negotiable instruments. (**1**)
2. State the legal characteristics of a negotiable instrument. (**1**)
3. What are the commercial advantages of using bills of exchange as a method of payment? (**3**)

4. Define a bill of exchange.   (**4**)

5. Explain the words (*a*) unconditional order and (*b*) a sum certain in money in the Bills of Exchange Act 1882, s.3(1).   (**5** and **10**).

6. What is an accommodation bill?   (**16**)

7. State and explain the three special features of consideration in relation to bills of exchange.   (**21**)

8. What is meant by a fictitious or non-existing payee of a bill of exchange? What is the effect of drawing a bill payable to such a payee?   (**23**)

9. What is the effect of a forged or unauthorised indorsement on a bill?   (**24**)

10. What is the effect of issuing an inchoate instrument?   (**25**)

11. Explain estoppel.   (**27**)

12. List the five circumstances in which a person may be prevented from denying the genuineness of some part of a bill of exchange. Give examples.   (**28**)

13. Define the terms (*a*) holder and (*b*) holder for value.   (**29–30**)

14. Who is a holder in due course?   (**31**)

15. Can a person taking an order bill under a forged indorsement become a holder in due course of the bill?   (**29** and **31**)

16. When is an indorsement considered to be irregular?   (**31**)

17. What is meant by good faith and defect in title under the Bills of Exchange Act 1882, s.29(1)?   (**31**)

18. Explain the meaning of holder in due course in the context of the Bills of Exchange Act 1882, s.55(2).   (**31**)

19. State the rights of a holder in due course.   (**31**)

20. What defences can be raised against a holder in due course?   (**31**)

21. List the conditions for incurring liability on a bill of exchange.   (**33**)

22. State and explain the nature of the liability of (*a*) the drawer, (*b*) the acceptor, and (*c*) an indorser to the holder of a bill of exchange.   (**35, 37–38**)

23. Explain the term transferor by delivery.   (**39**)

24. In what circumstances is presentment for acceptance necessary?   (**41**)

25. List the five possible types of qualified acceptance.   (**41**)

26. What is the effect of negotiating a bill of exchange?   (**42**)

27. Distinguish between general, special and restrictive indorsements, explaining the effect of each.   (**43**)

28. When is presentment for payment excused?   (**44**)

29. How is a bill of exchange dishonoured?   (**45**)

30. What is the effect of failing to give notice of dishonour?   (**45**)

31. What is meant by noting and protesting a bill? When is it necessary?   (**45**)

32. Explain acceptance and payment for honour.   (**45**)

33. List the ways in which a bill of exchange can be discharged. (**46**)

34. Define payment in due course.   (**46**)

35. When is an alteration of a bill material? Give examples. (**46**)

12
Cheques

Introduction

1. Definition. A cheque is a bill of exchange drawn on a banker payable on demand: Bills of Exchange Act 1882, s.73. To be a cheque, a document must therefore satisfy s.3(1) of the 1882 Act. It amounts to a written promise by the drawer that the banker on which it is drawn will pay to the payee on demand the amount stipulated.

NOTE: Besides being a negotiable instrument, a cheque is also (1) a *mandate* from the customer authorising and directing his banker to pay the holder, and (2) a *piece of property*—a chose in action—over which legal rights exist.

2. Cheques and the Bills of Exchange Act 1882, s.3(1).

(*a*) *Unconditional and conditional orders.* A cheque must contain an unconditional order to the drawee bank.

A conditional order to pay is not a cheque, e.g. an order to pay on condition that the receipt on the face or reverse of the instrument is signed: *Bavins* v. *London and South Western Bank* (1900) (*see* 11:5). Conditional orders are not negotiable.

However, a cheque which includes a receipt form and a statement that this must be signed is unconditional provided that the instruction is to the payee and is not made a prerequisite for payment by the bank.

Following a resolution by the Committee of London Clearing Bankers, a banker will not accept the responsibility of ensuring that the receipt is signed unless the cheque bears a large letter "R" near to the statement of the amount of the cheque. Customers are sometimes asked to sign an indemnity before their bank will agree to handle such cheques.

(b) *In writing*. This includes typewriting and printing. Cheques should be written in ink.

While a cheque can be written on anything capable of delivery (except metal), banks discourage the use of unusual cheques by imposing a substantial commission charge or by giving notice to close the account if they are frequently presented.

(c) *Addressed by one person to another*. Two separate parties must be involved and the cheque must be addressed by the drawer to a bank.

A bank draft (a draft drawn by a bank on its head office or on another branch payable to order on demand) is not a cheque because all branches and offices of a bank are a single legal entity.

(d) *Signed by the person giving it*. An agent can sign a cheque on behalf of his principal but he must make his representative capacity absolutely clear in order to avoid personal liability.

(e) *Payable on demand*. A cheque is payable when it is presented on the date it bears or within a reasonable time thereafter (*see* **4** below).

(f) *A sum certain in money*. A cheque stating the amount in words but lacking the amount in figures must be paid, although the payee will usually have filled in the figures: Bills of Exchange Act 1882, s.20.

Whether a cheque lacking the amount in words is returned will depend on the circumstances but cheques bearing a discrepancy between the amounts in figures and in words are normally returned marked "Words and figures differ".

(g) *Payable to or to the order of a specified person or to bearer*. Customers frequently draw "cheques" on their own banks payable to "Cash". Such instruments fail to satisfy the Bills of Exchange Act 1882, s.3(1), but they are valid orders to the bank to pay the stated amount from the customer's account. The same applies to "cheques" drawn to wages. Such instruments are not negotiable: *North and South Insurance Corporation* v. *National Provincial Bank* (1936).

A cheque made payable to a non-existing or fictitious payee is payable to bearer: Bills of Exchange Act 1882, s.7(3).

3. Cheques and other bills compared.

(a) *Introduction.* The provisions of the 1882 Act applicable to bills payable on demand apply equally to cheques unless otherwise provided: Bills of Exchange Act 1882, s.73.

(b) *Distinctions.*

(i) *Acceptance.* A cheque is never accepted by the bank on which it is drawn. Hence, the rules relating to acceptance of bills do not apply to cheques.

A banker is therefore never liable to the holder of a cheque if he does not pay. The drawer and any indorsers are the only parties liable on a cheque.

(ii) *Negotiation.* In practice, the rules relating to negotiation are of limited importance in relation to cheques since only a small proportion (about 3 per cent) are negotiated.

(iii) *Delay in presenting for payment.* Section 45(2) does not apply to the drawer of a cheque. He is not discharged by delay in presenting for payment unless he suffers actual damage through the delay. He is then discharged to the extent of the damage: Bills of Exchange Act 1882, s.74(1).

This would be the case where the bank on which the cheque was drawn fails when there would have been sufficient funds in the account to meet the cheque if its presentment had not been delayed.

Since the failure of a UK bank is most unlikely to happen today, for all practical purposes the drawer of a cheque remains liable on it for six years from its date or its date of issue, whichever is the later: Limitation Act 1980.

NOTE: Section 74 of the 1882 Act applies only to the drawer; indorsers are discharged by a delay in presenting for payment under s.45(2).

(iv) *Crossings.* The rules relating to crossings are confined to cheques (and certain other instruments mentioned in the Cheques Act 1957, s.4(2)); other bills cannot be crossed.

(v) *Forged and unauthorised indorsements.* In certain circumstances, an order cheque bearing a forged or unauthorised indorsement is discharged by the drawee bank making payment: Bills of Exchange Act 1882, s.60.

Payment under similar conditions by the acceptor of a bill does not discharge the bill.

(*vi*) "*Not negotiable*". The use of this phrase on a bill prevents the bill being *transferred*. On a cheque, it merely prevents the cheque being *negotiated* (*see* **8** below).

4. Stale and overdue cheques. A cheque is *stale* when it has been in circulation for a considerable period of time. It is usual for a bank to refuse to pay a cheque which is more than six months old.

A cheque is *overdue* when it has been in circulation for an unreasonable length of time. This is a question of fact in the circumstances: Bills of Exchange Act 1882, s.36(3). It is generally considered that, in the absence of special circumstances, a cheque is overdue if it is not presented within ten days of its issue. There are no modern decisions on this point.

Subject to s.74 of the Act (*see* **3** above), the drawer remains liable on an overdue cheque, but a person taking a transfer of a cheque when it is overdue cannot become a holder in due course: Bills of Exchange Act 1882, s.29(1).

5. Post-dated cheques. A post-dated cheque is not payable on demand and, therefore, strictly speaking, not a cheque at all.

A banker may pay a post-dated cheque when it falls due. However, he cannot debit his customer's account should he pay the cheque before the date that it bears, or if his customer stops the cheque, becomes insolvent or dies before this date. In such a situation, the banker would have to bear the loss himself.

NOTE: A person in possession of an undated cheque has *prima facie* authority to date it as he wishes: Bills of Exchange Act 1882, s.20(1) (*see* **11:25**). It is usual banking practice to refuse to pay undated cheques.

6. Cheques as evidence of payment. Both paid indorsed and unindorsed cheques are evidence that the payee has received payment.

Crossed cheques

7. Introduction. A crossing is a direction to the paying banker that the money should only be paid to another banker as agent of the holder and not directly to the holder himself. It therefore restricts payment.

Today, the main purpose of crossing cheques is to guard against fraud.

A crossing is a material part of a cheque: Bills of Exchange Act 1882, s.78. An unauthorised alteration of a crossing will therefore discharge the cheque: Bills of Exchange Act 1882, s.64. A bank should not pay a cheque which has been altered unless the alteration has been signed by the drawer.

A banker must not pay a cheque crossed *specially* (*see* below) to more than one banker except when one banker is acting as an agent for collection for the other: Bills of Exchange Act 1882, s.79(1).

A banker is liable to the true owner of a cheque for any loss caused by paying a cheque contrary to its crossing: Bills of Exchange Act 1882, s.79(2). He cannot debit his customer's account.

(A paying banker's protection in relation to crossed cheques is discussed in **13** below.)

NOTE: Bankers will allow their own customers, or their known agents, to cash crossed cheques over the counter. Sometimes the customer is required to open the crossing by writing "Please pay cash" and signing the opening but more usually an opening is not requested. The practice, although technically incorrect at law, is convenient and the risk involved slight.

8. Types of crossings.

(*a*) *General*. This consists of two transverse parallel lines across the face of the cheque, with or without the words "and Company" between the lines and with or without the words "not negotiable": Bills of Exchange Act 1882, s.76(1).

A cheque cossed generally can only be paid through a bank account; it cannot be paid directly to the holder.

(*b*) *Special*. This consists of the name of a particular bank to which payment must be made. The name itself is the crossing and, while they often appear, two transverse parallel lines are unnecessary: Bills of Exchange Act 1882, s.76(2).

The words "not negotiable" may be added to the crossing.

(*c*) *Not negotiable*. Where the words "not negotiable" are added to a crossing they deprive the cheque of its negotiability, i.e. a person taking the cheque does not receive and cannot give a better title to it than that of the person transferring it to him: Bills of Exchange Act

1882, s.81. The cheque is always transferred subject to any existing defects in title.

In short, while the cheque is still *transferable*, the words prevent a transferee from becoming a holder in due course.

(*d*) *Account payee*. These words are, strictly speaking, not part of any crossing. They are a direction to the collecting bank as to how the money must be dealt with after its receipt.

The words are, however, often encountered, usually in conjunction with a crossing. While they have no statutory significance, the courts recognise them as a warning to the collecting bank that collection of the cheque for a person other than the named payee without enquiry and sufficient explanation is *prima facie* proof of negligence.

The words do not affect the negotiability of a cheque.

9. Who may cross a cheque.

(*a*) The *drawer* may cross a cheque generally or specially, adding the words "not negotiable" if he wishes.

(*b*) The *holder* may cross an uncrossed cheque generally or specially. If it is crossed generally, he may cross it specially. In either case he may add the words "not negotiable".

(*c*) A *bank* to which a cheque has been specially crossed can cross it specially to another bank for collection. A bank may specially cross an uncrossed or generally crossed cheque sent to it for collection.

The paying banker

10. Introduction. A banker owes a contractual duty to pay a customer's cheques provided (*a*) they are properly drawn; (*b*) sufficient funds are available or an agreed overdraft facility exists; (*c*) there is no legal bar to payment; and (*d*) the customer has not revoked his authority to pay.

Payment in due course by the drawee bank discharges the cheque: Bills of Exchange Act 1882, ss.59 and 60.

11. Termination of authority to pay.

(*a*) *Countermand of payment*. Bills of Exchange Act 1882, s.75. A countermand must be (*i*) in writing, and (*ii*) absolutely unequivocal. It must also be communicated to the branch on which the cheque was drawn: *London Provincial and South Western Bank* v. *Buszard* (1919).

Only the drawer can countermand payment.

NOTE: A cheque "backed" by a cheque guarantee card in accordance with its conditions of use and within the current limit cannot be stopped.

Countermand by *telephone* entitles a banker to postpone payment or dishonour pending written confirmation. If the cheque is returned in the meantime, the banker must indicate that he is expecting confirmation of the countermand.

Written notice of countermand is not effective unless and until it comes to the actual attention of the bank.

EXAMPLE: In *Curtice* v. *London City and Midland Bank Ltd.* (1908), a telegram countermanding payment of a cheque was delivered after banking hours and left in the bank's letter box. The next day the countermand was accidently overlooked. It was found the following day, but by this time the cheque had already been paid. HELD: since the bank had no actual knowledge of the telegram, the countermand was ineffective and the bank was entitled to debit the plaintiff's account with the amount of the cheque.

The countermand must give complete details of the cheque, in particular (*i*) the payee's name; (*ii*) the amount of the cheque; and (*iii*) its number.

The *number of the cheque* to be countermanded is the most important detail to communicate. If the wrong number is given, a banker incurs no liability if he pays the cheque which his customer intended to stop: *Westminster Bank Ltd.* v. *Hilton* (1926).

A banker can still stop payment when a countermand is received after the cheque has been presented but before it has been paid.

NOTE: If, by mistake, a bank pays a cheque without a mandate, e.g. by overlooking its customer's countermand, it is *prima facie* entitled to recover payment from the payee unless he changes his position in good faith as a result of the payment.

(*b*) *Legal bar to payment.*

(*i*) *Garnishee order.* Following judgment against a debtor, a creditor may seek a garnishee order against a credit balance in the debtor's account. A bank must then pay the balance to the judgment creditor and cannot lawfully pay further cheques drawn on the account.

(*ii*) *Injunction.* An injunction may be issued by the court to freeze a bank account. Where, for example, the ownership of certain funds is disputed, an injunction will prevent them being paid away before ownership is determined in court.

> NOTE: In recent years, such injunctions have become known as *Mareva* injunctions after a 1975 case involving a company of that name. They are *interlocutory* injunctions, i.e. temporary injunctions granted while the case is pending in court and before final judgment is given. One will only be granted if (1) the plaintiff is likely to recover judgment, and (2) it is reasonably believed that the defendant has assets within the court's jurisdiction to meet the judgment but is likely to take steps to ensure that they are not available when judgment is given against him.

(*c*) *Notice of the customer's death.* Bills of Exchange Act 1882, s.75.

(*d*) *Notice of the customer's mental disorder.* The mental disorder must be such that it prevents the customer from managing his affairs.

If there is any doubt about his condition, the legal position can be determined by a judge appointed under the Mental Health Act 1983. An order made under the Act forbids any transaction on the account without the consent of the court.

(*e*) *Notice of a bankruptcy petition against the customer.* The protection afforded by the Insolvency Act 1985, s.131(4) to dispositions of property and payments of money made in the period between the presentation of the bankruptcy petition and the making of the bankruptcy order, only applies if made in good faith, for value and *without notice* of the petition (*see* 5:4).

(*f*) *The making of a bankruptcy order or winding-up order against the customer.* (A winding-up order would only apply to a customer who is a registered company.) It is the making of the order, not notice of it, which terminates the bank's authority to pay.

(*g*) *Knowledge of a defect in the presenter's title.* A banker may know, for example, that the presenter is an undischarged bankrupt. The cheque should not be paid in this case because the proceeds might belong to the presenter's trustee in bankruptcy.

NOTE: It is unusual for a banker to have knowledge of a defect in the presenter's title.

(*h*) *Where the cheque is a misapplication of funds.* If the banker either knows or should know that this is so, he is liable to his customer should he pay the cheque, e.g. where an official of a company signs company cheques for the purchase of its own shares (*see* 4:**14**).

12. Possible liability of a paying banker.

(*a*) *Wrongful debit of an account.* A banker is liable in damages to his customer if he wrongly debits his account. There are four situations in which he would do so.

(*i*) After his customer has countermanded payment (*see* **11** above).

(*ii*) Where he pays a post-dated cheque before the proper date for payment (*see* **5** above). His customer can stop the cheque before the payment date and an early payment could result in other cheques being dishonoured for apparent lack of funds.

(*iii*) Where his customer's signature on the cheque has been forged: Bills of Exchange Act 1882, s.24. Estoppel may, however, prevent the customer from denying its genuineness: *Greenwood* v. *Martins Bank Ltd.* (1932) (*see* 11:**28**).

NOTE: The holders of a joint account have both joint and several (independent) rights against the bank. Hence, on a "both to sign" mandate a banker is liable to the innocent account holder should he pay a cheque signed by one joint account holder who has forged the signature of the other: *Jackson* v. *White and Midland Bank Ltd.* (1967). Similarly, if he allows a withdrawal to be made by one account holder only, e.g. a transfer to another account, he is liable to the other, who can *independently* enforce repayment of the amount withdrawn: *Catlin* v. *Cyprus Finance Corporation (London) Ltd.* (1982).

(*iv*) Where the cheque has been materially altered without his customer's consent. Usually this would be a fraudulent increase in the amount of the cheque.

A cheque which has been visibly altered is void against all parties to it who have not consented to the alteration; but if the alteration is not apparent, a holder in due course is entitled to the original amount for which the cheque was drawn. Anybody else presenting the cheque is entitled to nothing: Bills of Exchange Act 1882, s.64(1).

Apart from the partial protection relating to crossings on cheques provided by ss.79 and 80 of the 1882 Act (*see* **13** below), a banker has no statutory protection if he pays a cheque which has been materially altered. This applies whether or not the alteration is apparent.

A customer does, however, owe a duty to draw cheques with reasonable care in order to avoid fraudulent alterations. A banker may debit his customer's account where the latter's negligence has facilitated the fraud: *London Joint Stock Bank* v. *Macmillan and Arthur* (1918) (*see* II:**28**).

NOTE: The protection of the Rule in *Macmillan and Arthur* (1918) only applies to (1) cheques; on which (2) the alteration is not apparent; and (3) where the customer's negligence facilitated the alteration.

In practice a banker will seldom be the innocent victim of a fraudulently altered cheque. If he pays a visibly altered cheque without confirmation of the alteration he has only himself to blame, and most non-apparent alterations will be the result of his customer's negligence, thereby enabling him to rely on the Rule in *Macmillan and Arthur* (1918).

(*b*) *Wrongful dishonour of a cheque.* Should this happen (it is very unusual), a banker is liable in damages to his customer for *breach of contract* and possibly *libel*.

An action for libel would be based on the argument that the words used in stating the reason for dishonour are defamatory. The phrase "Refer to drawer" could be defamatory because it has the generally accepted connotation that the drawer of the cheque has no money in his account and this, it is argued, causes him to be lowered in the estimation of others. Alternatively, and perhaps more realistically today, it could carry the connotation that the drawer has been acting dishonestly by using worthless cheques—in so far as he knows that they will be dishonoured—to obtain goods and services. (Consequently, it is advisable wherever possible to state a technical reason for returning a cheque.)

For breach of contract, a *trader* is entitled to reasonable compensation for injury to his reputation and credit without proof of actual damage. A *non-trader* must generally prove actual damage to be awarded more than nominal damages: *Gibbons* v. *Westminster Bank Ltd*. (1939).

If, however, the cheque was returned to its presenter stating a reason for dishonour which was subsequently held to be libellous, a non-trader's claim would not be limited to nominal damages.

In practice, litigation can usually be avoided by the bank admitting its mistake and making a prompt apology to its customer and the presenter of the cheque.

NOTE: Where there are insufficient funds in a current account to meet a cheque, but sufficient funds in a deposit account, a banker is not obliged to pay the cheque. He will normally do so, however, because he is entitled to a *lien* on the deposit account to the extent of the overdraft on the current account.

(*c*) *To the cheque's true owner*. Section 59 of the 1882 Act requires payment to be made to the holder of a cheque, in good faith and without notice of any defect in title. If a banker pays a person not entitled to the cheque, he is liable at common law for conversion of the cheque to its true owner.

NOTE: Conversion is committed where a person deals with property belonging to another in a manner which denies the owner's title and right to possess the property.

Such a position would be untenable in modern banking since a banker is seldom in a position to know whether the presenter of a cheque has a good title to it. Therefore, reasonable protection against the possibility of innocently committing conversion when paying cheques is necessary.

The protection is discussed in the next section but note that it will be lost, rendering him liable to the true owner, when he fails to fulfil the statutory prerequisites for it.

13. The paying banker's protection.

(*a*) *Payment in due course*. Bills of Exchange Act 1882, s.59. Payment by the banker (*i*) to the holder of the cheque; (*ii*) in good faith; and (*iii*) without notice of any defect in his title discharges the cheque.

All parties to the cheque are discharged.

(*b*) *Forged and unauthorised indorsements*. Section 60 of the 1882 Act protects a banker against liability to the holder (the true owner) if he pays a cheque (open or crossed) which bears a forged or unauthorised indorsement provided he pays in good faith and in the ordinary course of business.

(*i*) *In good faith.* Payment of a cheque knowing that an indorsement on it was a forgery would not be payment in good faith, but a *negligent payment* is protected by s.60: *Carpenters' Co.* v. *British Mutual Banking Co.* (1938). Payment in good faith therefore means an *honest* payment.

(*ii*) *In the ordinary course of business.* This is payment according to current banking practice and within normal banking hours. For example, a crossed cheque should only be paid through a bank account, and an open cheque cashed over the counter must appear to be properly indorsed.

NOTE: In *Baines* v. *National Provincial Bank Ltd.* (1927), it was held that a bank is allowed a reasonable period of time to complete its business after its advertised closing time. Thus, in this case the bank was allowed to debit its customer's account with a cheque cashed five minutes after closing time and a countermand the following morning was ineffective.

Payment of an open cheque to an unusual presenter, e.g. an "office boy", particularly if it is drawn for a substantial amount, would probably not be payment in the ordinary course of business. However, the payment of bills or cheques for large sums over the counter is not in itself outside the ordinary course of business: *Auchteroni* v. *Midland Bank Ltd.* (1928).

Payment under s.60 of the Act is deemed to be payment *in due course*. The cheque is therefore discharged as is the liability of the drawer on it. If the cheque actually or constructively reached the payee before its payment, the drawer will, in addition, be discharged from liability on the consideration for which the cheque was originally given, and he is not liable to make a second payment to him.

NOTE: Section 60 only applies to cheques and affords no protection if the drawer's signature is forged.

The Cheques Act 1957, s.1. (*see* below) has greatly reduced the practical significance of s.60 but it remains important wherever indorsement of a cheque is still necessary because a banker will seldom be in a position to know whether any indorsements on a cheque drawn by its customer are genuine or forged. Without, s.60's protection, a banker would have to make a second payment to the cheque's true owner, having already paid the person presenting it, but would not be able to debit the customer's account.

(c) *Crossed cheques.* Protection in relation to crossed cheques is provided by the proviso in s.79(2) and by s.80 of the 1882 Act.

The proviso in s.79(2) protects the payment of a cheque in good faith and without negligence on which the crossing is not apparent, or on which the crossing has been obliterated, added to or altered and this is not apparent.

Section 80 protects a banker against the liability to the true owner if he pays a cheque: (*i*) in good faith; (*ii*) without negligence, and (*iii*) in accordance with the crossing. A banker is placed in the same position under this section as if he had paid the true owner. He can, therefore, debit his customer's account with the amount of the cheque.

NOTE: The section provides no protection against other material alterations of a cheque. These render a cheque void: Bills of Exchange Act 1882, s.64(1). Protection is only afforded against alterations to crossings by s.79(2) and even here the alteration must not be apparent.

Once a crossed cheque has actually or constructively reached the payee, under s.80, the drawer is also regarded as being in the same position as if the true owner had been paid. He is discharged from liability on the original consideration given for the cheque. In other words, he cannot be made to pay again.

NOTE: The protection of s.80 has seldom, if ever, been relied on by a paying banker. A forged or unauthorised indorsement is by far the most likely defect on a cheque which will involve a banker and s.60 already provides adequate protection where this occurs. In practice, therefore, s.80 virtually duplicates the protection of s.60 while only applying to crossed cheques and requiring a banker to have acted without negligence.

(d) *Cheques not indorsed or irregularly indorsed.* Under the Cheques Act 1957, s.1(1), a banker who pays a cheque drawn on him which is not indorsed or which is irregularly indorsed is deemed to have paid it in due course provided he pays it: (*i*) in good faith; and (*ii*) in the ordinary course of business.

NOTE: The Cheques Act 1957 was passed following the report of the Mocatta Committee, its object being to dispense with the need for indorsement of cheques which were being paid directly into the payee's account.

Thus, if a paying banker fails to obtain an indorsement which he knows to be necessary, he cannot rely on the Cheques Act 1957, s.1(1), because he would not be paying in the ordinary course of business.

If, however, a cheque is indorsed as required, e.g. a negotiated order cheque, but the indorsement proves to be *irregular*, he may rely on s.1(1). If it proves to be *forged or unauthorised*, he may rely on the Bills of Exchange Act 1882, s.60.

An *irregular indorsement* is genuine enough, it merely does not conform to banking practice, while a *forged or unauthorised indorsement* is one written on the cheque without the holder's authority.

As with the Bills of Exchange Act 1882, s.60, payment under the Cheques Act 1957, s.1(1), is deemed to be payment in due course. Therefore it protects a paying banker from an action for conversion brought by the true owner of the cheque and entitles him to debit his customer's account.

The cheque is discharged, and if it actually or constructively reached the payee before being paid, the drawer is discharged from liability on the original consideration given for the cheque.

NOTE: Bankers have not fully relied on the Cheques Act 1957, s.1, and by a resolution of the Committee of London Clearing Bankers in 1957 the following instruments still require indorsement before payment. (1) Cheques and other instruments cashed at the counter. This includes the situation where the customer presents his own cheque for payment. If, however, the cheque is made payable to "Cash" or to "Wages", no indorsement is required. (2) Order cheques which are to be paid into an account other than that of the original payee, i.e. order cheques which have been negotiated. (3) Bills of exchange other than cheques. (4) Combined cheques and receipt forms marked "R". (5) Promissory notes. (6) Travellers' cheques.

14. Payment of conditional orders. The payment of an open conditional order which bears a forged or unauthorised indorsement is not protected by either the Bills of Exchange Act 1882, s.60, or the Stamp Act 1853, s.19 (its predecessor).

The protection of the Bills of Exchange Act 1882, s.80, is extended to the payment of crossed conditional orders by the Cheques Act 1957, s.5.

The Cheques Act 1957, s.1(2), protects the payment of a conditional order which is not indorsed, or which is irregularly indorsed. The section could also protect payment under a forged indorsement (but not an unauthorised one) if a forged indorsement was held to be no indorsement at all.

15. Payment of bankers' drafts. Protection against payment on a forged or unauthorised indorsement is provided by the Stamp Act 1853, s.19. (A banker's draft is not a cheque and therefore the Bills of Exchange Act 1882, s.60, does not apply.)

The protection of the Bills of Exchange Act 1882, s.80, is extended to the payment of crossed bankers' drafts by the Cheques Act 1957, s.5.

The Cheques Act 1957, s.1(2), protects the payment of a banker's draft which is not indorsed or which is irregularly indorsed.

16. Payment of dividend or interest warrants. These warrants are often drawn in the form of cheques, in which case the legal rules relating to cheques apply to them. These include the statutory protection afforded to a paying (and collecting) banker.

If the warrant is not a cheque, payment on a forged or unauthorised indorsement is protected by the Stamp Act 1853, s.19.

The crossed cheque sections of the Bills of Exchange Act 1882, including the protection of s.80, apply to such warrants: Bills of Exchange Act 1882, s.95.

17. Cheque cards. Cheque cards are a means of identification which (*a*) enable a customer to cash cheques up to a prescribed limit (at present £50) at branch banks other than the one at which he has his account; and (*b*) guarantee that a cheque taken in payment "backed" by the card will be honoured (subject to a prescribed limit—at present £50) whatever the state of the customer's account.

NOTE: (1) The use of cheque cards is now very common. In ordinary retail sales a cheque will frequently not be accepted in payment unless it is "backed" by a valid cheque card. (2) The misuse of a cheque card by a customer to obtain an unauthorised overdraft is an offence under the Theft Act 1968, s.16: *Metropolitan Police Commissioner* v. *Charles* (1976).

Whenever a cheque card is used, the cheque must be signed in the presence of the other party, and if taken in payment, the *payee* must write the number of the cheque card on the back of the cheque.

The use of cheque cards to "back" cheques involves two separate contracts, one between the banker and customer, and one between the banker and payee.

In the former, the customer agrees to use the card in accordance with the conditions of its issue and use, and acknowledges that he cannot countermand payment of a cheque guaranteed by the card. Subject to the current limit, the banker undertakes to honour any cheque drawn and delivered to the payee who takes it relying on the card.

In the latter, the banker undertakes to honour a cheque (up to the current limit) taken in payment provided the payee takes it relying on the card and according to the instructions printed on it.

Should the cheque be negotiated, the holder gains the benefit of the bank's undertaking and he can enforce payment against the bank. However, the bank's liability to pay is not based on the cheque itself, it is based on the contract created by the use of the cheque card.

The collecting banker

18. Possible liability of a collecting banker.

(*a*) *To his customer.* A banker acts as an agent when he presents cheques and other bills of exchange for payment on his customer's behalf.

If he fails to present an instrument for payment in accordance with the Bills of Exchange Act 1882, s.45 (*see* 11:**44**), and established banking practice, he will be liable to his customer for breach of contract.

He would incur similar liability as an agent if he fails to give notice of dishonour in accordance with the Bills of Exchange Act 1882, ss.48 and 49 (*see* 11:**45**).

(*b*) *To the cheque's true owner*. A banker commits the tort of conversion against its true owner if he collects a cheque on behalf of a customer who has no title to it.

NOTE: At common law, it is no defence in an action for conversion to establish that the tort was committed innocently. Thus, a banker cannot be expected to undertake the collection of cheques for his customers without reasonable protection from such liability.

19. A collecting banker's statutory protection.

(*a*) *The Cheques Act 1957, s.4*. This section applies where a banker in good faith and without negligence:

(*i*) receives payment for a customer of an instrument to which the section applies; or

(*ii*) having credited a customer's account with the amount of such an instrument, receives payment thereof for himself.

It provides that he incurs no liability to the true owner of the instrument where his customer has either a defective title or no title at all to the instrument merely because he received payment of it: Cheques Act 1957, s.4(1).

NOTE: The protection applies both when a banker collects as an agent and when he collects for himself (as holder of the cheque) having already credited the cheque to his customer's account.

The protection covers the collection of the following instruments: Cheques Act 1957, s.4(2):

(*i*) cheques;

(*ii*) documents issued by a customer which are valid mandates to his banker, but which are not bills of exchange, i.e. conditional orders, cheques payable to impersonal payees and dividend and interest warrants;

(*iii*) documents issued by a public officer which are intended to enable a person to obtain payment from the Paymaster General or the Queen's and Lord Treasurer's Remembrancer, but which are not bills of exchange, e.g. Paymaster General Warrants;

(*iv*) bankers' drafts.

The section applies to both crossed and uncrossed instruments, but it does not apply to bills of exchange other than cheques.

(*b*) *Conditions of protection*. A banker must act as follows:

(*i*) *For a customer*. A customer is a person who has entered into a contract with a banker for the opening of an account in his name (*see* 1:**1**).

(*ii*) *In good faith*. Honesty is required, but negligence is not evidence of bad faith: Bills of Exchange Act 1882, s.90. (Section 90 applies to the Cheques Act 1957, s.4, by virtue of s.6(1) of that Act.)

(*iii*) *Without negligence*. The Cheques Act 1957, s.4(3), provides that a banker is not to be treated as negligent purely because the instrument collected was not indorsed or was irregularly indorsed.

In all other cases, the banker must establish that he acted with reasonable care. This is because the true owner of the instrument is deprived of his common law right to compensation by the Cheques Act 1957, s.4.

The duty to act without negligence is owed to the person who would suffer loss if the collection proved to be unlawful, i.e. the true owner of the instrument: *Lloyds Bank Ltd.* v. *E. B. Savory & Co.* (1933). The *standard of care* required is that of the ordinary competent banker.

More recent decisions would seem to show a less severe judicial attitude to the possible negligence of bankers than rather older decisions; *Savory's Case* (1933) can be compared with the *Orbit Mining and Trading Co. Case* (1963) and *Marfani's Case* (1968) in this respect: *see* below.

Indeed, in *Marfani's Case* (1968) the Court of Appeal accepted the contention that the current practice of careful bankers is unlikely to be negligent. This suggests that when an instance of possible negligence arises, the courts will prefer to look for guidance to modern banking practice rather than to decisions made decades ago. This does not mean, however, that current banking practice will never itself be held to be negligent.

NOTE: A banker can plead the Law Reform (Contributory Negligence) Act 1945 in an action for conversion in a case within the Cheques Act 1957, s.4. A successful plea will reduce the damages awarded. The defence would be applicable where the owner of cheques carelessly left them lying around, facilitating their fraudulent use. It also applies where carelessly drawn cheques are fraudulently altered: *Lumsden & Co.* v. *London Trustee Savings Bank* (1971). (A collecting banker cannot avail himself of the Rule in *Macmillan and Arthur* (1918).)

(c) *Instances of negligence*. Each instance of negligence depends very much on its own facts, and decided cases should be viewed as *guides* rather than hard and fast rules. However, the common theme in decisions against bankers has been either absence of inquiry where it was reasonably called for, or the unsatisfactory nature of inquiries which were made.

(i) Failure to make reasonable inquiries before opening an account.

EXAMPLE: In *Ladbroke & Co.* v. *Todd* (1914), a cheque crossed "Account payee" was stolen in transit. The thief fraudulently indorsed the payee's name and opened an account with the cheque at the defendant bank posing as the payee. At his request the cheque was specially cleared and the next day he withdrew the proceeds and disappeared. HELD: while the thief had become a customer of the bank, it had been negligent in opening the account and therefore lost the protection of the Bills of Exchange Act 1882, s.82 (the predecessor of the Cheques Act 1957, s.4(1)).

References are probably not required where the prospective customer is already known to the bank as a suitable person, or introduced by a person of similar standing.

NOTE: Unless the referee is personally known to the bank, e.g. where he is an existing customer, the authenticity of the reference should be checked, e.g. through his own bank: *Hampstead Guardians* v. *Barclays Bank Ltd* (1923), confirmed in *Lumsden & Co.* v. *London Trustee Savings Bank* (1971).

The decision in *Marfani & Co. Ltd.* v. *Midland Bank Ltd.* (1968), indicates that while basic inquiries must be made, it is impossible to be categorical concerning the nature and extent of them.

FACTS: The plaintiff company's office manager prepared a cheque for £3,000 payable to Eliaszade, a firm with which the plaintiff did business, and obtained Marfani's signature upon it. The manager opened an account with the cheque at the defendant bank posing as Eliaszade, giving as a referee a person who knew him by this false name. Over the next two weeks the £3,000 was withdrawn and the plaintiff company brought an action against the bank for conversion of the cheque. HELD (C.A.): the defendant bank had not been negligent in opening the account and they were protected by the Cheques Act 1957, s.4(1). Evidence was given by other bankers that the defendants had acted as reasonable bankers and the following circumstances were held not to constitute negligence: (1) opening an account after only one reference had been received without further inquiries (the referee was a respected customer of six years' standing and the second referee's failure to reply was satisfactorily explained by the mobility of the ethnic community to which he belonged); (2) failure to ask the new customer to produce his passport (he was a Pakistani); and (3) clearing the cheque before receiving the reference.

(*ii*) Failure to check the information disclosed under the Business Names Act 1985 (*see* 3:**18**) before opening an account in a trade name.

NOTE: In *Smith and Baldwin* v. *Barclays Bank Ltd.* (1944), the defendant bank collected cheques payable to a firm for the private account of its customer after he had produced a certificate of registration (in the now defunct Register of Business Names) showing him to be its registered proprietor. The customer, however, was a partner in the firm and had been able to obtain the certificate because the partners collectively had not registered the firm name. HELD: the bank had not collected the cheques negligently. It was entitled to rely on the certificate produced by its dishonest customer. (This case can by analogy be applied to a situation where the requirements of the Business Names Act 1985 are not met by a firm, in particular, where the names of one or more partners have not been disclosed.)

(*iii*) Failure to obtain the name of its customer's employer or, in the case of married customers, the name of the spouse's employer.

EXAMPLE: In *Lloyds Bank Ltd.* v. *E. B. Savory & Co.* (1933), two stockbroker's clerks stole a number of crossed bearer cheques from their employers and paid them in at city branches of the defendant bank for accounts at country branches. One account was in the name of one clerk and one in the name of the other's wife. Neither branch had inquired as to who were the employers of the clerk in the one case, and the customer's husband in the other. The respondent sought damages for conversion of the cheques. HELD: the bank had been negligent and therefore was not protected by the Bills of Exchange Act 1882, s.82 (now the Cheques Act 1957, s.4).

NOTE: The common feature in the above instances is negligence in opening the account.

(*iv*) Crediting cheques payable to a company to the private account of an official of the company. This applies even where it is a one-man company: *A. L. Underwood* v. *Bank of Liverpool and Martins Ltd.* (1924).

NOTE: In *Orbit Mining and Trading Co. Ltd.* v. *Westminster Bank Ltd.* (1963), the defendant's customer, a co-director of the plaintiff company, had requested and obtained the other co-director's signature on a number of blank cheques, both signatures being required on the account. These he completed to "Cash or order" and countersigned them with his own virtually illegible signature. He paid them into an existing private account at the defendant bank, the bank being ignorant of his employment with the company. The company sought damages for conversion. HELD: the defendant bank had not been negligent. On the facts, the circumstances did not warrant inquiry. (N.B. The decision is also authority for the proposition that merely failing to observe internal rules does not necessarily constitute negligence. The rules may be *counsels of perfection*, and exceed the standard of reasonable care.)

(*v*) Crediting a private account of an agent or of an employee with cheques drawn by him on the account of his principal or employer.

EXAMPLE: In *Midland Bank Ltd.* v. *Reckitt* (1933), the bank were held to have acted negligently in collecting for the personal account of a solicitor cheques drawn by him on the account of a customer for whom he acted as attorney. A relevant factor was that the bank had previously asked him to reduce his overdraft. The customer's power of attorney did not remove the need to make inquiries.

(*vi*) Crediting an agent's private account with cheques expressly payable to him in his capacity as an agent.

EXAMPLE: In *Marquess of Bute* v. *Barclays Bank Ltd.* (1955), the bank was held to have acted negligently in collecting for the private account of an agent three warrants made payable to him because in brackets on the cheques were the words "for Marquess of Bute".

(*vii*) Crediting cheques payable to the holder of a public office to his private account: *Ross* v. *London City Westminster and Parr's Bank Ltd*. (1919).

NOTE: The instances of negligence in (*iv–vii*) above all concern negligence in collecting cheques where the customer has broken his fiduciary duty to the drawer of payee of the cheque. The instances below are examples of cheques being collected without sufficient inquiry where *unusual circumstances demanded particular care*.

(*viii*) Collecting without satisfactory explanation a cheque payable to a limited company for the account of another company: *London & Montrose Shipbuilding & Repairing Co*. v. *Barclays Bank Ltd*. (1926).

NOTE: Collection in such circumstances is permissible if the payee company specially indorsed the cheque to the other company, or where general instructions exist concerning such credits.

(*ix*) Collecting without satisfactory explanation cheques, particularly third party cheques, for amounts inconsistent with its customer's activities.

EXAMPLE: In *Nu-Stilo Footwear Ltd*. v. *Lloyds Bank Ltd*. (1956), the plaintiff's company secretary opened an account in an assumed name. He gave his real name as referee. The first cheque paid in was drawn in his own favour and for a modest sum but the second cheque was a third party cheque for £550. While the bank was held not to have been negligent in opening the account, nor in collecting the first cheque, it had been negligent in collecting the second and other subsequent cheques, some of which were also third party cheques, because the amounts were inconsistent with its customer's stated occupation as an agent newly started in business.

(*x*) Collecting without satisfactory explanation third party cheques where the customer had previously proved to be unreliable.

EXAMPLE: In *Motor Traders Guarantee Corporation Ltd*. v. *Midland Bank Ltd*. (1937), a customer had induced the plaintiff to draw a cheque crossed "Not negotiable" in favour of a firm of car dealers, purportedly in payment for a car. He forged the firm's indorsement and paid the cheque into his own account at the defendant's bank. The cashier accepted his explanation that the cheque had been negotiated to him. On the facts the bank had acted negligently because in the six months that the account had been open some thirty-five cheques had been dishonoured. In addition the branch rules required that the manager should have decided whether the cheque was to be accepted for the credit of the customer.

(*xi*) Collecting third party cheques without sufficient inquiry where the circumstances demand it.

EXAMPLE: In *Baker* v. *Barclays Bank Ltd*. (1955), the defendant bank acted negligently in not making sufficient inquiries before paying cheques payable to a partnership and indorsed by one of two partners into its customer's previously dormant account. The manager had accepted the customer's explanation that the indorser was the sole proprietor of the firm and that he (the customer) was helping him in the business with a view to joining him in a partnership.

(*xii*) Collecting without sufficient explanation "Account payee" cheques for someone other than the named payee: *House Property Co. of London Ltd. & others* v. *London County & Westminster Bank Ltd*. (1915). The effect of the words is, however, merely to put the banker on inquiry, if his inquiries are reasonably answered he retains the protection of the Cheques Act 1957, s.4.

NOTE: There is no duty on a banker to make inquiries where he collects a cheque crossed "Not negotiable": *Crumplin* v. *London Joint Stock Bank* (1913).

(*xiii*) Negligence when a banker both pays and collects a cheque. A banker acting as both paying and collecting banker must satisfy the statutory requirements for protection in *both* capacities to avoid liability in conversion to the true owner of the cheque. That is, he must satisfy the requirements of the Cheques Act 1957, s.4(1), when collecting the cheque, and those of the Bills of Exchange Act 1882, s.60 (or the Cheques Act 1957, s.1, plus those of the Bills of Exchange Act 1882, s.80, if the cheque is crossed), when paying the cheque.

EXAMPLE: In *Carpenters' Co.* v. *British Mutual Banking Co. Ltd*.

(1938), the defendant's customer stole cheques drawn by the company, his employer, payable to third parties. He forged the indorsements of the payees and paid them into his own account, the company's account also being held at the same office of the bank, in fact the bank's sole office. HELD: although the bank's payment satisfied the Bills of Exchange Act 1882, s.60, it was negligent in failing to inquire why its customer was paying his employer's cheques into his own account and could not, therefore, rely on the Cheques Act 1957, s.4. This being so, it forfeited the protection of the Bills of Exchange Act 1882, s.60.

20. Protection as holder in due course.

(*a*) *Introduction.* The Cheques Act 1957, s.4(1), protects a banker when he acts as agent for his customer, merely receiving payment for him, or receiving payment for himself after crediting his customer's account.

If, however, he gives value (consideration) for the cheque, he will be collecting for himself as holder for value of the cheque and not as an agent. Consequently, he will not be protected by the Cheques Act 1957, s.4(1).

Establishing himself as holder in due course of a cheque in such circumstances gives a banker an alternative and perfect defence to an action for conversion of the cheque—at law he is the *true owner* of the instrument.

The defence has the advantage of applying even where the banker may have acted negligently but it has the disadvantage of not being available where he took the cheque under a forged indorsement, for this prevents the banker from becoming a holder. The protection of the Cheques Act 1957, s.4(1), is not lost in this latter situation.

In addition, the bank as holder in due course acquires the right to enforce the cheque against all prior parties (*see* 11:**31**). The Cheques Act 1957, s.4(1), only provides a defence.

(*b*) *Instances of giving value.*

(*i*) Allowing the customer to draw against the cheque before it has been cleared. There must, however, be an express or implied contract permitting him to do so: *A. L. Underwood Ltd.* v. *Bank of Liverpool and Martins* (1924).

A statement on a paying-in slip reserving the right to postpone or refuse payment of cheques drawn against uncleared effects prevents a banker from becoming a holder for value in such circumstances.

NOTE: No consideration is given by merely crediting the account before receiving payment.

(*ii*) Where the cheque is paid in specifically, i.e. permanently, to reduce or discharge an existing overdraft, and not in the ordinary course of business as an overdrawn account: Bills of Exchange Act 1882, s.27(1)(b).

(*iii*) Where the banker "buys" the cheque, e.g. where he cashes a cheque drawn by a third party for his customer, or where he cashes a cheque drawn on another branch by a customer of that branch without open credit arrangements.

(*iv*) Where the banker has a lien on the cheque, he is the holder for value of the cheque to the extent of the sum for which he has a lien: Bills of Exchange Act 1882, s.27(3).

A lien would arise if a cheque sent for payment by a banker acting as agent for his customer is returned unpaid and debiting his account with the cheque creates an overdraft.

NOTE: A lien is lost if a banker even temporarily gives up possession of the cheque to which the lien relates: *Westminster Bank* v. *Zang* (1966).

(*c*) *Indorsement*. The Cheques Act 1957, s.2, provides that a banker is to be considered the holder of a cheque payable to order for which he has given value, or on which he has a lien, although the previous holder delivers it to him for collection without indorsing it.

The provision is necessary because under the Bills of Exchange Act 1882, s.31(3), an order bill can only be negotiated by indorsement completed by delivery but the Cheques Act 1957, s.1, removed the need for indorsement of an order cheque paid straight into the payee's account. This section does not increase a banker's protection but merely preserves his rights as a holder when he collects a cheque which is unindorsed. Thus, the banker is then in a position to establish himself as a holder for value/holder in due course, providing he can comply with the Bills of Exchange Act 1882, ss.27 or 29, as the case may be.

The Cheques Act 1957, s.2, also applies where the holder of a cheque pays it in for the credit of a third party's account without indorsing it: *Westminster Bank Ltd.* v. *Zang* (1966).

NOTE: The Cheques Act 1957, s.2, only applies to cheques and does not confer the status of holder on a banker where a cheque is irregularly indorsed—it refers only to the absence of an indorsement.

(*d*) *The Bills of Exchange Act 1882, s.29(1)*. To be a holder in due course of a cheque received from a customer for collection, a banker must satisfy this section of the 1882 Act (*see* 11:**31**).

21. Collection of postal orders and money orders. Neither order is a negotiable instrument, and neither the Bills of Exchange Act 1882 nor the Cheques Act 1957 apply to them. If, however, they are crossed, payment will only be made to a bank in accordance with the crossing.

The Post Office Act 1953 protects a banker collecting a postal order for a principal from liability to anyone except the principal.

There is no statutory protection covering the collection of money orders. The Post Office, moreover, has the right to return a money order to a bank and deduct the amount from any money which may become due to the bank if it discovers that the order was wrongly paid. The bank can then debit an equivalent amount to its customer's account.

Progress test 12

1. Define a cheque. (**1**)
2. What is a bank draft? (**2**)
3. Are cheques made payable to impersonal payees negotiable? Give reasons. (**2**)
4. State the distinctions between cheques and other bills of exchange. (**3**)
5. When is a cheque (*a*) stale, (*b*) overdue? (**4**)
6. What is a crossing on a cheque? (**7**)
7. List the different types of crossings and explain the effect of each. (**8**)
8. Why are the words "Account payee" on a cheque not part of any crossing? What is the significance of the words? (**8**)

9. List the circumstances in which a banker's authority to pay a cheque is terminated. (**11**)

10. List the situations in which a paying banker could wrongly debit his customer's account. (**12**)

11. Explain why a banker could possibly commit libel if he wrongly dishonoured a cheque. (**12**)

12. Explain the nature of the protection afforded to a banker by (*a*) s.60, and (*b*) s.80 of the Bills of Exchange Act 1882. (**13**)

13. What is meant by "good faith" in the Bills of Exchange Act 1882, s.60? (**13**)

14. What protection does the Cheques Act 1957, s.1, give to a banker and why has s.1. reduced the practical importance of the Bills of Exchange Act 1882, s.60? (**13**)

15. What protection has a banker if he pays a crossed cheque on which the crossing has been altered? (**13**)

16. List the instruments on which an indorsement is still required before payment is made. (**13**)

17. To what extent does a paying banker's protection in relation to cheques apply to the payment of (*a*) conditional orders, (*b*) bankers' drafts, (*c*) dividend or interest warrants? (**14–16**)

18. Explain the importance of cheque cards. (**17**)

19. In what circumstances will a banker incur liability to his customer when collecting a cheque for him? (**18**)

20. Explain the protection afforded to a collecting banker by the Cheques Act 1957, s.4. (**19**)

21. Explain and illustrate three possible instances of negligence when opening an account. (**19**)

22. Explain and illustrate ten possible instances of negligence in collecting cheques for an existing account. (**19**)

23. List the situations in which a banker will be holder for value of a cheque which he collects. (**20**)

24. State two advantages to a collecting banker of being able to establish himself as holder in due course of a cheque. (**20**)

25. Outline a collecting banker's protection in relation to postal orders and money orders. (**21**)

Appendix 1
Bills of Exchange Act 1882

45 & 46 Vict. Ch. 61

PART I

Preliminary

1. This Act may be cited as the Bills of Exchange Act 1882.

2. In this Act, unless the context otherwise requires:

"Acceptance" means an acceptance completed by delivery or notification.

"Action" includes counter claim and set-off.

"Banker" includes a body of persons whether incorporated or not who carry on the business of banking.

"Bankrupt" includes any person whose estate is vested in a trustee or assignee under the law for the time being in force relating to bankruptcy.

"Bearer" means the person in possession of a bill or note which is payable to bearer.

"Bill" means bill of exchange and "note" means promissory note.

"Delivery" means transfer of possession, actual or constructive, from one person to another.

"Holder" means the payee or indorsee of a bill or note who is in possession of it, or the bearer thereof.

"Indorsement" means an indorsement completed by delivery.

"Issue" means the first delivery of a bill or note, complete in form to a person who takes it as a holder.

"Person" includes a body of persons whether incorporated or not.

"Value" means valuable consideration.

"Written" includes printed, and "writing" includes print.

PART II

BILLS OF EXCHANGE

Form and Interpretation

3. (1) A bill of exchange is an unconditional order in writing, addressed by one person to another, signed by the person giving it, requiring the person to whom it is addressed to pay on demand or at a fixed or determinable future time a sum certain in money to or to the order of a specified person, or to bearer.

(2) An instrument which does not comply with these conditions, or which orders any act to be done in addition to the payment of money, is not a bill of exchange.

(3) An order to pay out of a particular fund is not unconditional within the meaning of this section; but an unqualified order to pay, coupled with (*a*) an indication of a particular fund out of which the drawee is to re-imburse himself or a particular account to be debited with the amount, or (*b*) a statement of the transaction which gives rise to the bill, is unconditional.

(4) A bill is not invalid by reason:

(*a*) That it is not dated;

(*b*) That it does not specify the value given, or that any value has been given therefor;

(*c*) That it does not specify the place where it is drawn or the place where it is payable.

4. (1) An inland bill is a bill which is or on the face of it purports to be (*a*) both drawn and payable within the British Islands, or (*b*) drawn within the British Islands upon some person resident therein. Any other bill is a foreign bill.

For the purposes of this Act "British Islands" mean any part of the United Kingdom of Great Britain and Ireland, the islands of Man, Guernsey, Jersey, Alderney, and Sark, and the islands adjacent to any of them being part of the dominions of Her Majesty.

(2) Unless the contrary appears on the face of the bill the holder may treat it as an inland bill.

5. (1) A bill may be drawn payable to, or to the order of, the drawer; or it may be drawn payable to, or to the order of, the drawee.

(2) Where in a bill drawer and drawee are the same person, or where the drawee is a fictitious person or a person not having capacity to contract, the holder may treat the instrument, at his option, either as a bill of exchange or as a promissory note.

6. (1) The drawee must be named or otherwise indicated in a bill with reasonable certainty.

(2) A bill may be addressed to two or more drawees whether they are partners or not, but an order addressed to two drawees in the alternative or to two or more drawees in succession is not a bill of exchange.

7. (1) Where a bill is not payable to bearer, the payee must be named or otherwise indicated therein with reasonable certainty.

(2) A bill may be payable to two or more payees jointly, or it may be made payable in the alternative to one of two, or one or some of several payees. A bill may also be made payable to the holder of an office for the time being.

(3) Where the payee is a fictitious or non-existing person the bill may be treated as payable to bearer.

8. (1) When a bill contains words prohibiting transfer, or indicating an intention that it should not be transferable, it is valid as between the parties thereto, but is not negotiable.

(2) A negotiable bill may be payable either to order or to bearer.

(3) A bill is payable to bearer which is expressed to be so payable, or on which the only or last indorsement is an indorsement in blank.

(4) A bill is payable to order which is expressed to be so payable, or which is expressed to be payable to a particular person, and does not contain words prohibiting transfer or indicating an intention that it should not be transferable.

(5) Where a bill, either originally or by indorsement, is expressed to be payable to the order of a specified person, and not to him or his order, it is nevertheless payable to him or his order at his option.

9. (1) The sum payable by a bill is a sum certain within the meaning of this Act, although it is required to be paid:

(*a*) With interest.

(*b*) By stated instalments.

(*c*) By stated instalments, with a provision that upon default in payment of any instalment the whole shall become due.

(*d*) According to an indicated rate of exchange or according to a rate of exchange to be ascertained as directed by the bill.

(2) Where the sum payable is expressed in words and also in figures, and there is a discrepancy between the two, the sum denoted by the words is the amount payable.

(3) Where a bill is expressed to be payable with interest, unless the instrument otherwise provides, interest runs from the date of the bill, and if the bill is undated from the issue thereof.

10. (1) A bill is payable on demand:

(*a*) Which is expressed to be payable on demand, or at sight, or on presentation; or

(*b*) In which no time for payment is expressed.

(2) Where a bill is accepted or indorsed when it is overdue, it shall, as regards the acceptor who so accepts, or any indorser who so indorses it, be deemed a bill payable on demand.

11. A bill is payable at a determinable future time within the meaning of this Act which is expressed to be payable:

(1) At a fixed period after date or sight.

(2) On or at a fixed period after the occurrence of a specified event which is certain to happen, though the time of happening may be uncertain.

An instrument expressed to be payable on a contingency is not a bill, and the happening of the event does not cure the defect.

12. Where a bill expressed to be payable at a fixed period after date is issued undated, or where the acceptance of a bill payable at a fixed period after sight is undated, any holder may insert therein the true date of issue or acceptance, and the bill shall be payable accordingly.

Provided that (1) where the holder in good faith and by mistake inserts a wrong date, and (2) in every case where a wrong date is inserted, if the bill subsequently comes into the hands of a holder in due course the bill shall not be avoided thereby, but shall operate and be payable as if the date so inserted had been the true date.

13. (1) Where a bill or an acceptance or any indorsement on a bill is dated, the date shall, unless the contrary be proved, be deemed to be the true date of the drawing, acceptance, or indorsement, as the case may be.

(2) A bill is not invalid by reason only that it is ante-dated or post-dated, or that it bears date on a Sunday.

14. Where a bill is not payable on demand the day on which it falls due is determined as follows:

(1) The bill is due and payable in all cases on the last day of the time of payment as fixed by the bill or, if that is a non-business day, on the succeeding business day.

(This new sub-section was inserted, replacing the original sub-section, by the Banking and Financial Dealings Act 1979, s.3(2).)

(2) Where a bill is payable at a fixed period after date, after sight, or after the happening of a specified event, the time of payment is determined by excluding the day from which the time is to begin to run and by including the day of payment.

(3) Where a bill is payable at a fixed period after sight, the time begins to run from the date of the acceptance if the bill be accepted, and from the date of noting or protest if the bill be noted or protested for non-acceptance, or for non-delivery.

(4) The term "month" in a bill means calendar month.

15. The drawer of a bill and any indorser may insert therein the name of a person to whom the holder may resort in case of need, that is to say, in case the bill is dishonoured by non-acceptance or non-payment. Such person is called the referee in case of need. It is in the option of the holder to resort to the referee in case of need or not as he may think fit.

16. The drawer of a bill, and any indorser, may insert therein an express stipulation:

(1) Negativing or limiting his own liability to the holder;

(2) Waiving as regards himself some or all of the holder's duties.

17. (1) The acceptance of a bill is the signification by the drawee of his assent to the order of the drawer.

(2) An acceptance is invalid unless it complies with the following conditions, namely:

(*a*) It must be written on the bill and be signed by the drawee. The mere signature of the drawee without additional words is sufficient.

(*b*) It must not express that the drawee will perform his promise by any other means than the payment of money.

18. A bill may be accepted:

(1) Before it has been signed by the drawer, or while otherwise incomplete;

(2) When it is overdue, or after it has been dishonoured by a previous refusal to accept, or by non-payment;

(3) When a bill payable after sight is dishonoured by non-acceptance, and the drawee subsequently accepts it, the holder, in the absence of any different agreement, is entitled to have the bill accepted as of the date of first presentment to the drawee for acceptance.

19. (1) An acceptance is either (*a*) general or (*b*) qualified.

(2) A general acceptance assents without qualification to the order of the drawer. A qualified acceptance in express terms varies the effect of the bill as drawn.

In particular an acceptance is qualified which is:

(*a*) Conditional, that is to say, which makes payment by the acceptor dependent on the fulfilment of a condition therein stated;

(*b*) Partial, that is to say, an acceptance to pay part only of the amount for which the bill is drawn;

(*c*) Local, that is to say, an acceptance to pay only at a particular specified place.

An acceptance to pay at a particular place is a general acceptance, unless it expressly states that the bill is to be paid there only and not elsewhere;

(*d*) Qualified as to time;

(*e*) The acceptance of some one or more of the drawees, but not of all.

20. (1) Where a simple signature on a blank [stamped] paper is delivered by the signer in order that it may be converted into a bill, it operates as a prima facie authority to fill it up as a complete bill for any amount [the stamp will cover,] using the signature for that of the drawer, or the acceptor, or an indorser; and, in like manner, when a bill is wanting in any material particular, the person in possession of it has a prima facie authority to fill up the omission in any way he thinks fit. (Words in square brackets deleted by the Finance Act 1970.)

(2) In order that any such instrument when completed may be enforceable against any person who became a party thereto prior to its completion, it must be filled up within a reasonable time, and strictly in accordance with the authority given. Reasonable time for this purpose is a question of fact.

Provided that if any such instrument after completion is negotiated to a holder in due course it shall be valid and effectual for all purposes in his hands, and he may enforce it as if it had been filled up within a reasonable time and strictly in accordance with the authority given.

21. (1) Every contract on a bill, whether it be the drawer's, the acceptor's, or an indorser's, is incomplete and revocable, until delivery of the instrument in order to give effect thereto.

Provided that where an acceptance is written on a bill, and the drawee gives notice to or according to the directions of the person entitled to the bill that he has accepted it, the acceptance then becomes complete and irrevocable.

(2) As between immediate parties, and as regards a remote party other than a holder in due course, the delivery:

(*a*) In order to be effectual must be made either by or under the authority of the party drawing, accepting, or indorsing, as the case may be:

(*b*) May be shown to have been conditional or for a special purpose only, and not for the purpose of transferring the property in the bill.

But if the bill be in the hands of a holder in due course a valid delivery of the bill by all parties prior to him so as to make them liable to him is conclusively presumed.

(3) Where a bill is no longer in the possession of a party who has signed it as drawer, acceptor, or indorser, a valid and unconditional delivery by him is presumed until the contrary is proved.

Capacity and Authority of Parties

22. (1) Capacity to incur liability as a party to a bill is coextensive with capacity to contract.

Provided that nothing in this section shall enable a corporation to make itself liable as drawer, acceptor, or indorser of a bill unless it is competent for it so to do under the law for the time being in force relating to corporations.

(2) Where a bill is drawn or indorsed by an infant, minor, or corporation having no capacity or power to incur liability on a bill, the drawing or indorsement entitles the holder to receive payment of a bill, and to enforce it against any other party thereto.

23. No person is liable as drawer, indorser, or acceptor of a bill who has not signed it as such: Provided that:

(1) Where a person signs a bill in a trade or assumed name, he is liable thereon as if he had signed it in his own name;

(2) The signature of the name of a firm is equivalent to the signature by the person so signing of the names of all persons liable as partners in that firm.

24. Subject to the provisions of this Act, where a signature on a bill is forged or placed thereon without the authority of the person whose signature it purports to be, the forged or unauthorised signature is wholly inoperative, and no right to retain the bill or to give a discharge therefor or to enforce payment thereof against any party thereto can be acquired through or under that signature, unless the party against whom it is sought to retain or enforce payment of the bill is precluded from setting up the forgery or want of authority.

Provided that nothing in this section shall affect the ratification of an unauthorised signature not amounting to a forgery.

25. A signature by procuration operates as notice that the agent has but a limited authority to sign, and the principal is only bound by such signature if the agent in so signing was acting within the actual limits of his authority.

26. (1) Where a person signs a bill as a drawer, indorser, or acceptor, and adds words to his signature, indicating that he signs for or on behalf of a principal, or in a representative character, he is not personally liable thereon; but the mere addition to his signature of words describing him as an agent, or as filling a representative character, does not exempt him from personal liability.

(2) In determining whether a signature on a bill is that of the principal or that of the agent by whose hand it is written, the construction most favourable to the validity of the instrument shall be adopted.

The Consideration for a Bill

27. (1) Valuable consideration for a bill may be constituted by:

(*a*) Any consideration sufficient to support a simple contract;

(*b*) An antecedent debt or liability. Such a debt or liability is deemed valuable consideration whether the bill is payable on demand or at a future time.

(2) Where value has at any time been given for a bill the holder is deemed to be a holder for value as regards the acceptor and all parties to the bill who became parties prior to such time.

(3) Where the holder of a bill has a lien on it, arising either from contract or by implication of law, he is deemed to be a holder for value to the extent of the sum for which he has a lien.

28. (1) An accommodation party to a bill is a person who has signed a bill as drawer, acceptor, or indorser, without receiving value therefore, and for the purpose of lending his name to some other person.

(2) An accommodation party is liable on the bill to a holder for value; and it is immaterial whether, when such holder took the bill, he knew such party to be an accommodation party or not.

29. (1) A holder in due course is a holder who has taken a bill, complete and regular on the face of it, under the following conditions; namely:

(*a*) That he became the holder of it before it was overdue, and without notice that it had been previously dishonoured, if such was the fact;

(*b*) That he took the bill in good faith and for value, and that at the time the bill was negotiated to him he had no notice of any defect in the title of the person who negotiated it.

(2) In particular the title of a person who negotiates a bill is defective within the meaning of this Act when he obtained the bill, or the acceptance thereof, by fraud, duress, or force and fear, or other unlawful means, or for an illegal consideration, or when he negotiates it in breach of faith, or under such circumstances as amount to a fraud.

(3) A holder (whether for value or not), who derives his title to a bill through a holder in due course, and who is not himself a party to any fraud or illegality affecting it, has all the rights of that holder in due course as regards the acceptor and all parties to the bill prior to that holder.

30. (1) Every party whose signature appears on a bill is prima facie deemed to have become a party thereto for value.

(2) Every holder of a bill is prima facie deemed to be a holder in due course; but if in an action on a bill it is admitted or proved that the acceptance, issue, or subsequent negotiation of the bill is affected with fraud, duress, or force and fear, or illegality, the burden of proof is shifted, unless and until the holder proves that, subsequent to the alleged fraud or illegality, value has in good faith been given for the bill.

Negotiation of Bills

31. (1) A bill is negotiated when it is transferred from one person to another in such a manner as to constitute the transferee the holder of the bill.

(2) A bill payable to bearer is negotiated by delivery.

(3) A bill payable to order is negotiated by the indorsement of the holder completed by delivery.

(4) Where the holder of a bill payable to his order transfers it for value without indorsing it, the transfer gives the transferee such title as the transferor had in the bill, and the transferee in addition acquires the right to have the indorsement of the transferor.

(5) Where any person is under obligation to indorse a bill in a representative capacity, he may indorse the bill in such terms as to negative personal liability.

32. An indorsement in order to operate as a negotiation must comply with the following conditions, namely:

(1) It must be written on the bill itself and be signed by the indorser. The simple signature of the indorser on the bill, without additional words, is sufficient.

An indorsement written on an allonge, or on a "copy" of a bill issued or negotiated in a country where "copies" are recognised, is deemed to be written on the bill itself.

(2) It must be an indorsement of the entire bill. A partial indorsement, that is to say, an indorsement which purports to transfer to the indorsee a part only of the amount payable, or which purports to transfer the bill to two or more indorsees severally, does not operate as a negotiation of the bill.

(3) Where a bill is payable to the order of two or more payees or indorsees who are not partners all must indorse, unless the one indorsing has authority to indorse for the others.

(4) Where, in a bill payable to order, the payee or indorsee is wrongly designated, or his name is mis-spelt, he may indorse the bill as therein described, adding, if he think fit, his proper signature.

(5) Where there are two or more indorsements on a bill, each indorsement is deemed to have been made in the order in which it appears on the bill, until the contrary is proved.

(6) An indorsement may be made in blank or special. It may also contain terms making it restrictive.

33. Where a bill purports to be indorsed conditionally the condition may be disregarded by the payer, and payment to the indorsee is valid whether the condition has been fulfilled or not.

34. (1) An indorsement in blank specifies no indorsee, and a bill so indorsed becomes payable to bearer.

(2) A special indorsement specifies the person to whom, or to whose order, the bill is to be payable.

(3) The provisions of this Act relating to a payee apply with the necessary modifications to an indorsee under a special indorsement.

(4) When a bill has been indorsed in blank, any holder may convert the blank indorsement into a special indorsement by writing above the indorser's signature a direction to pay the bill to or to the order of himself or some other person.

35. (1) An indorsement is restrictive which prohibits the further negotiation of the bill or which expresses that it is a mere authority to deal with the bill as thereby directed and not a transfer of the ownership thereof, as, for example, if a bill be indorsed "Pay D only," or "Pay D for the account of X," or "Pay D or order for collection."

(2) A restrictive indorsement gives the indorsee the right to receive payment of the bill and to sue any party thereto that his indorser could have sued, but gives him no power to transfer his rights as indorsee unless it expressly authorises him to do so.

(3) Where a restrictive indorsement authorises further transfer, all subsequent indorsees take the bill with the same rights and subject to the same liabilities as the first indorsee under the restrictive indorsement.

36. (1) Where a bill is negotiable in its origin it continues to be negotiable until it has been (*a*) restrictively indorsed or (*b*) discharged by payment or otherwise.

(2) Where an overdue bill is negotiated, it can only be negotiated subject to any defect of title affecting it at its maturity, and thenceforward no person who takes it can acquire or give a better title than that which the person from whom he took it had.

(3) A bill payable on demand is deemed to be overdue within the meaning, and for the purposes, of this section, when it appears on the face of it to have been in circulation for an unreasonable length of time. What is an unreasonable length of time for this purpose is a question of fact.

(4) Except where an indorsement bears date after the maturity of the bill, every negotiation is prima facie deemed to have been effected before the bill was overdue.

(5) Where a bill which is not overdue has been dishonoured any person who takes it with notice of the dishonour takes it subject to any defect of title attaching thereto at the time of dishonour, but nothing in this sub-section shall affect the rights of a holder in due course.

37. Where a bill is negotiated back to the drawer, or to a prior indorser or to the acceptor, such party may, subject to the provisions of this Act, re-issue and further negotiate the bill, but he is not entitled to enforce payment of the bill against any intervening party to whom he was previously liable.

38. The rights and powers of the holder of a bill are as follows:

(1) He may sue on the bill in his own name:

(2) Where he is a holder in due course, he holds the bill free from any defect of title of prior parties, as well as from mere personal defences available to prior parties among themselves, and may enforce payment against all parties liable on the bill:

(3) Where his title is defective (*a*) if he negotiates the bill to a holder in due course, that holder obtains a good and complete title to the bill, and (*b*) if he obtains payment of the bill the person who pays him in due course gets a valid discharge for the bill.

General duties of the Holder

39. (1) Where a bill is payable after sight, presentment for acceptance is necessary in order to fix the maturity of the instrument.

(2) Where a bill expressly stipulates that it shall be presented for acceptance, or where a bill is drawn payable elsewhere than at the residence or place of business of the drawee it must be presented for acceptance before it can be presented for payment.

(3) In no other case is presentment for acceptance necessary in order to render liable any party to the bill.

(4) Where the holder of a bill, drawn payable elsewhere than at the place of business or residence of the drawee, has not time, with the exercise of reasonable diligence, to present the bill for acceptance before presenting it for payment on the day that it falls due, the delay caused by presenting the bill for acceptance before presenting it for payment is excused, and does not discharge the drawer and indorsers.

40. (1) Subject to the provisions of this Act, when a bill payable after sight is negotiated, the holder must either present it for acceptance or negotiate it within a reasonable time.

(2) If he does not do so, the drawer and all indorsers prior to that holder are discharged.

(3) In determining what is a reasonable time within the meaning of this section, regard shall be had to the nature of the bill, the usage of trade with respect to similar bills, and the facts of the particular case.

41. (1) A bill is duly presented for acceptance which is presented in accordance with the following rules:

(*a*) The presentment must be made by or on behalf of the holder to the drawee or to some person authorised to accept or refuse acceptance on his behalf at a reasonable hour on a business day and before the bill is overdue;

(*b*) Where a bill is addressed to two or more drawees, who are not partners, presentment must be made to them all, unless one has authority to accept for all, then presentment may be made to him only;

(*c*) Where the drawee is dead presentment may be made to his personal representative;

(*d*) Where the drawee is bankrupt, presentment may be made to him or to his trustee;

(*e*) Where authorised by agreement or usage, a presentment through the post office is sufficient.

(2) Presentment in accordance with these rules is excused, and a bill may be treated as dishonoured by non-acceptance:

(*a*) Where the drawee is dead or bankrupt, or is a fictitious person or a person not having capacity to contract by bill;

(*b*) Where, after the exercise of reasonable diligence, such presentment cannot be effected;

(*c*) Where, although the presentment has been irregular, acceptance has been refused on some other ground.

(3) The fact that the holder has reason to believe that the bill, on presentment, will be dishonoured does not excuse presentment.

42. (1) When a bill is duly presented for acceptance and is not accepted within the customary time, the person presenting it must treat it as dishonoured by non-acceptance. If he does not, the holder shall lose his right of recourse against the drawer and indorsers.

43. (1) A bill is dishonoured by non-acceptance:

(*a*) When it is duly presented for acceptance, and such an acceptance as is prescribed by this Act is refused or cannot be obtained; or

(*b*) When presentment for acceptance is excused and the bill is not accepted.

(2) Subject to the provisions of this Act when a bill is dishonoured by non-acceptance, an immediate right of recourse against the drawer and indorsers accrues to the holder, and no presentment for payment is necessary.

44. (1) The holder of a bill may refuse to take a qualified acceptance, and if he does not obtain an unqualified acceptance may treat the bill as dishonoured by non-acceptance.

(2) Where a qualified acceptance is taken, and the drawer or an indorser has not expressly or impliedly authorised the holder to take a qualified acceptance, or does not subsequently assent thereto, such drawer or indorser is discharged from his liability on the bill.

The provisions of this sub-section do not apply to a partial acceptance, whereof due notice has been given. Where a foreign bill has been accepted as to part, it must be protested as to the balance.

(3) When the drawer or indorser of a bill receives notice of a qualified acceptance, and does not within a reasonable time express his dissent to the holder he shall be deemed to have assented thereto.

45. Subject to the provisions of this Act a bill must be duly presented for payment. If it be not so presented the drawer and indorsers shall be discharged.

A bill is duly presented for payment which is presented in accordance with the following rules:

(1) Where the bill is not payable on demand, presentment must be made on the day it falls due.

(2) Where the bill is payable on demand, then, subject to the provisions of this Act, presentment must be made within a reasonable time after its issue in order to render the drawer liable, and within a reasonable time after its indorsement, in order to render the indorser liable.

In determining what is a reasonable time, regard shall be had to the nature of the bill, the usage of trade with regard to similar bills, and the facts of the particular case.

(3) Presentment must be made by the holder or by some person authorised to receive payment on his behalf at a reasonable hour on a business day, at the proper place as hereinafter defined, either to the person designated by the bill as payer, or to some person authorised

to pay or refuse payment on his behalf if with the exercise of reasonable diligence such person can there be found.

(4) A bill is presented at the proper place:

(*a*) Where a place of payment is specified in the bill and the bill is there presented.

(*b*) Where no place of payment is specified, but the address of the drawee or acceptor is given in the bill, and the bill is there presented.

(*c*) Where no place of payment is specified and no address given, and the bill is presented at the drawee's or acceptor's place of business if known, and if not, at his ordinary residence if known.

(*d*) In any other case if presented to the drawee or acceptor wherever he can be found, or if presented at his last known place of business or residence.

(5) Where a bill is presented at the proper place, and after the exercise of reasonable diligence no person authorised to pay or refuse payment can be found there, no further presentment to the drawee or acceptor is required.

(6) Where a bill is drawn upon, or accepted by two or more persons who are not partners, and no place of payment is specified, presentment must be made to them all.

(7) Where the drawee or acceptor of a bill is dead, and no place of payment is specified, presentment must be made to a personal representative, if such there be, and with the exercise of reasonable diligence he can be found.

(8) Where authorised by agreement or usage a presentment through the post office is sufficient.

46. (1) Delay in making presentment for payment is excused when the delay is caused by circumstances beyond the control of the holder, and not imputable to his default, misconduct, or negligence. When the cause of delay ceases to operate presentment must be made with reasonable diligence.

(2) Presentment for payment is dispensed with:

(*a*) Where, after the exercise of reasonable diligence presentment, as required by this Act, cannot be effected.

The fact that the holder has reason to believe that the bill will, on presentment, be dishonoured, does not dispense with the necessity for presentment.

(*b*) Where the drawee is a fictitious person.

(*c*) As regards the drawer where the drawee or acceptor is not bound, as between himself and the drawer, to accept or pay the bill, and the drawer has no reason to believe that the bill would be paid if presented.

(*d*) As regards an indorser, where the bill was accepted or made for the accommodation of that indorser, and he has no reason to expect that the bill would be paid if presented.

(*e*) By waiver of presentment, express or implied.

47. (1) A bill is dishonoured by non-payment (*a*) when it is duly presented for payment and payment is refused or cannot be obtained, or (*b*) when presentment is excused and the bill is overdue and unpaid.

(2) Subject to the provisions of this Act, when a bill is dishonoured by nonpayment, an immediate right of recourse against the drawer and indorsers accrues to the holder.

48. Subject to the provisions of this Act, when a bill has been dishonoured by non-acceptance or by non-payment, notice of dishonour must be given to the drawer and each indorser, and any drawer or indorser to whom such notice is not given is discharged; Provided that:

(1) Where a bill is dishonoured by non-acceptance, and notice of dishonour is not given, the rights of a holder in due course subsequent to the omission, shall not be prejudiced by the omission.

(2) Where a bill is dishonoured by non-acceptance and due notice of dishonour is given, it shall not be necessary to give notice of a subsequent dishonour by nonpayment unless the bill shall in the meantime have been accepted.

49. Notice of dishonour in order to be valid and effectual must be given in accordance with the following rules:

(1) The notice must be given by or on behalf of the holder, or by or on behalf of an indorser who, at the time of giving it, is himself liable on the bill.

(2) Notice of dishonour may be given by an agent either in his own name, or in the name of any party entitled to give notice whether that party be his principal or not.

(3) Where the notice is given by or on behalf of the holder, it enures for the benefit of all subsequent holders and all prior indorsers who have a right of recourse against the party to whom it is given.

(4) Where notice is given by or on behalf of an indorser entitled to give notice as hereinbefore provided, it enures for the benefit of the holder and all indorsers subsequent to the party to whom notice is given.

(5) The notice may be given in writing or by personal communication, and may be given in any terms which sufficiently identify the bill, and intimate that the bill has been dishonoured by non-acceptance or non-payment.

(6) The return of a dishonoured bill to the drawer or an indorser is, in point of form, deemed a sufficient notice of dishonour.

(7) A written notice need not be signed, and an insufficient written notice may be supplemented and validated by verbal communication. A misdescription of the bill shall not vitiate the notice unless the party to whom the notice is given is in fact misled thereby.

(8) Where notice of dishonour is required to be given to any person, it may be given either to the party himself, or to his agent in that behalf.

(9) Where the drawer or indorser is dead, and the party giving notice knows it, the notice must be given to a personal representative if such there be, and with the exercise of reasonable diligence he can be found.

(10) Where the drawer or indorser is bankrupt, notice may be given either to the party himself or to the trustee.

(11) Where there are two or more drawers or indorsers who are not partners, notice must be given to each of them, unless one of them has authority to receive such notice for the others.

(12) The notice may be given as soon as the bill is dishonoured and must be given within a reasonable time thereafter.

In the absence of special circumstances notice is not deemed to have been given within a reasonable time, unless:

(*a*) Where the person giving and the person to receive notice reside in the same place, the notice is given or sent off in time to reach the latter on the day after the dishonour of the bill.

(*b*) Where the person giving and the person to receive notice reside in different places, the notice is sent off on the day after the dishonour of the bill, if there be a post at a convenient hour on that day, and if there be no such post on that day then by the next post thereafter.

(13) Where a bill when dishonoured is in the hands of an agent, he may either himself give notice to the parties liable on the bill, or he may give notice to his principal. If he gives notice to his principal, he must do so within the same time as if he were the holder, and the principal upon receipt of such notice has himself the same time for giving notice as if the agent had been an independent holder.

(14) Where a party to a bill receives due notice of dishonour, he has after the receipt of such notice the same period of time for giving notice to antecedent parties that the holder has after the dishonour.

(15) Where a notice of dishonour is duly addressed and posted, the sender is deemed to have given due notice of dishonour, notwithstanding any miscarriage by the post office.

50. (1) Delay in giving notice of dishonour is excused where the delay is caused by circumstances beyond the control of the party giving notice, and not imputable to his default, misconduct, or negligence. When the cause of the delay ceases to operate the notice must be given with reasonable diligence.

(2) Notice of dishonour is dispensed with:

(*a*) When, after the exercise of reasonable diligence, notice as required by this Act cannot be given to or does not reach the drawer or indorser sought to be charged;

(*b*) By waiver express or implied. Notice of dishonour may be waived before the time of giving notice has arrived, or after the omission to give due notice;

(*c*) As regards the drawer in the following cases, namely, (1) where drawer and drawee are the same person, (2) where the drawee is a fictitious person or a person not having capacity to contract, (3) where the drawer is the person to whom the bill is presented for payment, (4) where the drawee or acceptor is as between himself and the drawer under no obligation to accept or pay the bill, (5) where the drawer has countermanded payment;

(*d*) As regards the indorser in the following cases, namely, (1) where the drawee is a fictitious person or a person not having capacity to contract and the indorser was aware of the fact at the time he indorsed the bill, (2) where the indorser is the person to whom the bill is presented for payment, (3) where the bill was accepted or made for his accommodation.

51. (1) Where an inland bill has been dishonoured it may, if the holder thinks fit, be noted for non-acceptance or non-payment, as the case may be; but it shall not be necessary to note or protest any such bill in order to preserve the recourse against the drawer or indorser.

(2) Where a foreign bill, appearing on the face of it to be such, has been dishonoured by non-acceptance it must be duly protested for non-acceptance, and where such a bill, which has not been previously dishonoured by non-acceptance, is dishonoured by non-payment it must be duly protested for non-payment. If it be not so protested the drawer and indorsers are discharged. Where a bill does not appear on the face of it to be a foreign bill, protest thereof in case of dishonour is unnecessary.

(3) A bill which has been protested for non-acceptance may be subsequently protested for non-payment.

(4) Subject to the provisions of this Act, when a bill is noted or protested, [it may be noted on the day of its dishonour, and must be noted not later than the next succeeding business day]. When a bill has been duly noted, the protest may be subsequently extended as of the date of the noting. (Original wording amended by the Bill of Exchange (Time of Noting) Act 1917, s.1.)

(5) Where the acceptor of a bill becomes bankrupt or insolvent or suspends payment before it matures, the holder may cause the bill to be protested for better security against the drawer and indorsers.

(6) A bill must be protested at the place where it is dishonoured: Provided that:

(*a*) When a bill is presented through the post office, and returned by post dishonoured, it may be protested at the place to which it is returned and on the day of its return if received during business hours, and if not received during business hours, then not later than the next business day;

(*b*) When a bill drawn payable at the place of business or residence of some person other than the drawee, has been dishonoured by non-acceptance, it must be protested for non-payment at the place where it is expressed to be payable, and no further presentment for payment to, or demand on, the drawee is necessary.

(7) A protest must contain a copy of the bill, and must be signed by the notary making it, and must specify:

(*a*) The person at whose request the bill is protested;

(*b*) The place and date of protest, the cause or reason for protesting the bill, the demand made, and the answer given, if any, or the fact that the drawee or acceptor could not be found.

(8) Where a bill is lost or destroyed, or is wrongly detained from the person entitled to hold it, protest may be made on a copy or written particulars thereof.

(9) Protest is dispensed with by any circumstance which would dispense with notice of dishonour. Delay in noting or protesting is excused when the delay is caused by circumstances beyond the control of the holder, and not imputable to his default, misconduct, or negligence. When the cause of delay ceases to operate the bill must be noted or protested with reasonable diligence.

52. (1) When a bill is accepted generally presentment for payment is not necessary in order to render the acceptor liable.

(2) When by the terms of a qualified acceptance presentment for payment is required, the acceptor, in the absence of an express stipulation to that effect, is not discharged by the omission to present the bill for payment on the day that it matures.

(3) In order to render the acceptor of a bill liable it is not necessary to protest it, or that notice of dishonour should be given to him.

(4) Where the holder of a bill presents it for payment, he shall exhibit the bill to the person from whom he demands payment, and when a bill is paid the holder shall forthwith deliver it up to the party paying it.

Liabilities of Parties

53. (1) A bill, of itself, does not operate as an assignment of funds in the hands of the drawee available for the payment thereof, and the drawee of a bill who does not accept as required by this Act is not liable on the instrument. This sub-section shall not extend to Scotland.

(2) In Scotland, where the drawee of a bill has in his hands funds

available for the payment thereof, the bill operates as an assignment of the sum for which it is drawn in favour of the holder, from the time when the bill is presented to the drawee.

54. The acceptor of a bill, by accepting it:

(1) Engages that he will pay it according to the tenor of his acceptance;

(2) Is precluded from denying to a holder in due course:

(a) The existence of the drawer, the genuineness of his signature, and his capacity and authority to draw the bill;

(b) In the case of a bill payable to the drawer's order, the then capacity of the drawer to indorse, but not the genuineness or validity of his indorsement;

(c) In the case of a bill payable to the order of a third person, the existence of the payee and his then capacity to indorse, but not the genuineness or validity of his indorsement.

55. (1) The drawer of a bill by drawing it:

(a) Engages that on due presentment it shall be accepted and paid according to its tenor, and that if it be dishonoured he will compensate the holder or any indorser who is compelled to pay it, provided that the requisite proceedings on dishonour be duly taken;

(b) Is precluded from denying to a holder in due course the existence of the payee and his then capacity to indorse.

(2) The indorser of a bill by indorsing it:

(a) Engages that on due presentment it shall be accepted and paid according to its tenor, and that if it be dishonoured he will compensate the holder or a subsequent indorser who is compelled to pay it, provided that the requisite proceedings on dishonour be duly taken;

(b) Is precluded from denying to a holder in due course the genuineness and regularity in all respects of the drawer's signature and all previous indorsements;

(c) Is precluded from denying to his immediate or a subsequent indorsee that the bill was at the time of his indorsement a valid and subsisting bill, and that he had then a good title thereto.

56. Where a person signs a bill otherwise than as drawer or acceptor, he thereby incurs the liabilities of an indorser to a holder in due course.

57. Where a bill is dishonoured, the measure of damages, which shall be deemed to be liquidated damages, shall be as follows:

(1) The holder may recover from any party liable on the bill, and the drawer who has been compelled to pay the bill may recover from the acceptor, and an indorser who has been compelled to pay the bill may recover from the acceptor or from the drawer, or from a prior indorser:

(*a*) The amount of the bill;

(*b*) Interest thereon from the time of presentment for payment if the bill is payable on demand, and from the maturity of the bill in any other case;

(*c*) The expenses of noting, or, when protest is necessary, and the protest has been extended, the expenses of protest.

(2) (Repealed by the Administration of Justice Act 1977, s.4.)

(3) Where by this Act interest may be recovered as damages, such interest may, if justice require it, be withheld wholly or in part, and where a bill is expressed to be payable with interest at a given rate, interest as damages may or may not be given at the same rate as interest proper.

58. (1) Where the holder of a bill payable to bearer negotiates it by delivery without indorsing it, he is called a "transferor by delivery."

(2) A transferor by delivery is not liable on the instrument.

(3) A transferor by delivery who negotiates a bill thereby warrants to his immediate transferee being a holder for value that the bill is what it purports to be, that he has a right to transfer it, and that at the time of transfer he is not aware of any fact which renders it valueless.

Discharge of Bill

59. (1) A bill is discharged by payment in due course by or on behalf of the drawee or acceptor.

"Payment in due course" means payment made at or after the maturity of the bill to the holder thereof in good faith and without notice that his title to the bill is defective.

(2) Subject to the provisions hereinafter contained, when a bill is paid by the drawer or an indorser it is not discharged; but

(*a*) Where a bill payable to, or to the order of, a third party is paid by the drawer, the drawer may enforce payment thereof against the acceptor, but may not re-issue the bill.

(*b*) Where a bill is paid by an indorser, or where a bill payable to the drawer's order is paid by the drawer, the party paying it is remitted to his former rights as regards the acceptor or antecedent parties, and he may, if he thinks fit, strike out his own and subsequent indorsements, and again negotiate the bill.

(3) Where an accommodation bill is paid in due course by the party accommodated the bill is discharged.

60. When a bill payable to order on demand is drawn on a banker, and the banker on whom it is drawn pays the bill in good faith and in the ordinary course of business, it is not incumbent on the banker to show that the indorsement of the payee or any subsequent indorsement was made by or under the authority of the person whose indorsement it purports to be, and the banker is deemed to have paid the bill in due course, although such indorsement has been forged or made without authority.

61. When the acceptor of a bill is or becomes the holder of it at or after its maturity, in his own right, the bill is discharged.

62. (1) When the holder of a bill at or after its maturity absolutely and unconditionally renounces his rights against the acceptor the bill is discharged.

The renunciation must be in writing, unless the bill is delivered up to the acceptor.

(2) The liabilities of any party to a bill may in like manner be renounced by the holder before, at, or after its maturity; but nothing in this section shall affect the rights of a holder in due course without notice of the renunciation.

63. (1) Where a bill is intentionally cancelled by the holder or his agent, and the cancellation is apparent thereon, the bill is discharged.

(2) In like manner any party liable on a bill may be discharged by the intentional cancellation of his signature by the holder or his agent. In such case any indorser who would have had a right of recourse against the party whose signature is cancelled, is also discharged.

(3) A cancellation made unintentionally, or under a mistake, or without the authority of the holder is inoperative; but where a bill or any signature thereon appears to have been cancelled the burden of proof lies on the party who alleges that the cancellation was made unintentionally, or under a mistake, or without authority.

64. (1) Where a bill or acceptance is materially altered without the assent of all parties liable on the bill, the bill is avoided except as against a party who has himself made, authorised, or assented to the alteration, and subsequent indorsers.

Provided that,

Where a bill has been materially altered, but the alteration is not apparent, and the bill is in the hands of a holder in due course, such holder may avail himself of the bill as if it has not been altered, and may enforce payment of it according to its original tenor.

(2) In particular the following alterations are material, namely, any alteration of the date, the sum payable, the time of payment, the place of payment, and, where a bill has been accepted generally, the addition of a place of payment without the acceptor's assent.

Acceptance and Payment for Honour

65. (1) Where a bill of exchange has been protested for dishonour by non-acceptance, or protested for better security, and is not overdue, any person, not being a party already liable thereon, may, with the consent of the holder, intervene and accept the bill supra protest, for the honour of any party liable thereon, or for the honour of the person for whose account the bill is drawn.

(2) A bill may be accepted for honour for part only of the sum for which it is drawn.

(3) An acceptance for honour supra protest in order to be valid must:

(*a*) Be written on the bill, and indicate that it is an acceptance for honour;

(*b*) Be signed by the acceptor for honour.

(4) Where an acceptance for honour does not expressly state for whose honour it is made, it is deemed to be an acceptance for the honour of the drawer.

(5) Where a bill payable after sight is accepted for honour, its maturity is calculated from the date of the noting for non-acceptance, and not from the date of the acceptance for honour.

66. (1) The acceptor for honour of a bill by accepting it engages that he will, on due presentment, pay the bill according to the tenor of his acceptance, if it is not paid by the drawee, provided it has been duly presented for payment, and protested for non-payment, and that he receives notice of these facts.

(2) The acceptor for honour is liable to the holder and to all parties to the bill subsequent to the party for whose honour he has accepted.

67. (1) Where a dishonoured bill has been accepted for honour supra protest, or contains a reference in case of need, it must be protested for non-payment before it is presented for payment to the acceptor for honour, or referee in case of need.

(2) Where the address of the acceptor for honour is in the same place where the bill is protested for non-payment, the bill must be presented to him not later than the day following its maturity; and where the address of the acceptor for honour is in some place other than the place where it was protested for non-payment, the bill must be forwarded not later than the day following its maturity for presentment to him.

(3) Delay in presentment or non-presentment is excused by any circumstance which would excuse delay in presentment for payment or non-presentment for payment.

(4) When a bill of exchange is dishonoured by the acceptor for honour it must be protested for non-payment by him.

68. (1) Where a bill has been protested for non-payment, any person may intervene and pay it supra protest for the honour of any party liable thereon, or for the honour of the person for whose account the bill is drawn.

(2) Where two or more persons offer to pay a bill for the honour of

different parties, the person whose payment will discharge most parties to the bill shall have the preference.

(3) Payment for honour supra protest, in order to operate as such and not as a mere voluntary payment, must be attested by a notarial act of honour which may be appended to the protest or form an extension of it.

(4) The notarial act of honour must be founded on a declaration made by the payer for honour, or his agent in that behalf, declaring his intention to pay the bill for honour, and for whose honour he pays.

(5) Where a bill has been paid for honour, all parties subsequent to the party for whose honour it is paid are discharged, but the payer for honour is subrogated for, and succeeds to, both the rights and duties of the holder as regards the party for whose honour he pays, and all parties liable to that party.

(6) The payer for honour on paying to the holder the amount of the bill and the notarial expenses incidental to its dishonour is entitled to receive both the bill itself and the protest. If the holder does not on demand deliver them up he shall be liable to the payer for honour in damages.

(7) Where the holder of a bill refuses to receive payment supra protest he shall lose his right of recourse against any party who would have been discharged by such payment.

Lost Instruments

69. Where a bill has been lost before it is overdue, the person who was the holder of it may apply to the drawer to give him another bill of the same tenor, giving security to the drawer if required to indemnify him against all persons whatever in case the bill alleged to have been lost shall be found again.

If the drawer on request as aforesaid refuses to give such duplicate bill, he may be compelled to do so.

70. In any action or proceeding upon a bill, the court or a judge may order that the loss of the instrument shall not be set up, provided an indemnity be given to the satisfaction of the court or judge against the claims of any other person upon the instrument in question.

Bill in a Set

71. (1) Where a bill is drawn in a set, each part of the set being numbered, and containing a reference to the other parts, the whole of the parts constitute one bill.

(2) Where the holder of a set indorses two or more parts to different persons, he is liable on every such part, and every indorser subsequent to him is liable on the part he has himself indorsed as if the said parts were separate bills.

(3) Where two or more parts of a set are negotiated to different holders in due course, the holder whose title first accrues is as between such holders deemed the true owner of the bill; but nothing in this sub-section shall affect the rights of a person who in due course accepts or pays the part first presented to him.

(4) The acceptance may be written on any part, and it must be written on one part only.

If the drawee accepts more than one part, and such accepted parts get into the hands of different holders in due course, he is liable on every such part as if it were a separate bill.

(5) When the acceptor of a bill drawn in a set pays it without requiring the part bearing his acceptance to be delivered up to him, and that part at maturity is outstanding in the hands of a holder in due course, he is liable to the holder thereof.

(6) Subject to the preceding rules, where any one part of a bill drawn in a set is discharged by payment or otherwise, the whole bill is discharged.

Conflict of Laws

72. Where a bill drawn in one country is negotiated, accepted, or payable in another, the rights, duties, and liabilities of the parties thereto are determined as follows:

(1) The validity of a bill as regards requisites in form is determined by the law of the place of issue, and the validity as regards requisites in form of the supervening contracts, such as acceptance, or indorsement, or acceptance supra protest, is determined by the law of the place where such contract was made.

Provided that:

(*a*) Where a bill is issued out of the United Kingdom it is not invalid by reason only that it is not stamped in accordance with the law of the place of issue;

(*b*) Where a bill, issued out of the United Kingdom, conforms, as regards requisites in form, to the law of the United Kingdom, it may, for the purpose of enforcing payment thereof, be treated as valid as between all persons who negotiate, hold, or become parties to it in the United Kingdom.

(2) Subject to the provisions of this Act, the interpretation of the drawing, indorsement, acceptance, or acceptance supra protest of a bill, is determined by the law of the place where such contract is made.

Provided that where an inland bill is indorsed in a foreign country the indorsement shall as regards the payer be interpreted according to the law of the United Kingdom.

(3) The duties of the holder with respect to presentment for acceptance or payment and the necessity for or sufficiency of a protest or notice of dishonour, or otherwise, are determined by the law of the place where the act is done or the bill is dishonoured.

(4) (Repealed by the Administration of Justice Act 1977, s.4.)

(5) Where a bill is drawn in one country and is payable in another, the due date thereof is determined according to the law of the place where it is payable.

PART III

Cheques on a Banker

73. A cheque is a bill of exchange drawn on a banker payable on demand.

Except as otherwise provided in this Part, the provisions of this Act applicable to a bill of exchange payable on demand apply to a cheque.

74. Subject to the provisions of this Act:

(1) Where a cheque is not presented for payment within a reasonable time of its issue, and the drawer or the person on whose account it is drawn had the right at the time of such presentment as between him and the banker to have the cheque paid and suffers actual damage through the delay, he is discharged to the extent of such damage, that is to say, to the extent to which such drawer or person

is a creditor of such banker to a larger amount than he would have been had such cheque been paid.

(2) In determining what is a reasonable time regard shall be had to the nature of the instrument, the usage of trade and of bankers, and the facts of the particular case.

(3) The holder of such cheque as to which such drawer or person is discharged shall be a creditor, in lieu of such drawer or person, of such banker to the extent of such discharge, and entitled to recover the amount from him.

75. The duty and authority of a banker to pay a cheque drawn on him by his customer are determined by:

(1) Countermand of payment;

(2) Notice of the customer's death.

Crossed Cheques

76. (1) Where a cheque bears across its face an addition of:

(*a*) The words "and company" or any abbreviation thereof between two parallel transverse lines, either with or without the words "not negotiable"; or

(*b*) Two parallel transverse lines simply, either with or without the words "not negotiable";

that addition constitutes a crossing, and the cheque is crossed generally.

(2) Where a cheque bears across its face an addition of the name of a banker, either with or without the words "not negotiable," that addition constitutes a crossing, and the cheque is crossed specially and to that banker.

77. (1) A cheque may be crossed generally or specially by the drawer.

(2) Where a cheque is uncrossed, the holder may cross it generally or specially.

(3) Where a cheque is crossed generally the holder may cross it specially.

(4) Where a cheque is crossed generally or specially, the holder may add the words "not negotiable."

(5) Where a cheque is crossed specially, the banker to whom it is

crossed may again cross it specially to another banker for collection.

(6) Where an uncrossed cheque, or a cheque crossed generally, is sent to a banker for collection, he may cross it specially to himself.

78. A crossing authorised by this Act is a material part of the cheque; it shall not be lawful for any person to obliterate or, except as authorised by this Act, to add to or alter the crossing.

79. (1) Where a cheque is crossed specially to more than one banker except when crossed to an agent for collection being a banker, the banker on whom it is drawn shall refuse payment thereof.

(2) Where the banker on whom a cheque is drawn which is so crossed nevertheless pays the same, or pays a cheque crossed generally otherwise than to a banker, or if crossed specially otherwise than to the banker to whom it is crossed, or his agent for collection being a banker, he is liable to the true owner of the cheque for any loss he may sustain owing to the cheque having been so paid.

Provided that where a cheque is presented for payment which does not at the time of presentment appear to be crossed, or to have had a crossing which has been obliterated, or to have been added to or altered otherwise than as authorised by this Act, the banker paying the cheque in good faith and without negligence shall not be responsible or incur any liability, nor shall the payment be questioned by reason of the cheque having being crossed, or of the crossing having been obliterated or having been added to or altered otherwise than as authorised by this Act, and of payment having been made otherwise than to a banker or to the banker to whom the cheque is or was crossed, or to his agent for collection being a banker, as the case may be.

80. Where the banker, on whom a crossed cheque is drawn, in good faith and without negligence pays it, if crossed generally, to a banker, and if crossed specially, to the banker to whom it is crossed, or his agent for collection being a banker, the banker paying the cheque, and, if the cheque has come into the hands of the payee, the drawer, shall respectively be entitled to the same rights and be placed in the same position as if payment of the cheque had been made to the true owner thereof.

81. Where a person takes a crossed cheque which bears on it the words "not negotiable," he shall not have and shall not be capable of giving a better title to the cheque than that which the person from whom he took it had.

82. (Repealed by the Cheques Act 1957, see now s.4 of that Act.)

PART IV

PROMISSORY NOTES

83. (1) A promissory note is an unconditional promise in writing made by one person to another signed by the maker, engaging to pay, on demand or at a fixed or determinable future time, a sum certain in money, to, or to the order of, a specified person or to bearer.

(2) An instrument in the form of a note payable to the maker's order is not a note within the meaning of this section unless and until it is indorsed by the maker.

(3) A note is not invalid by reason only that it contains also a pledge of collateral security with authority to sell or dispose thereof.

(4) A note which is, or on the face of it purports to be, both made and payable within the British Islands is an inland note. Any other note is a foreign note.

84. A promissory note is inchoate and incomplete until delivery thereof to the payee or bearer.

85. (1) A promissory note may be made by two or more makers, and they may be liable thereon jointly, or jointly and severally according to its tenor.

(2) Where a note runs "I promise to pay" and is signed by two or more persons it is deemed to be their joint and several note.

86. (1) Where a note payable on demand has been indorsed, it must be presented for payment within a reasonable time of the indorsement. If it be not so presented the indorser is discharged.

(2) In determining what is a reasonable time, regard shall be had

to the nature of the instrument, the usage of trade, and the facts of the particular case.

(3) Where a note payable on demand is negotiated, it is not deemed to be overdue, for the purpose of affecting the holder with defects of title of which he had no notice, by reason that it appears that a reasonable time for presenting it for payment has elapsed since its issue.

87. (1) Where a promissory note is in the body of it made payable at a particular place, it must be presented for payment at that place in order to render the maker liable. In any other case, presentment for payment is not necessary in order to render the maker liable.

(2) Presentment for payment is necessary in order to render the indorser of a note liable.

(3) Where a note is in the body of it made payable at a particular place, presentment at that place is necessary in order to render an indorser liable; but when a place of payment is indicated by way of memorandum only, presentment at that place is sufficient to render the indorser liable, but a presentment to the maker elsewhere, if sufficient in other respects, shall also suffice.

88. The maker of a promissory note by making it:

(1) Engages that he will pay it according to its tenor;

(2) Is precluded from denying to a holder in due course the existence of the payee and his then capacity to indorse.

89. (1) Subject to the provisions of this part and, except as by this section provided, the provisions of this Act relating to bills of exchange apply, with the necessary modifications, to promissory notes.

(2) In applying those provisions the maker of a note shall be deemed to correspond with the acceptor of a bill, and the first indorser of a note shall be deemed to correspond with the drawer of an accepted bill payable to drawer's order.

(3) The following provisions as to bills do not apply to notes; namely, provisions relating to:

(*a*) Presentment for acceptance;

(*b*) Acceptance;

(c) Acceptance supra protest;

(d) Bills in a set.

(4) Where a foreign note is dishonoured, protest thereof is unnecessary.

PART V

SUPPLEMENTARY

90. A thing is deemed to be done in good faith, within the meaning of this Act, where it is in fact done honestly, whether it is done negligently or not.

91. (1) Where, by this Act, any instrument or writing is required to be signed by any person, it is not necessary that he should sign it with his own hand, but it is sufficient if his signature is written thereon by some other person by or under his authority.

(2) In the case of a corporation, where, by this Act, any instrument or writing be required to be signed, it is sufficient if the instrument or writing be sealed with the corporate seal.

But nothing in this section shall be construed as requiring the bill or note of a corporation to be under seal.

92. Where, by this Act, the time limited for doing any act or thing is less than three days, in reckoning time, non-business days are excluded.

"Non-business days" for the purposes of this Act mean:

(a) [Saturday,] Sunday, Good Friday, Christmas Day;

(b) A bank holiday under the [Banking and Financial Dealings Act 1971];

(c) A day appointed by Royal proclamation as a public fast or thanksgiving day. [A day declared by an order under s.2 of the Banking and Financial Dealings Act 1971, to be a non-business day.]

Any other day is a business day.

(Words in square brackets inserted by the Banking and Financial Dealings Act 1971.)

93. For the purposes of this Act, where a bill or note is required to be protested within a specified time or before some further proceeding is taken, it is sufficient that the bill has been noted for protest before the expiration of the specified time or the taking of the proceeding; and the formal protest may be extended at any time thereafter as of the date of the noting.

94. Where a dishonoured bill or note is authorised or required to be protested, and the services of a notary cannot be obtained at the place where the bill is dishonoured, any householder or substantial resident of the place may, in the presence of two witnesses, give a certificate, signed by them, attesting the dishonour of the bill, and the certificate shall in all respects operate as if it were a formal protest of the bill.

The form given in Schedule 1 to this Act may be used with necessary modifications, and if used shall be sufficient.

95. The provisions of this Act as to crossed cheques shall apply to a warrant for payment of dividend.

96. (Repealed by the Statute Law Revision Act 1898.)

97. (1) The rules in bankruptcy relating to bills of exchange, promissory notes, and cheques, shall continue to apply thereto notwithstanding anything in this Act contained.

(2) The rules of common law including the law merchant, save in so far as they are inconsistent with the express provisions of this Act, shall continue to apply to bills of exchange, promissory notes, and cheques.

(3) Nothing in this act or in any repeal effected thereby shall affect:

(*a*) [The provisions of the Stamp Act 1870, or Acts amending it, or] any law or enactment for the time being in force relating to the revenue;

(*b*) The provisions of the Companies Act 1862, or Acts amending it, or any Act relating to joint stock banks or companies;

(*c*) The provisions of any Act relating to or confirming the privileges of the Bank of England or the Bank of Ireland respectively;

(*d*) The validity of any usage relating to dividend warrants, or the indorsements thereof.

(Words in square brackets repealed by the Statute Law Revision Act 1898.)

98. Nothing in this Act or in any repeal effected thereby shall extend or restrict, or in any way alter or affect the law and practice in Scotland in regard to summary diligence.

99. Where any Act or document refers to any enactment repealed by this Act, the Act or document shall be construed, and shall operate, as if it referred to the corresponding provisions of this Act.

100. In any judicial proceeding in Scotland, any fact relating to a bill of exchange, bank cheque, or promissory note, which is relevant to any question of liability thereon, may be proved by parole evidence: Provided that this enactment shall not in any way affect the existing law and practice whereby the party who is, according to the tenor of any bill of exchange, bank cheque, or promissory note, debtor to the holder in the amount thereof, may be required, as a condition of obtaining a sist of diligence, or suspension of a charge, or threatened charge, to make such consignation, or to find such caution as the court or judge before whom the cause is depending may require.

[This section shall not apply to any case where the bill of exchange, bank cheque, or promissory note has undergone the sesennial prescription.]

(Words in square brackets repealed by the Prescription and Limitation (Scotland) Act 1973, s. 16(2).)

FIRST SCHEDULE

Form of protest which may be used when the services of a notary cannot be obtained.

Know all men that I, *A.B.* [householder], of   in the county of   in the United Kingdom, at the request of *C.D.*, there being no notary public available, did on the   day of   198   at   demand payment [*or acceptance*] of the bill of exchange hereunder written, from *E.F.*, to which demand he made answer [state answer, if any] wherefore I now, in the presence of *G.H.* and *J.K.* do protest the said bill of exchange.

(Signed)   *A.B.*

          G.H.   Witnesses

          J.K.

   N.B. The bill itself should be annexed, or a copy of the bill and all that is written thereon should be underwritten.

SECOND SCHEDULE

(Repealed by the Statute Law Revision Act 1898.)

Appendix 2
Cheques Act 1957

5 & 6 Eliz. 2 Ch. 36

1. (1) Where a banker in good faith and in the ordinary course of business pays a cheque drawn on him which is not indorsed or is irregularly indorsed, he does not, in doing so, incur any liability by reason only of the absence of, or irregularity in, indorsement, and he is deemed to have paid it in due course.

(2) Where a banker in good faith and in the ordinary course of business pays any such instrument as the following, namely:

(*a*) A document issued by a customer of his which, though not a bill of exchange, is intended to enable a person to obtain payment from him of the sum mentioned in the document;

(*b*) A draft payable on demand drawn by him upon himself, whether payable at the head office or some other office of his bank;

he does not, in doing so, incur any liability by reason only of the absence of, or irregularity in, indorsement, and the payment discharges the instrument.

2. A banker who gives value for, or has a lien on, a cheque payable to order which the holder delivers to him for collection without indorsing it, has such (if any) rights as he would have had if, upon delivery, the holder had indorsed it in blank.

3. An unindorsed cheque which appears to have been paid by the banker on who it is drawn is evidence of the receipt by the payee of the sum payable by the cheque.

4. (1) Where a banker, in good faith and without negligence:

(*a*) Receives payment for a customer of an instrument to which this section applies; or

(*b*) Having credited a customer's account with the amount of such an instrument, receives payment thereof for himself;

and the customer has no title, or a defective title, to the instrument, the banker does not incur any liability to the true owner of the instrument by reason only of having received payment thereof.

(2) This section applies to the following instruments, namely:

(*a*) Cheques;

(*b*) Any document issued by a customer of a banker which, though not a bill of exchange, is intended to enable a person to obtain payment from that banker of the sum mentioned in the document;

(*c*) Any document issued by a public officer which is intended to enable a person to obtain payment from the Paymaster General or the Queen's and Lord Treasurer's Remembrancer of the sum mentioned in the document but is not a bill of exchange;

(*d*) Any draft payable on demand drawn by a banker upon himself, whether payable at the head office or some other office of his bank.

(3) A banker is not to be treated for the purposes of this section as having been negligent by reason only of his failure to concern himself with absence of, or irregularity in, indorsement of an instrument.

5. The provisions of the Bills of Exchange Act 1882, relating to crossed cheques shall, so far as applicable, have effect in relation to instruments (other than cheques) to which the last foregoing section applies as they have effect in relation to cheques.

6. (1) This Act shall be construed as one with the Bills of Exchange Act 1882.

(2) The foregoing provisions of this Act do not make negotiable any instrument which, apart from them, is not negotiable.

(3) (Repealed by the Statute Law (Repeals) Act 1974.)

7. This Act extends to Northern Ireland, but, for the purposes of section six of the Government of Ireland Act 1920, so much of the provisions of this Act as relates to, or affects, instruments other than negotiable instruments shall be deemed to be provisions of an Act passed before the appointed day within the meaning of that section.

8. (1) This Act may be cited as the Cheques Act 1957.

(2) This Act shall come into operation at the expiration of a period of three months beginning with the day on which it is passed.

SCHEDULE

(Repealed by the Statute Law (Repeals) Act 1974.)

Appendix 3
Specimen questions

Chapter 2

1. To what extent, if at all, can an agent delegate his authority to another person?

2.(a) Normally the principal alone is liable on a contract made by his agent with a third party. In some circumstances, however, the agent can become personally liable on the contract. Outline these circumstances.

(b) X engages Y as his agent to obtain a second mortgage on his behalf. Y arranges mortgage facilities with Z Finance Ltd., but does not disclose to X that he has received a commission of £100 from the company. Discuss the legal position.

3.(a) State the various ways in which termination of agency may occur.

(b) Rashleigh has authority to sign "per pro" on his wife's current account with the Metropolitan Bank. The bank has been informed that a receiving order was made against Rashleigh last week. What action, if any, should the bank take?

Chapter 3

1. Whilst, A, B, C and D are in partnership together, the following events occur:

(i) A accepts a bill of exchange in the firm's name;

(ii) B opens a bank account saying that, as he is the only partner resident in Extown, the account had better be in his name. This is done, and the account is subsequently allowed to become overdrawn;

(*iii*) C seeks to introduce his son into the partnership;

(*iv*) D is convicted of travelling on the London Underground without a ticket.

Explain the legal implications of each of these events so far as the other partners are concerned.

2.(*a*) X, Y and Z have been carrying on business as a firm, which has recently been made bankrupt. The firm's debts are £25,000 and its assets are £7,000. X has private debts of £10,000 and private assets of £8,000. Y has neither private debts nor private assets. Z has private debts of £12,000 and private assets of £15,000.

Explain the legal rules which apply in this case, and state what the final outcome will be as regards the creditors of the firm and of the partners.

(*b*) What course of action should a bank take if it discovers that one of its customers is an undischarged bankrupt?

3.(*a*) Explain the meaning of "novation" and show its relevance in the context of partnership.

(*b*) Pip, Squeak and Wilfred are partners in a firm whose bank account is substantially overdrawn. Pip, who is about to retire, is the wealthiest of the partners and the bank is anxious that he should remain liable for the overdraft. What steps should the bank take and why?

Chapter 4

1. State the five clauses which will be set out in the memorandum of association of a recently incorporated company limited by shares. To what extent and by what method can these clauses be altered?

2. In relation to companies, what is meant by the *ultra vires* doctrine? Is it true to say that the doctrine has lost much of its significance in recent years?

3. Advise the Grand Bank as to what legal aspects regarding borrowing powers it should consider when asked to make an advance of £20,000 to each of the following:

(*i*) Hammond Brothers, a firm operating motor lorries.

(*ii*) Michael, Stephen and Henry, a firm of medical practitioners.

(*iii*) Wyatt Construction Ltd., which was formed two years ago and includes Clause 79 of Table A in its articles of association. At present the company has an authorised share capital of £30,000, of which £25,000 is issued, and, although there are no debentures, there are outstanding directors' loans to the company of £10,000.

(*iv*) The Foundation Ltd., a non-trading company, limited by guarantee and not having a share capital.

4. The East Bank has been worried for some time about the overdraft of its customer, Go-Slow Ltd. On 1 February, 1985, under pressure from the bank, the company gave an unlimited debenture to the bank to secure its overdraft, then £35,000. The debenture contained a fixed first charge on the company's factory, and a first floating charge on all other assets. On 1 July, 1985, the company passed an extraordinary resolution to wind up voluntarily because it could not, by reason of its liabilities, continue in business. At that time the company owed the bank £45,000.

There were also:

(*i*) unpaid wages and salaries totalling £6,000;

(*ii*) two years' arrears of taxes totalling £4,500 (being £2,500 for the earlier year, and £2,000 for the more recent year);

(*iii*) unpaid rates for the previous 12 months totalling £1,000;

(*iv*) ordinary trade creditors amounting to £55,000.

Assume that the liquidation expenses will be £500, the factory will fetch £25,000, and the remaining assets £30,000. State the order of priority of the various claims.

What difference, if any, would it make if the liquidator was able to prove that the company was already insolvent on 1 February, 1985?

5. Debentures issued by a company are often secured by a fixed and a floating charge. Explain the differences between these types of charge and show the disadvantages for a bank of a debenture which contains only a floating charge over the assets of the company.

6. Titanic Shipping Ltd., created a debenture, containing a fixed and a floating charge, in favour of the Grand Bank as security for its overdraft. When the company's financial position deteriorated, the bank appointed a receiver. Subseqently another creditor presented a winding-up petition, which resulted in the appointment of a liquidator. Explain the respective roles of the receiver and the liquidator.

Chapter 5

1. The South Bank is today given notice that a bankruptcy order has been made against its customer, John Doe, a small trader. His account is overdrawn by £19,000 against the following security:

(*i*) a legal mortgage on his premises, valued at £15,000;

(*ii*) quoted stocks and shares in his name deposited together with blank transfers, their current market value being £2,000;

(*iii*) A guarantee by Richard Roe for £3,000.

What immediate action should the bank take, and what alternatives has the bank as regards proof?

2. Desmond Doolittle is a customer of the North Bank. On 14 January 1987, a bankruptcy petition was presented against him and on the 12 February a bankruptcy order is made against him, the bank being informed of the order in the afternoon of that day. Advise the bank of the legal position as regards the following transactions:

(*ii*) on 10 January a direct debit was made to his account in respect of the payment of a life policy premium;

(*ii*) on 28 January his monthly salary was received by bank giro and was credited to his account;

(*iii*) on 29 January his wife was allowed to cash a cheque drawn by him for £50;

(*iv*) on 12 February, shortly after the bank opened, he was allowed to cash a cheque for £30 for urgent living expenses.

Chapter 6

1. Under s.1 of the Law of Property Act 1925, only two legal estates in land may now be created. Describe these briefly, and also state the two methods by which a legal mortgage on each of them may be effected.

2. What registration, if any, should (*a*) a legal mortgagee, and (*b*) an equitable mortgagee make in order to protect the mortgage in the case of (*i*) registered land, and (*ii*) unregistered land?

Chapter 7

1. Why are searches an important part of the procedure for

mortgaging land? What searches should be made by a bank when taking a mortgage of (*i*) registered land; and (*ii*) unregistered land?

When is it advisable to make a "surplus proceeds search"?

2. What registration, if any, should (*a*) a legal mortgagee, and (*b*) an equitable mortgagee make in order to protect the mortgage in the case of (*i*) registered land, and (*ii*) unregistered land?

3. Outline the remedies available in the event of default by a mortgagor of land where the mortgagee holds:

(*a*) a legal mortgage;

(*b*) an equitable mortgage under seal;

(*c*) an equitable mortgage under hand.

4.(*a*) In relation to mortgages of land, explain what is meant by: (*i*) consolidation, and (*ii*) foreclosure.

(*b*) Jason has an overdraft limit of £10,000 at the Argonaut Bank, the only security being a first legal mortgage on his house, valued at £15,000. When the debit balance on his account is £8,000, the bank receives notice from the Golden Fleece Finance Co. Ltd. that Jason has just executed a second legal mortgage on the house in favour of the company. The bank contacts Jason, who admits that he has given the second mortgage, but claims that he is entitled to draw cheques on his account for a further £2,000 since his mortgage to the bank covers "all moneys due or to become due to the bank". What action should the bank take and why?

Chapter 8

1.(*a*) Summarise the advantages of life policies as security for bankers' advances. Are there any drawbacks to them as securities?

(*b*) Just before he left on a motoring tour, Alfred called at his bank branch, where he had an overdraft, and handed his life policy (which was for a substantial amount) to the manager, saying: "This is security for my account. I might need to draw some more money whilst I'm on holiday, and I will sign any necessary forms when I return." On his way home at the close of his holiday, Alfred was killed in a road accident. Advise the bank of the legal position concerning the life policy.

2. Consider the legal position in respect of the following life policies recently issued by the Titanic Assurance Co. Ltd.:

(*i*) to Philip, who did not inform the company that he is a gliding enthusiast;

(*ii*) to Philippa, who understated her age by five years;

(*iii*) to Quentin, who gave a legal mortgage of the policy to his bank as security for an advance. Yesterday, owing to business worries, he committed suicide.

Chapter 9

1. James is seeking substantial overdraft facilities from his bank, but the only security he can offer is his shareholding in John Ltd., a small and prosperous private company of which he is a director. In what ways might the bank obtain a charge on his shares, and would there be any particular defects in them as security?

2. Advise the Omega Bank of its legal position concerning the following securities:

(*a*) Customer A applied for a short-term advance, and as security handed the bank a certificate for £1,000 Imperial Chemical Industries Limited Ordinary Stock in his name. His request was agreed, and A overdrew his account. In view of the temporary nature of the overdraft, the bank did not ask A to sign any documents, though a memorandum of the arrangement was made by the manager. Before he could repay the overdraft, A was killed in a road accident.

(*b*) Customer B, a stockbroker, pledged certain bearer securities to the bank to cover an advance made to him. It now transpires that the securities were the property of his client, C, and the stockbroker had no authority to pledge them.

Chapter 10

1. Advise the Hilltop Bank in the following circumstances:

(*a*) Jack and his wife, Jill, have an overdrawn joint account, secured by a legal mortgage by Jack on the house where they live and by a guarantee for £5,000 by Jill's father. The bank has been pressing for reductions for some time and, with the debt at £10,000 the guarantor informs the bank that the couple are about to separate. He states that, although he is ready to discharge his guarantee liability, he would prefer to pay off the whole debt provided the bank will transfer the mortgage to him.

(b) Tom has guaranteed the account of Jerry, a local trader. The debit balance is at present £3,500 and the guarantee is for £5,000. Tom now calls at the bank and asks to see three cheques drawn by Jerry, of which he gives the cheque numbers and amounts, because he says they have been issued by Jerry in settlement of gambling debts.

2.(a) A, B, C and D are directors of Z Ltd., and have agreed to give to the South Bank their joint and several guarantee to secure the company's borrowing. A, B and C have signed the guarantee. D is to sign it on his return from a business trip abroad. As the company wishes to make a quick purchase of raw materials, the bank allows the overdraft. The aeroplane on which D is returning crashes and he is killed. Discuss the legal position as regards the guarantee.

(b) (i) Would it make any difference if D returned safely but then decided not to sign the guarantee?

(ii) If D returned and signed the guarantee, but then a year later, when the company's account was still overdrawn, resigned his directorship and asked to be released from the guarantee, what advice would you give the bank?

3. Discuss the legal position of the Dales Bank and the sureties in the following situations:

(a) The bank holds a guarantee by X for the indebtedness of its customer, A. As A failed to make payment on demand, the bank claimed upon X, only to find that he had died six months previously. At that time notice of his death had been received by the bank, but had been inadvertently filed away before any action had been taken in respect of it.

(b) Customer B has an overdraft with the bank secured by (i) a guarantee in the sum of £2,000 by C; and (ii) certain bonds valued at £1,000 and deposited by D. Repayment was demanded from B when his overdraft was £2,500 but he managed only to reduce it to £1,800. C now offers the bank £1,800 under his guarantee and asks for the bonds to be delivered to him.

Chapter 11

1. Consider whether or not documents containing the following wording are valid bills of exchange (assuming that they are otherwise complete in every detail):

(*a*) Pay Arthur Bailey or order £2,000 three months after sight and charge the same against the consignment of champagne shipped m.v. Denise.

(*b*) Pay Charles Dawson or order £2,000 six months after date and debit my Estate Maintenance A/c.

(*c*) Pay either Eric Fox or Ernest Fox £2,000 four months after date.

(*d*) Pay George Hand or order £2,000 four months after sight with interest at 9 per cent per annum.

(*e*) Pay Ivor Jones or order £2,000 in four equal instalments due 31 October, 1978; 31 January, 1979; 30 April, 1979; and 31 July, 1979.

(*f*) Pay Anna Brown or order £2,000 when she shall marry. (Anna was married last Saturday.)

2. How would you distinguish between inland and foreign bills of exchange? Why is the difference between them important in the event of dishonour?

3. In the context of bills of exchange and cheques, distinguish between:

(*i*) a holder and a wrongful possessor;

(*ii*) a holder for value and a holder in due course.

Can the payee of a cheque be a holder in due course?

4. Explain the term "transferor by delivery" as used in the context of bills of exchange. What liability, if any, does such a person incur?

5.(*a*) When is a bill of exchange deemed to be overdue, and what significance does this have as regards its negotiation?

(*b*) On 20 January, 1978 Oswald drew a bill of exchange for £500 on Philip payable to bearer three months after date. Whilst being sent to Philip, the bill was amongst items of mail stolen by thieves, who threw it away. It was found by Roger, who passed it on to Sam in settlement for goods supplied. When Sam presented the bill to Philip at maturity, it was dishonoured. Advise Sam as to his legal rights, if any.

6. A draws a bill of exchange on B payable to C. The bill is in proper form and falls due three months after date. B accepts the bill and A then sends it to C, who indorses it and hands it to X in settlement of a debt.

Outline the respective promises or engagements of A, B and C as regards the bill.

Can any of them, when signing the bill, add "sans recours" and, if so, what effect would these words have?

Chapter 12

1. (a) (i) Explain the meaning and effect of the phrases "A/c Payee" and "Not negotiable" which often appear on crossed cheques.

(ii) Does "Not negotiable" have any significance if it appears on a bill of exchange other than a cheque?

(b) Charles Dickens, a customer of the Fenland Bank, wishes to pay in for the credit of his account a cheque crossed "A/c Payee" and drawn by a well-known insurance company for £750 in favour of Mrs Sarah Gamp. He explains that the payee is an elderly relative, who does not have a bank account of her own. Are there any risks involved if the bank collects the cheque?

2.(a) As regards consideration, does the law relating to bills of exchange differ at all from the law relating to contracts generally?

(b) On her 18th birthday Amy is given a cheque for £25 by her father, Bill, and later that day she uses it to buy clothes from Cecil's boutique. The next day, before the cheque has been presented, Bill has a violent argument with his daughter and countermands payment of the cheque at the bank. Advise Amy, Bill and Cecil as to their legal position.

3. What statutory protection is afforded to a banker when paying cheques drawn by customers? Outline the circumstances in which this protection may be lost. Does the legal position alter at all if the paying banker is also the collecting banker?

4.(a) What protection, if any, has a bank if it pays a cheque on which either (i) the drawer's signature, or (ii) the payee's indorsement has been forged?

(b) Mr Grouser, who is a customer of the Toytown branch of the Omega Bank, draws a cheque for £50 in payment for an old coin at a coin-dealer's shop, where he purchases items from time to time. When he examines this particular coin at home, he is not satisfied with it, and telephones his branch with instructions to stop payment of the relevant cheque. He is asked to confirm by post his countermand of payment, but does not do so. However, three days later he calls at the branch and hands in a letter confirming the counter-mand, whereupon the bank finds that the cheque had in fact been debited to his account on the day after receipt of his telephone instruction. Discuss the position of the bank.

5. Codd visits the Dogger Bank with his friend, who is posing as Bloater, a famous television personality, whom he closely resembles. Codd asks to open a current account offering "Bloater" as a referee. Thereupon "Bloater" gives a favourable reference in respect of Codd, which the bank accepts without further inquiry. Codd then pays in a cheque for a large amount and, after it has been cleared, he withdraws almost all the proceeds. The true owner of this cheque now claims its value from the bank, and Codd cannot be found. Advise the bank.

Would you change your advice if in fact the bank had allowed Codd to draw against the cheque whilst still uncleared, and payment of it was stopped by the drawer?

6.(a) Cheque books often contain a statement to the effect that the bank reserves the right to refuse payment of the cheques drawn against uncleared items. What is the reason for this statement?

Are there any circumstances in which it may be to a bank's advantage to have specifically agreed with a customer that he may draw cheques against uncleared items?

(b) Is there any legal significance if:

(i) a bank cashes or exchanges a third-party cheque for a customer, instead of insisting that he pays it in to the credit of his account and then withdraws the amount;

(ii) a bank takes a cheque from a customer for the express purpose of reducing his overdraft, instead of merely crediting it to his account, which happens to be overdrawn at the time?

Appendix 4
Examination technique

Revision

1. Introduction. All students have their own particular methods of revision, and you will certainly have yours. This method will be tried and tested but it is very likely that you will gain positive benefit by devoting a few minutes to carefully reading this short guide to methods of revision.

Provided that you have studied the text thoroughly, you will have understood the *Law of Banking*. However, the examination is not passed purely by understanding the law; you must also learn it and be able to apply the law in the examination questions.

Hence, your revision of the *Law of Banking* should have three main aims:

—complete *understanding* of the law;
—*retention and recall* of the law;
—the ability to *explain and apply* the law.

You need not feel daunted by these aims because *understanding* is the key to both the learning and the use of a subject. Thus, it is understanding which is crucial to examination success, and your revision should be designed above all else to *reinforce* understanding.

You must have discovered in your previous studies that no matter how much a subject may interest you when you actually study it, learning it for an examination can at best be tedious and at worst boring. You must try to lessen this effect.

2. Revision programme. Tedium in revision is caused mainly by reading the same original notes over and over again. This is also

```
                                          ┌─ Definition
                                          ├─ Bills of Exchange Act 1882, s.3(1)
                           ┌─ Introduction ┼─ Cheques and other bills
                           │              ├─ Stale and overdue cheques
                           │              ├─ Post-dated cheques
                           │              └─ Cheques as evidence of payment
                           │
                           │              ┌─ Introduction
                           ├─ Crossed     ┼─ Types of crossing
                           │  Cheques     └─ Who may cross
                           │
                           │              ┌─ Introduction
                           │              ├─ Termination of authority
                           │              ├─ Possible liability
  CHEQUES ─────────────────┤  The Paying  ├─ Protection
                           ├─ Banker      ┼─ Conditional orders
                           │              ├─ Bankers' drafts
                           │              ├─ Divident and interest warrants
                           │              └─ Cheque cards
                           │
                           │              ┌─ Possible liability
                           │  The         ├─ Statutory protection
                           └─ Collecting  ┼─ As holder in due course
                              Banker      └─ Postal and money orders
```

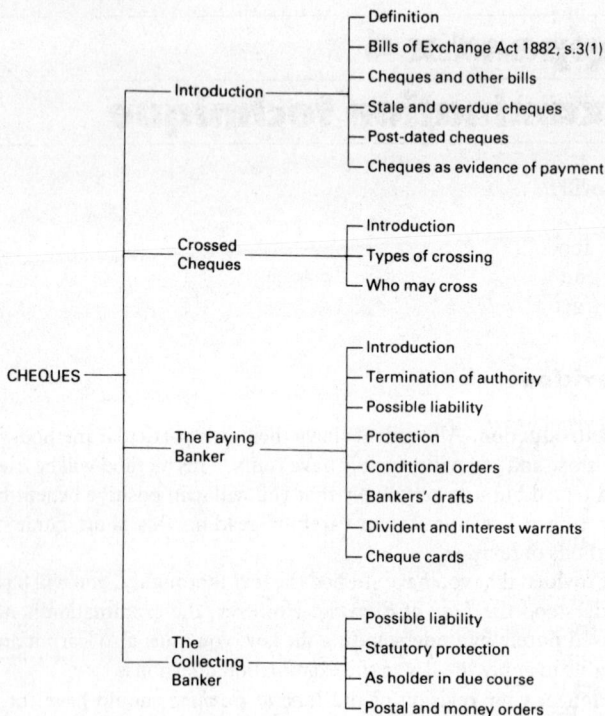

Fig. 3 *Diagram as a revision aid.*

unproductive. After the initial re-read of your notes you will already know much of what you are reading and progressively more of your time will be wasted each time you repeat the exercise. It is far better to adopt a *positive revision* programme, one which uses your time profitably and enables you to teach yourself. Your Handbook is the perfect basis for such a programme.

Revision should be done a chapter at a time. Try adopting the following sequence.

(*a*) *Re-read* the chapter thoroughly.

(*b*) *Make revision notes.* These can consist of no more than the headings in the text with a very brief note about important principles and the names of leading cases.

Your summary notes can subsequently be used in the following way. Take each note in turn and try to recall and explain the subject matter. If you can, proceed to the next; if you cannot, look in your Handbook. By doing this, you will revise, test your knowledge and spend your time profitably by concentrating your revision on those aspects of the subject with which you are least familiar. In addition, you will have an excellent last-minute revision aid.

(c) Construct a chart for each topic using the headings in your Handbook. (An example is drawn for you in Fig. 3.) Many people respond well to diagrammatic explanations and summaries, it often helps actually to see how different aspects of a subject relate to each other.

Constructing diagrams is a particularly useful form of positive revision. Besides providing an extremely quick and efficient means of revision, diagrams are an excellent last minute revision aid. You need to think how best to construct them, thus in doing so you teach yourself and better understand the subject.

If you find this method works for you, you could construct diagrams of specific aspects of a main topic, breaking the law down further than the headings in the text.

Two tips: do not try to include too much on each diagram; and do not try to economise on paper. The impact and usefulness of a diagram depends very much on its visual simplicity. The same applies to revision notes.

(d) Prepare concise explanations of key principles and cases that you are likely to need in the examination. Try to include an actual example of their operation. An obvious case to prepare is *Clayton's Case* (1816), this is almost certain to be required in at least one question.

This exercise is also particularly useful because you are revising positively and thinking about the subject matter. In addition, you may save 2 or 3 minutes on each question in the examination simply because you do not have to think about how to explain something which you probably know well but cannot easily put into words there and then. Multiplied five times, this is a considerable saving in time—how often have you wished for 10–15 minutes more time in an examination?

(e) Answer the progress tests again. You should find a significant improvement in the number of questions that you can answer immediately. This exercise will primarily test your ability to recall and explain the law.

(*f*) Plan answers to the specimen examination questions in the back of the Handbook and any others set by the Institute of Bankers. (Booklets of questions with suggested answers can be purchased from the Institute.)

Planning answers is often a more useful exercise than actually writing the answer out in full. In planning you have in effect answered the question and writing it out is a largely mechanical exercise. If, however, you feel that you need the practice in essay writing, answer some fully.

Read the notes on answering questions (*see* **3** below) before planning any answers.

This suggested revision sequence is not a substitute for hard work, only a positive and logical approach to it. No matter how good your tuition, you are by yourself in the examination room. However, if you follow the suggested programme, you will at least be well prepared for it.

The examination

Provided you have thoroughly revised, you need not fear the examination. You will have a comprehensive knowledge and under-standing of the Law of Banking, and it is unlikely that the paper set will contain a single question that you cannot answer. Do not, however, underestimate the examination.

3. Examination technique.

(*a*) Read the examination instructions carefully.

(*b*) Thoroughly read through the questions and provisionally mark which questions to answer. Take care over your choice. An apparently simple question might have a hidden twist—do not get caught out. Similarly, never decide to answer a question which is in two or more parts on the strength of the first part alone. Make sure that you can answer *all* parts.

(*c*) Make sure you have selected the right number of questions—you get no extra marks for answering more!

(*d*) Divide your time equally between questions. Answer one too few questions and you have immediately lost 20 per cent. Plan to leave time for a final check through your answers.

(e) Everyone suffers from examination nerves and you are unlikely to perform at your best for the first fifteen minutes or so of the examination. Consequently, it is often a good practice to answer your best question second or third. By that time you will be thoroughly relaxed and working well.

(f) Plan all your answers—this is *absolutely vital*.

(g) Check through your answers; a few minutes spent doing this can eliminate many minor errors and give a final "polish" to your answers.

4. Types of questions. These can be divided into two broad categories: "textbook" questions and "problems".

(a) *Textbook questions.* Such questions are designed to test your ability to recall, explain and/or comment upon a particular aspect of the Law of Banking. They are usually fairly straightforward but your answer must be planned very carefully in order to make it *accurate*, *relevant* and *concise*.

Resist the temptation to stray from the question where you know rather more about the subject than the question actually requires as an answer.

(b) *Problem questions.* Such questions are designed to test your ability to apply the law to a hypothetical situation. They are usually more complicated than text book questions but high marks can be attained by applying a simple planning formula.

Your answer should contain the following four elements (but not necessarily in the order illustrated).

(i) Identification of the exact legal *problem(s)* posed by the question. (N.B. This is not whether X will succeed or fail in his action against Y.)

(ii) Statement and explanation of the relevant legal *principle(s)* involved.

(iii) Reference to relevant *precedents* or *Acts of Parliament*. (N.B. Always give a brief outline of the facts of any case which you are going to use as part of your argument.)

(iv) Application of legal principle and "Authority" to the facts of the question in a *conclusion*. Always argue this thoroughly, considering both sides of the situation where necessary. (N.B. Bear in mind the way in which the question is phrased, e.g. "advise" or "discuss".)

The formula can be applied to any problem, and you will find that with practice you develop a "feel" for deciding the arrangement of these four elements depending upon the exact question set.

Index